Lecture Notes in Artificial Intelligence   3550

Edited by J. G. Carbonell and J. Siekmann

Subseries of Lecture Notes in Computer Science

Torsten Eymann   Franziska Klügl
Winfried Lamersdorf   Matthias Klusch
Michael N. Huhns (Eds.)

Multiagent System Technologies

Third German Conference, MATES 2005
Koblenz, Germany, September 11-13, 2005
Proceedings

 Springer

Series Editors

Jaime G. Carbonell, Carnegie Mellon University, Pittsburgh, PA, USA
Jörg Siekmann, University of Saarland, Saarbrücken, Germany

Volume Editors

Torsten Eymann
Universität Bayreuth, Wirtschaftsinformatik (BWL VII)
Universitätsstrasse 30, 95440, Bayreuth, Germany
E-mail: eymann@uni-bayreuth.de

Franziska Klügl
Universität Würzburg
Department of Artificial Intelligence and Applied Computer Science
Am Hubland, 97074 Würzburg, Germany
E-mail: kluegl@informatik.uni-wuerzburg.de

Winfried Lamersdorf
Universität Hamburg
Department of Informatics, Distributed and Information Systems (VSIS)
Vogt-Kölln-Str. 30, 22527 Hamburg, Germany
E-mail: lamersd@informatik.uni-hamburg.de

Matthias Klusch
DFKI, German Research Center for Artificial Intelligence
Stuhlsatzenhausweg 3, 66123 Saarbrücken, Germany
E-mail: klusch@dfki.de

Michael N. Huhns
University of South Carolina, Department of Computer Science and Engineering
Columbia, SC 29208, USA
E-mail: huhns@sc.edu

Library of Congress Control Number: 2005931591
CR Subject Classification (1998): I.2.11, I.2, C.2.4, D.2.12, D.1.3, J.1

ISSN   0302-9743
ISBN-10   3-540-28740-X Springer Berlin Heidelberg New York
ISBN-13   978-3-540-28740-7 Springer Berlin Heidelberg New York

Springer is a part of Springer Science+Business Media

springeronline.com

© Springer-Verlag Berlin Heidelberg 2005
Printed in Germany

Typesetting: Camera-ready by author, data conversion by Scientific Publishing Services, Chennai, India
Printed on acid-free paper   SPIN: 11550648   06/3142   5 4 3 2 1 0

Preface

After two successful MATES conferences in Erfurt 2003 and 2004, the 3rd German conference on Multi-agent System Technologies (MATES 2005) took place in Koblenz, Germany, in September 2005, and was co-located with the 28th German Conference on Artificial Intelligence (KI 2005).

Building on other agent-related events in Germany in the past, and organized by the GI German Special Interest Group on Distributed Artificial Intelligence, the MATES conference series aims at promoting the theory and applications of agents and multiagent systems. Incorporating the 9th International Workshop on Cooperative Information Agents (CIA 2005), the topics of interest for MATES 2005 also covered the fields of intelligent information agents and systems for the Internet and the (Semantic) Web.

As in recent years, MATES 2005 provided a distinguished, lively and interdisciplinary forum for researchers, users, and developers of agent technology, to present and discuss the latest advances of research and development in the area of autonomous agents and multiagent systems. Accordingly, the topics of MATES 2005 covered the whole range from the theory to applications of agent- and multiagent technology. The technical program included a total of 24 scientific talks, and demonstrations of selected running agent systems, and both the MATES 2005 Best Paper and the CIA 2005 System Innovation awards.

The international Program Committee for MATES 2005 selected carefully 14 out of 54 submissions from all over the world to be accepted as full papers, and an additional 5 short papers as well as 5 posters to be presented. The program also included four distinguished invited speakers: Karl Aberer (EPF Lausanne, Switzerland), John-Jules C. Meyer (Utrecht University, The Netherlands), Steffen Staab (Universität Koblenz, Germany), and jointly with KI 2005, Luc Steels (SONY Computer Science Lab Paris and Free University of Brussels), as well as a doctoral colloquium and a mentoring program.

Finally, as general co-chairs and PC co-chairs, and in the name of all members of the Steering Committee, we would like to thank all authors of submitted papers and all invited speakers for their contributions, all members of the Program Committee as well as other reviewers for their careful, critical, and thoughtful reviews, and all local conference organizers and others involved in helping to make MATES 2005 a success. In addition, we would like to explicitly thank our sponsors AgentLink III, Whitestein Technologies, Siemens, and the German Computer Society (GI), whose financial support helped to make this event possible.

We hope the attendees enjoyed MATES 2005 and the Koblenz conference site both scientifically and socially and will continue to support MATES as a conference series with many more successful events to come in the future!

June 2005   Torsten Eymann, Franziska Klügl, Winfried Lamersdorf,
               Michael Huhns, Matthias Klusch

Organization

General Co-chairs

Matthias Klusch   DFKI Saarbrücken, Germany
Michael Huhns   University of South Carolina, USA

Program Co-chairs

Torsten Eymann   Bayreuth University, Germany
Franziska Klügl   Würzburg University, Germany
Winfried Lamersdorf   Hamburg University, Germany

Program Committee

Karl Aberer   EPF Lausanne, Switzerland
Elisabeth Andre   University of Augsburg, Germany
Bernhard Bauer   University of Augsburg, Germany
Wolfgang Benn   TU Chemnitz, Germany
Monique Calisti   Whitestein Technologies AG, Zürich, Switzerland
Cristiano Castelfranchi   CNR, Italy
Thomas Christaller   Fraunhofer AIS, Germany
Rosaria Conte   NRC Rome, Italy
Stephen Cranefield   University of Otago, New Zealand
Mehdi Dastani   University of Utrecht, The Netherlands
Yves Demazeau   Leibniz/IMAG, France
Jörg Denziger   University of Calgary, Canada
Klaus Fischer   DFKI Saarbrücken, Germany
Ana Garcia Serrano   TU Madrid, Spain
Fausto Giunchiglia   University of Trento, Italy
Marie-Pierre Gleizes   IRIT Toulouse, France
Rune Gustavsson   TH Blekinge, Sweden
Heikki Helin   TeliaSonera, Helsinki, Finland
Heinrich Hussmann   Universität München, Germany
Toru Ishida   University of Kyoto, Japan
Stefan Kirn   Uiversität Hohenheim, Germany
Ryszard Kowalczyk   TU Swinburne, Australia
Daniel Kudenko   University of York, UK
Jürgen Lind   AgentLab München, Germany
Gabriela Lindemann   HU Berlin, Germany
Jiming Liu   Hong Kong Baptist University, China

Table of Contents

Invited Contributions

Workflows and Group Interaction

Reasoning about Utility

The Dynamics of Knowledge

Methodology and Simulation

Agent Tools and Agent Education

Short Papers

Posters

On the Convergence of Structured Search, Information Retrieval and Trust Management in Distributed Systems⋆

Karl Aberer, Philippe Cudré-Mauroux, and Zoran Despotovic

School of Computer and Communication Sciences,
EPFL, Lausanne, Switzerland
{karl.aberer, philippe.cudre-mauroux, zoran.despotovic}@epfl.ch

Abstract. The database and information retrieval communities have long been recognized as being irreconcilable. Today, however, we witness a surprising convergence of the techniques used by both communities in decentralized, large-scale environments. The newly emerging field of reputation based trust management, borrowing techniques from both communities, best demonstrates this claim. We argue that incomplete knowledge and increasing autonomy of the participating entities are the driving forces behind this convergence, pushing the adoption of probabilistic techniques typically borrowed from an information retrieval context. We argue that using a common probabilistic framework would be an important step in furthering this convergence and enabling a common treatment and analysis of distributed complex systems. We will provide a first sketch of such a framework and illustrate it with examples from our previous work on information retrieval, structured search and trust assessment.

1 Introduction

The database and information retrieval communities have long been perceived as being irreconcilable. The different ways of how data is represented, interpreted and processed are at the core of the divergence in focus of these communities.

The main problem addressed by the database community can be stated as the efficient management of data represented in some first order logic language and the efficient evaluation of queries specifying information needs unambiguously through logical expressions. Recently this model has been extended in the context of the Semantic Web to deal with distributed, heterogeneous information sources by using shared first order conceptual models (ontologies) and a common Web-based infrastructure.

⋆ The work presented in this paper was supported (in part) by the National Competence Center in Research on Mobile Information and Communication Systems (NCCR-MICS) and by the Computational Reputation Mechanisms for Enabling Peer-to-Peer Commerce in Decentralized Networks Project, both supported by the Swiss National Science Foundation under grant number 5005-67322 and 20512-105287/1 respectively.

T. Eymann et al. (Eds.): MATES 2005, LNAI 3550, pp. 1–14, 2005.

On the other hand, the information retrieval community focuses on finding models for retrieving documents in response to incompletely or ambiguously specified information needs by exploiting document features and user relevance feedback. Web search engines are the most prominent incarnation of these techniques for assessing relevance of documents in response to user requests for information, using both textual content of documents and user feedback derived from the link structure of the Web.

Attempts to reconcile the two communities reach far back in history. Even a conference series, the International Conference on Information and Knowledge Management (CIKM), is dedicated to this goal. We were interested to see to which extent the interaction among the communities progressed, and analyzed the program of the years 2003 and 2004. The result is not too impressive. Among 120 research papers we could identify 10 that are at the borderline of databases and information retrieval, whereas the others are quite clearly belonging to the fields of classical database, information retrieval or knowledge management. In 2004, two sessions on databases and information retrieval have been organized. The topics addressed by the borderline papers are on storage management for retrieval systems, processing of XML documents and similarity search in databases. The last two areas in fact indicate one reason why the boundary between the database view of structured data processing and the information retrieval view of content-oriented processing is starting to dissolve. It is the result of processing specific data types that require both structural and content-oriented processing.

In this paper, we argue that recent developments in diverse areas, such as the Semantic Web, peer-to-peer computing, sensor networks, agent technologies and Web retrieval, indicate that the "semantic gap" between traditional logic-based knowledge presentation and processing and the probabilistic approach taken in information retrieval will be rapidly closing, for a very fundamental reason, that goes beyond the requirement of processing specific data types.

In a distributed environment of autonomous information sources, information and information needs can no longer be expressed concisely, as expected by database and semantic web technologies, but have to deal with *numerous sources of uncertainty*, thus requiring a probabilistic view in the processing of data. In information retrieval, one deals with one specific kind of uncertainty, uncertainty about users information needs. We claim that in distributed environments, qualitatively different sources of uncertainty have to be dealt with as well. This will require a structured framework to represent and process the different sources of uncertainty to provide insightful answers to users information needs. This requirement goes well beyond existing capabilities of both database and information retrieval techniques and systems.

We will illustrate this convergence process by providing several important examples of how the uncertainty resulting from autonomy and incomplete knowledge in distributed environments affects information processing. These examples are taken both from our own work and from some typical results found in the literature. We will provide short summaries of these techniques and illustrate by a simple example of a search problem how each of these techniques affects the information processing task for satisfying the search task. By doing this we illustrate how using a probabilistic framework makes it possible to integrate different ways of dealing with uncertainty, just as first order logic is being used as an integration framework for structured representation and reasoning over distributed information sources. This example-based analysis will allow us to derive some basic conclusions on requirements and issues for extending the current Web infrastructure for dealing with uncertainty in a systematic and integrated way.

2 Running Example: Getting Newspaper Articles About Hot Days in Switzerland

To illustrate our claims, we introduce an example which is in our opinion representative of the current challenges emerging in information management today. The example starts as a simple SQL query posed against a relational database but will be enriched throughout the paper as new sources of uncertainty are introduced.

From June to August 2003, unusually high temperatures were reported across Europe, including Switzerland. Imagine a journalist wanting to retrieve all newspaper articles about hot days in Switzerland which appeared exactly on one of those days. In a standard relational databases scenario, this could translate to a SQL query like the following:

```
SELECT article.text
FROM articles, weather WHERE
    article.text like %hot summer days%
    and article.date = weather.date
    and weather.temperature  > 30
```

The query contains three predicates, q_1, q_2 and q_3 representing some condition on the content of articles, their publication date and some temperature record respectively.

From a logical perspective, such a query can be considered as a logical expression q for which we have to find all objects d contained in a database such that the implication $d \rightarrow q$ is true.

Expressing an information need in this form reflects several basic assumptions being made, including the ability of the user to precisely express her information need, the correct interpretation of the schematic information provided by the database and the correctness of the data stored in the database. In practice, as we will demonstrate in the following, none of these assumptions can be taken for granted in realistic, distributed information systems.

3 Uncertainty on Users' Information Needs

Since long it has been recognized that logics is not an appropriate framework for information search when it comes to searching documents with textual content. Boolean retrieval has been an early attempt to apply logics for text search, which has soon found its limitations. Due to the ambiguity of natural language, there exists no strict relationship between queries expressed in natural language against documents containing natural language text. Thus the discipline of information retrieval has developed a rich set of models for assessing the relevance of documents for a given query. These models introduce an element of *uncertainty* into the search process, since result objects are no more included into the result set by virtue of a decidable property (a predicate) but whenever there is indication that they might be relevant to some degree to the users information need. These observations clearly apply to the clause q_1 == `article.text like` `%hot summer days%` of our example query, which in a current database system (ideally) would not be resolved at the syntactic level searching for the exact phrase, but using an underlying text retrieval system.

3.1 Running Example: Accounting for the Uncertainty on Information Needs Through Probabilistic Retrieval

Since we are aiming at a probabilistic framework for dealing with uncertainty in modern information systems, we provide here a short overview of information retrieval from a probabilistic perspective, which follows the exposition given by [5]. From a logical perspective, answering a query q with document d amounts to proving that the implication $d \rightarrow q$ is true. In Boolean retrieval this means that all terms of a (conjunctive) query q would appear in d. In contrast, probabilistic retrieval adopts the following notion for answering a query q: the conditional probability $P(q|d)$ indicates of how relevant document d is to query q.

For computing this probability usually a concept space C of disjoint concepts $c \in C$ is introduced with a probability density function $P(.)$ over C. Queries and documents are considered as concept sets. Then the query answer can be represented as follows:

$$P(q|d) = \frac{P(q \cap d)}{P(d)}, \ P(d) = \sum_{c \in d} P(c), \ P(q \cap d) = \sum_{c \in q, c \in d} P(c)$$

A popular type of concepts are terms taken from a vocabulary. Since the concepts are considered as being independent we can further derive

$$P(q|d) = \frac{P(q \cap d)}{P(d)} = \frac{\sum_{c \in C} P(d \cap q \cap c)}{P(d)} = \frac{\sum_{c \in C} P(d \cap q|c)P(c)}{P(d)}$$

If the concept space consists of the terms of a vocabulary, we may assume that the probabilities $P(d|c)$ and $P(q|c)$ are known from analyzing the text collection. For computing a query answer, a standard assumption that is made in probabilistic retrieval is the *maximum entropy principle*, which states the following independence:

$$P(d \cap q|c) = P(d|c)P(q|c).$$

Using this assumption we get

$$P(q|d) = \frac{\sum_{c \in C} P(d \cap q|c)P(c)}{P(d)}$$

$$= \frac{\sum_{c \in C} P(d|c)P(q|c)P(c)}{P(d)}$$

$$= \sum_{c \in C} P(q|c)P(c|d)$$

The last expression can be interpreted as the classical model of vector space retrieval, the predominant model for modern text retrieval. Under this interpretation, $P(c|d)$ corresponds to the term weight for a document representation, which is typically computed using a (heuristic) tf-idf scheme and gives the probability that a term is characteristic for a given document. $P(q|c)$ corresponds to the query term weight and gives the probability that a term is characteristic for the result set of query q.

In summary, a predicate such as q_1 == article.text like %hot summer days% corresponds in a search model that is considering uncertainty on users' information needs to a random variable q_1 for which we have a method to compute $P(q_1|d)$, the probability that a document is relevant to the predicate. The method to compute this probability relies on an intermediary concept (or feature) space C, for which we assume to have probabilistic models for $P(q_1|c)$ and $P(c|d)$ for a random variable c over the concept space. The computation of $P(q_1|d)$ is then performed by marginalization of the joint probability distribution $P(q_1, c, d)$ exploiting the separation of the random variables q_1 and d through c.

From a practical perspective, using a retrieval engine within a logics-based query language such as SQL poses the question of how to reflect the probabilistic evaluation of $q1$ into the query result. Two solutions are applicable: either only result documents are included that exceed a certain threshold probability. This seems to be problematic with respect to the interpretation of the result. Alternatively the probability values are included into the result table. This might raise efficiency concerns as the result set might become unacceptably large. As we will show in the following, this is a problem that is not confined to the case of dealing with users' uncertainty on information need, but with dealing with uncertainty in general.

4   Uncertainty on Knowledge Conceptualizations

Traditionally, knowledge representations have been based on subsets of first-order logic in computer science. Indeed, it is widely recognized that knowledge can be efficiently captured by characterizing classes of objects and their interrelationships. Databases have long used dialects derived from first-order logic to represent or query data, while description logic, a subset of first-order logic, has been chosen to back-up standards for the Semantic Web.

These representations have proven to be extremely useful for dealing with knowledge bases or providing sound semantics to query processing. Until recently, most information-processing tasks took place in controlled environments where one had full control over the definitions of entities in the universe of discourse. When semantic heterogeneity occurred, for examples when multiple schemas or ontologies had to be merged together, some higher-order element (e.g., an integrated schema) was statically introduced to consolidate knowledge in a consistent manner. Thus, some well-known techniques such as Global-As-View and Local-as-View to integrate heterogeneous databases and rewrite queries in deterministic ways have been developed.

Today, however, with the advent of the Internet and the democratization of Semantic Web tools facilitating knowledge elicitation in machine-processable formats, the situation is quickly evolving. One cannot rely on global, centralized schemas anymore as knowledge creation and consumption are getting more and more dynamic and decentralized. In such settings, one has to account for the fact that new knowledge and knowledge representations can appear on a continual basis without any central coordination, while well-known sources might well disappear without prior notice. As a corollary, it is getting more and more difficult to get any kind of certainty about knowledge coming from heterogeneous and dynamic sources over which one has little control.

In this context, uncertainty over knowledge gets particularly critical when one considers agreement on knowledge conceptualizations. Traditionally, only relevant information adhering to specific schemas, taxonomies or ontologies was returned as result of a structured search. As more and more conceptualizations get available from heterogeneous sources, one has to take into consideration the tradeoff between maximizing the precision of the results (by focusing on well-known information sources only) and the total number of relevant results (by considering as many information sources as possible). Many different (semi-) automatic schema mapping schemes have been explored recently. In most cases, some probabilistic value can be returned indicating whether or not the outcome of the mapping process makes sense. One could hence take advantage of these probabilistic values upon deciding whether or not to include an information source for a given structured query.

4.1   Running Example: Accounting for the Uncertainty on Shared Conceptualizations Through Semantic Gossiping

To come back to our running example, let us imagine that the journalist has access to various newspaper databases on the web. Each database was developed independently of the other ones. All databases consider some sort of representation to encode the date on which a particular newspaper article was published. However, some call this date *published_date*, while other might call it *dateDePublication* or *pd_field*. Due to the fact that the schemas are continually evolving, appearing or disappearing without any central coordination, maintaining a global schema from / to which all individual databases could be mapped is arguably impracticable. Instead, translation links (e.g., schema mappings, views) are defined between pairs of schemas. Those pairwise links permit to iteratively propagate a query posed against a specific schema to other databases. This approach has been taken in the new field of peer-to-peer data management.

The problem lies here in the fact that those links might be created (semi-) automatically, or might not be able to guarantee the outcome of a query mapping deterministically. Different cases may occur in practice. For example, *publication_date* might be erroneously mapped onto *deletion_date* or could be imperfectly mapped onto a *publicationWeek* attribute of a weekly newspaper (coarser degree of granularity for storing publication dates). Thus, we cannot expect the outcome of a query mapping to be one hundred percent faithful to the original query.

We engineered heuristics to quantify the degree to which a translated query differs from the intended query. We termed these techniques *Semantic Gossiping* [1,2] as they rely on gossiping a query through the various translation links for deriving probabilistic guarantees on the translation process. From a high-level perspective, our methods work as follows: after propagating queries throughout the network of translations, we collect feedback information f, both from the analysis of transitive closures of the query translation processes and from the results received from other databases.

We illustrate how such an approach introduces uncertainty into query answering for one specific type of approach when analyzing feedback received from issuing queries to a peer-to-peer schema mapping network. Given a cycle of mappings $m, m_1, \ldots, m_n$ and assuming all mappings are correct the composite mapping results in a partial identity function. We call this positive feedback f^+. We denote with m_i a random (Bernoulli) variable for a mapping m_i being correct and assume a prior probability ϵ of a mapping m_i being incorrect $P(m_i = 1) = 1 - \epsilon$. Furthermore we assume the probability δ of a mapping error to be compensated in the last step of the cycle by another mapping error to be known. Then we can derive the probability of receiving positive feedback, e.g.,

$$P(f^+|m = 1) = (1 - \epsilon)^n + (1 - (1 - \epsilon)^{n-1})\delta$$

Similarly, other probabilities, e.g. $P(f^+|m = 0, \epsilon, \delta)$ can be computed. We assume that we obtain a set of positive feedbacks $\mathcal{F}^+ = \{f_1^+, \ldots, f_n^+\}$ and of negative feedbacks $\mathcal{F}^- = \{f_1^-, \ldots, f_m^-\}$, $\mathcal{F} = \mathcal{F}^- \cup \mathcal{F}^+$ and want to determine the probability $P(m|\mathcal{F})$ of mapping m being correct under these observations. Assuming independence of feedbacks (which in fact is an oversimplification for a real mapping graph) we have

$$P(m|\mathcal{F}) = \prod_{f \in \mathcal{F}} P(m|f).$$

From there, and from the assumption that we have no prior knowledge on m (applying the maximum entropy principle implies $P(m = 1) = P(m = 0)$) we get

$$P(m|f) = \frac{P(f|m)P(m)}{\sum_{m \in \{0,1\}} P(f|m)}$$

Thus, we can determine the conditional probability $P(m|\mathcal{F})$ of a mapping m being correct given some feedback information $\mathcal{F}$. Applying this to our problem, we can determine the probability $P(q_2|\mathcal{F})$ of the date predicate being semantically preserved after applying a mapping m for obtaining the date value, based on feedback information about that mapping:

$$P(q_2|\mathcal{F}) = \frac{\sum_{m \in \{0,1\}} P(q_2, \mathcal{F}|m)P(m)}{P(\mathcal{F})} = \sum_{m \in \{0,1\}} P(q_2|m)P(m|\mathcal{F})$$

making use of the independence assumption $P(q_2, \mathcal{F}|m) = P(q_2|m)P(\mathcal{F}|m)$.

5   Uncertainty on Assertions

The quality or pertinence of assertions may greatly vary in decentralized settings. Putting aside trust-related issues (see below for a discussion on this topic), we can expect an ever increasing proportion of automatically-generated assertions in large-scale environments. Fuzzy logic, probabilistic or machine-learning approaches will certainly all contribute at deriving new assertions from existing ones.

Also of interest, the emerging field of sensor networks providing streams of raw data from sensor measurements. Sensors cannot deliver continuous data on extended periods of time due to energy constraints: In fact, there is a well-know trade-off between the precision of sensor data on the one hand, and the battery life of the sensors on the other hand. This implies the necessity of accounting for uncertainty while processing assertions derived from a data acquisition network. The question is, again, how to capture the degree of uncertainty related to the new assertions and how to take advantage of these degrees to get meaningful answers to queries.

5.1   Running Example: Accounting for the Uncertainty on Sensor Measurements in Data Acquisition Networks

Recently, a few probabilistic approaches appeared for processing queries in sensor networks. BBQ [3], for example, introduces the concept of model-based querying. The approach is based on a probabilistic model that captures the correlations among measurements of spatially and temporally correlated sensors, e.g., temperature sensors, to support query answering. The probabilistic model is derived from historical sensor measurements. For query answering, available sensor readings are used to answer user queries by computing the posterior probabilities of the measurement variables from the probabilistic model of the sensor network. In this way missing or faulty readings can be interpolated by the probabilistic model and opportunities for optimizing the physical cost of operating sensor networks can be taken advantage of, such as optimization of energy consumption and reduction of deployment and maintenance cost. We provide in the following a somewhat simplified high-level description of this approach.

Let us assume that the temperatures in `weather.temperature` (q_3) are gathered by a data acquisition network consisting of n fixed sensors, scattered all around Switzerland. They periodically transfer some temperature measurements s_i to a central server. From historical measurements a probability density function $P(s_1, \ldots, s_n)$ is derived. This function captures correlations of temperature measurements due to spatial vicinity of sensors. The model has been extended to also consider temporal correlations. In the case of BBQ this probability density function is a multivariate Gaussian function. The temperature in Switzerland is then defined as the average value of the currently measured values, i.e. $t = \frac{1}{n} \sum_{i=1}^{n} s_i$. If $P(s_1, \ldots, s_n)$ is a multivariate Gaussian, $P(t)$ follows a Gaussian distribution also.

Assume now that a probably incomplete set of raw observations from a subset of all sensors is available, $\mathcal{S} = \{s_j = s_j^o, j \in O\}, O \subseteq \{1, \ldots, n\}$. Then the average temperature can be determined by marginalization as follows

$$P(t|\mathcal{S}) = \int P(s_1, \ldots, s_n|\mathcal{S}) I_t \Big(\frac{1}{n} \sum_{i=1}^{n} s_i\Big) ds_1 \ldots ds_n$$

where $I_t(.)$ is the indicator function and

$$P(s_1, \ldots, s_n|\mathcal{S}) = \frac{P(\bar{s}_1, \ldots, \bar{s}_n)}{P(\mathcal{S})}$$

where $\bar{s}_j = s_j^o$ for $j \in O$ and $\bar{s}_j = s_j$ otherwise.

For evaluating predicate q_3 we can derive from

$$P(q_3|t) = \begin{cases} 0 \text{ if } t \le 30 \\ 1 \text{ if } t > 30 \end{cases}$$

in a now familiar way a probabilistic value for the predicate q_3 being correctly evaluated giving a set of raw measurements s gathered by sensors:

$$P(q_3|\mathcal{S}) = \int \frac{P(q_3, \mathcal{S}|t)P(t)}{P(\mathcal{S})} dt = \int P(q_3|t)P(t|\mathcal{S}) dt.$$

6   Reputation-Based Trust Management in Decentralized Settings

Up to this point we have considered the uncertainties resulting from interpreting factual data (stored in some database) with respect to the intended semantics of a user query. These models exploited intrinsic properties of the data objects being searched for and their associated schemas. These intrinsic properties directly pertain to the query and data objects under consideration. In different applications it can be observed that in addition to these intrinsic features also extrinsic features derived from the context in which the data objects are being used may have an important impact on the search. Trust is a typical example of such extrinsic features. Going back to our running example, we might wonder whether a given article with the content describing hot summer days can be trusted or not. More precisely, only if the newspaper that published the article can be trusted with a sufficiently high probability then we would like to see the article included in the result set.

6.1   Running Example: Accounting for the Uncertainty on Trustworthiness of the Information Providers

Imagine the following scenario. An article from a specific newspaper has been reported as containing information on "hot summer days", so the predicate `q1 == article.text like %hot summer days%` seems to be satisfied. It happened that the user read many articles from that newspaper and was always satisfied with the accuracy of their content. It is intuitively clear that the content from a new article will be accepted by the user. Similarly, the user may use her predominantly negative experiences with the newspaper to conclude that the returned article has to be rejected. Both of these two cases are very extreme in the sense that user *knows* whether to rely on the article content or not; there is little uncertainty here. But the reality is normally somewhere in between.

First, the user may have some positive and some negative experiences with the concerned newspaper. It becomes now unclear whether the predicate is satisfied or not. Second, the user may have never heard about the newspaper, in which case the problem becomes even more severe.

Along the previous discussion, we believe that the problem can be viewed in the following way. Newspapers might be inclined to write in specific ways. For example some may accurately transfer the factual information they collect. Some may exaggerate so that a warm day becomes "very hot." Some may lie deliberately. The readers can behave similarly when reporting on how they view specific newspapers. Their experiences with the newspaper constitute what we call the newspaper's reputation. But any given newspaper has many readers and the notion of reputation normally extends to the entire readers community. The readers can share their opinions, even newspapers can write in favor of some other ones etc. So, technically, a whole graph may emerge that encodes the readers' opinions about newspapers, eventual newspapers' statements about other newspapers, even readers' opinions about other readers are possible, they may say a lot about whether a specific reader is bad-mouthing a newspaper for a reason different than the quality of its articles.

There are many approaches that operate on such structures and try to establish trust of the involved entities. In our example this would mean that they can predict how exactly a given newspaper writes. Three fields, web search, semantic web and P2P systems offer good examples of such approaches. [6] presents a well-known technique to rank web pages based on the web link structure. A page is highly ranked if it has many incoming links and/or if the referring pages are themselves highly ranked. The notion of trust is just implicitly present here, in the relative order of the pages. Thus it is hard to talk about a probability of being trustworthy given a link structure. The same holds for [8], which provide a characterization of a class of algorithms to efficiently compute the relative order of the involved semantic statements. In our previous work [4], we establish the link between reputation and trust in the probabilistic sense. We assume that specific joint probability distributions determine the behavior of all involved entities, in our example readers and newspapers, and derive their associated trust as probability distributions over their possible performances.

As a simple example, let us assume that readers report the trustworthiness of the newspapers they happen to read. Thus any newspaper gets associated with a set $\mathcal{R} = \{r_1, r_2, \ldots, r_n\}$, $r_i \in \{0, 1\}$, with the following meaning: ith $(1 \le i \le n)$ reader claims that the newspaper's trustworthiness is r_i, where 1 stands for "trustworthy" and 0 "untrustworthy." Consider now a reader who wants to make use of this information to decide whether the newspaper can be trusted or not. Having read a number of other newspapers and being able to compare her own opinions about them with those of other readers our reader can assess the probability that the rest of the reader population actually misreports. Let λ denote this quantity. Denoting by θ the unknown probability that the newspaper is trustworthy we can write the probability of receiving the reports $\mathcal{R}$:

$$L(\theta) = [\lambda\theta + (1 - \lambda)(1 - \theta)]^{\sum_{i=1}^{n} r_i}[\lambda(1 - \theta) + \theta(1 - \lambda)]^{n - \sum_{i=1}^{n} r_i}.$$

It is also called the likelihood of the sample set $\mathcal{R}$. Note that it is a function of the unknown probability θ only, all other variables are known. We wonder now what θ maximizes $L(\theta)$ given our sample set. This value, denote it θ^*, is called the maximum likelihood estimate of the unknown probability θ. In this example we assumed that the newspapers can be either trustworthy or not. Refinements that cover more outcomes are also possible.

Therefore, trust for a specific newspaper becomes a random Bernoulli variable, denoted by tr and taking values 0 and 1, derived from directly observable reputation reports $\mathcal{R}$. From the maximum likelihood estimation we have a probabilistic model for $P(tr|\mathcal{R})$. Assuming that only results from trusted resources should be included into the result we can state $P(q_1|d, tr) = P(q1|d)$ if $tr = 1$ and $P(q_1|d, tr) = 0$ otherwise. Thus we get making the usual independence assumption $P(q_1, \mathcal{R}|tr) = P(q_1|tr)P(\mathcal{R}|tr)$

$$P(q_1|d, \mathcal{R}) = \frac{\sum_{tr \in \{0,1\}} P(q_1, \mathcal{R}|d, tr)P(tr)}{P(\mathcal{R})} = P(q_1|d)P(tr = 1|\mathcal{R}).$$

7   Search Under Uncertainty

As illustrated in the previous sections, the example search problem, formulated in a logical framework originally, has a good likelihood to turn into a probabilistic formulation in a distributed setting due to various sources of uncertainty involved in the interpretation of data and user query formulations. Thus, answering the original query, which we formulated as the conjunction of three predicates q_1, q_2, and q_3, results on computing the marginals of a joint probability distribution $P(q, q_1, q_2, q_3, d, c, \mathcal{R}, tr, \mathcal{F}, m, \mathcal{S}, t)$. Finding an answer to the

Fig. 1. A Bayesian Network summarizing the conditional dependencies for our running example

search problem then corresponds to assessing the relevance of the query q when $d, \mathcal{R}, \mathcal{F}, \mathcal{S}$ have been observed. By making independence assumptions on the sources of uncertainty, we can write the joint probability distribution as

$$P(q, q_1, q_2, q_3, d, c, \mathcal{R}, tr, \mathcal{F}, m, \mathcal{S}, t) =$$
$$P(q|q_1, q_2, q_3)P(q_1|c, tr)P(c|d)P(d)P(tr|\mathcal{R})P(\mathcal{R})$$
$$P(q_2|m)P(m|\mathcal{F})P(\mathcal{F})P(q_3|t)P(t|\mathcal{S})P(\mathcal{S})$$

The situation can be summarized in a graphical form, e.g., with the Bayesian Network from Fig. 1 below[1]. For each source of uncertainty, we derive a model from a set of observations. The model is in turn used to derive probabilistic guaranties on the predicates of the query being satisfied or not. In the end, the probability on the query being correctly evaluated for a given document and sets of observations $P(q = true|d, \mathcal{R}, \mathcal{F}, \mathcal{S})$ can be computed as

$$P(q = true|d, \mathcal{R}, \mathcal{F}, \mathcal{S})$$
$$= \sum_{Q_1, Q_2, Q_3} P(q = true|q_1, q_2, q_3, d, \mathcal{R}, \mathcal{F}, \mathcal{S})P(q_1, q_2, q_3|d, \mathcal{R}, \mathcal{F}, \mathcal{S})$$
$$= \sum_{Q_1, Q_2, Q_3} P(q = true|q_1, q_2, q_3)P(q_1|d, \mathcal{R})P(q_2|\mathcal{F})P(q_3|\mathcal{S})$$
$$= P(q_1 = true|d, \mathcal{R})P(q_2 = true|\mathcal{F})P(q_3 = true|\mathcal{S})$$

with $P(q_1|d, \mathcal{R})$, $P(q_2|\mathcal{F})$ and $P(q_3|\mathcal{S})$ derived as above, Q_1, Q_2, Q_3 ranging over $\{true, false\}$ for q_1, q_2, q_3 and $P(q = true|q_1, q_2, q_3) = 1$ if $(q_1 = true) \wedge (q_2 = true) \wedge (q_3 = true)$ and 0 otherwise. These derivations can be efficiently handled using well-known techniques such as Belief Propagation or Message-Passing schemes.

Some of our independence assumptions might however not hold in general: for example, trusting (tr) a source might well influence our model on the correctness on its mappings (m) or vice-versa. Also, detection of correct mappings might depend on sensor data, while considering a specific document might be

---

[1] Note that various Bayesian Networks can be derived from the aforementioned independence assumptions. For a discussion on causality, we refer the interested readers to [7].

dependant on the trustworthiness of its source, etc. Handling complex conditional relationships between various sources of uncertainty and their models is way beyond the scope of this paper, but might play a crucial role in deriving sufficiently precise heuristics in practice.

8   Conclusions

By now it should have become evident that a systematic treatment of uncertainty in the management of distributed, autonomous information sources will become (or already is) a necessity. We see this as a particularly urgent problem for the emerging field of the Semantic Web which aims at supporting semantically rich information representation for allowing more meaningful information processing, both by humans and machines. Interpretation of data is inherently affected with uncertainty.

A first and critical step for enabling management of uncertainty is the development of and agreement on shared abstractions for representing and handling uncertainty. This is similar to the step that has been taken by the Semantic Web community in agreeing on common logical foundations. Description logics with its many variants has been identified as the proper framework for at least the following reasons. On the one hand it captures the essential elements of conceptual data models used in data management and knowledge representation, on the other hand it provides a computationally tractable framework for reasoning.

Similar issues will have to be taken into account in the search for a common abstraction framework for reasoning under uncertainty. It is a well known fact that complete, probabilistic reasoning is as computationally intractable as reasoning in full first order logic is. AI has a long tradition in developing formalism for reasoning under uncertainty, for example with research lines along Bayesian networks or fuzzy logic. Choosing the proper one has to account for issues of computational feasibility as well as for the possibility to bridge the gap between existing approaches for information processing, such as logical reasoning, machine-learning or information retrieval. We foresee in particular the general extension of usual model-theoretic constructs to take into account uncertainty as an important step to improve structured search results in decentralized settings. This has deep consequences, down to Tarski's Truth definition. The question is: can we provide precise semantics to various probabilistic interpretations in decentralized settings while still developing pertinent, down-to-hearth heuristics for combining or deriving data?

Having selected a proper framework of abstraction, a syntactic representation compatible with existing and evolving Semantic Web standards, such as RDF and OWL, has to be found. This appears to be a comparably trivial task at the first glance. However, a challenge might also be hidden here. As we pointed out earlier, current reasoning techniques for handling uncertainty have typically be developed for isolated problems, and probabilistic statements are consolidated only at the very end of processing queries, as illustrated for our example. As soon as correlations among different aspects of uncertainty are considered, quite surprising problems might occur, which appear to be similar in nature to problems that have been addressed in developing Semantic Web languages, such as RDF, and their processing. How can information on correlations of probabilistic variables, respectively probabilistic statements, be represented in a distributed framework? We can view correlations as the equivalent of relationships, whereas probabilistic variables can be considered as the equivalent of entities. In a distributed setting, managing relationships introduces problems of addressing, assigning responsibilities for storage and management and interoperating with existing infrastructures, all of which would also have to be addressed if probabilistic correlations are managed in a distributed setting.

In summary, we believe that we are seeing today only the very first steps towards an information processing infrastructure that truly accounts for the inherent uncertainty in distributed information processing. Substantial research and development will be required, and both challenging theoretical questions and practical problems have to be mastered. The convergence of developments in different fields such as information retrieval, databases and the Semantic Web will be the main drivers for this development. The reward will be better qualified responses to our ever increasing information needs.

References

1. K. Aberer, P. Cudré-Mauroux, and M. Hauswirth. Start making sense: The Chatty Web approach for global semantic agreements. *Journal of Web Semantics*, 1(1), 2003.
2. K. Aberer, P. Cudré-Mauroux, and M. Hauswirth. The Chatty Web: Emergent Semantics Through Gossiping. In *International World Wide Web Conference (WWW)*, 2003.
3. A. Deshpande, C. Guestrin, S. Madden, J. M. Hellerstein, and W. Hong. Model-Driven Data Acquisition in Sensor Networks. In *Very Large DataBases (VLDB)*, pages 588–599, 2004.
4. Z. Despotovic and K. Aberer. A Probabilistic Approach to Predict Peers' Performance in P2P Networks. In *Eighth International Workshop on Cooperative Information Agents, CIA 2004*, Erfurt, Germany, 2004.
5. N. Fuhr. Models in Information Retrieval. In *European Summer School in Information Retrieval (ESSIR)*, 2000.
6. L. Page, S. Brin, R. Motwani, and T. Winograd. The PageRank Citation Ranking: Bringing Order to the Web. Technical report, Stanford University, Stanford, CA, 1998.
7. J. Pearl. *Causality: Models, Reasoning, and Inference*. Cambridge University Press, 2000.
8. M. Richardson, R. Agrawal, and P. Domingos. Trust management for the semantic web. In *Proceedings of the Second International Semantic Web Conference*, pages 351–368, Sanibel Island, FL, 2003.

Semantic Methods for P2P Query Routing

Alexander Löser[1], Steffen Staab[2], and Christoph Tempich[3]

[1] CIS, University of Technology Berlin, Einsteinufer 17, 10587 Berlin, Germany
aloeser@cs.tu-berlin.de
[2] ISWeb, University of Koblenz Landau 56016 Koblenz, Germany
staab@uni-koblenz.de
[3] AIFB, University of Karlsruhe 76128 Karlsruhe, Germany
tempich@aifb.uni-karlsruhe.de

Abstract. Knowledge sharing in a virtual organization requires a knowledge life cycle including knowledge provisioning, terminology alignment, determination of resource location, query routing, and query answering. In this talk we focus on the issue of determining a relevant resource in a completely decentralized setting such as necessitated by peer-to-peer knowledge management in virtual organizations. Requirements for this task include, e.g., full autonomy of peers as well as full control over own resources and therefore preclude prominent resource location and query routing schemes such as distributed hash tables. In order to tackle given requirements we use a resource location and query routing approach that exploits social metaphors of topical experts and experts' experts as well as semantic similarity of queries and information sources. The approach has been fully tested in simulation runs and partially implemented in the system Bibster (http://bibster.semanticweb.org).

1 Introduction

Finding relevant information from a heterogeneous set of information resources is a longstanding problem in computing. In everyday life we observe that there are successful strategies for finding relevant information in a social network of people. Studies of social networks show that the challenge of finding relevant information may be reduced to asking the 'right' people. 'The right people' generally are the ones who either have the desired piece of information and can directly provide the relevant content or the ones who can recommend 'the right people'. Milgram's [11] and Kleinbergs [8] experiments illustrated that people with only local knowledge of the network (i.e. their immediate acquaintances) were quite successful at constructing acquaintance chains of short length, leading to 'small world' networks. In such a network, a query is forwarded along that out going link which takes it 'closest' to the destination. We observe that such mechanisms in social networks work although

- people may not always be available to respond to requests,
- people may shift their interests and attention,
- people may not have exactly the 'right' knowledge, but only knowledge which is *semantically close.*

T. Eymann et al. (Eds.): MATES 2005, LNAI 3550, pp. 15–26, 2005.

I.e., the real-world social network is *highly dynamic* with regard to availability of peers and with regard to expertise about topics and it needs *semantic similarity* in order to determine 'the right person'.

Inspired by these observations and focussed by the requirements of semantic search in the setting of distributed autonomous information sources, we have conceived INGA a novel peer-to-peer algorithm where each peer plays the role of a person in a social network. In INGA , facts are stored and managed locally on each peer constituting the 'topical knowledge' of the peer. A peer responds to a query by providing an answer matching the query or by forwarding the query to what he deems to be the most appropriate peers. For the purpose of determining the most appropriate peers, each peer maintains a *personal semantic shortcut index*. The index is created and maintained in our highly dynamic setting in a lazy manner, i.e. by analyzing the queries that are initiated by users of the peer-to-peer network and that happen to pass through the peer.

The personal semantic shortcut index maintained at each peer reflects that a peer may play the following four different roles for the other peers in the network (in decreasing order of utility):

- The best peers to query are always those that already have answered the query or a semantically similar query in the past successfully. We call such peers *content providers*.
- If no content providers are known, peers are queried that have *issued semantically similar queries* in the past. The assumption is that this peer has been successful in getting matching answers and now we can directly learn from him about suitable content providers. We call such peers *recommenders*.
- If we do not know either of the above we query peers that have established a good social network to other persons over a variety of general domains. Such peers form a *bootstrapping network*.
- If we fail to discover any of the above we fall back to the default layer of neighboring peers. To avoid overfitting to peers already known we occasionally select random peers for a query. We call this the *default network*.

Seen from a local perspective, each peer maintains in its index information about some peers, about what roles these peers play for which topic and how useful they were in the past. Seen from a global perspective, each of the four roles results in a network layer of peers that is independent from the other layers.

Contributions and Paper Organisation. In this paper, we propose an improved shortcut selection strategy able to identify and semantical group peers with similar interests efficiently in a dynamic setting. To our best knowledge, this is the first approach simulating volatile shortcut networks without any static peers. To adapt to the dynamics of the networks and to bound the local index we present an index update policy combining temporal, semantic and community locality. To further boost performance and enhance recall in a dynamic setting we introduce in INGA recommender and bootstrapping overlays. We have built a network simulator and conducted extensive experiments under realistic conditions. Results show that INGA outperforms other state-of-the-art approaches significantly while it displays small world characteristics.

We describe the infrastructure to maintain the index and the semantic similarity function to select peers in section 2. Section 3 shows the index structure and update strategy for each type of shortcut. Section 4 presents our dynamic routing model. Section 5 describes our simulation methodology and the results of our simulations.

2   System Architecture

Our peer selection strategies described in section 3 are implemented independent on top of any unstructured P2P network. For evaluation purposes, though we use the SWAP infrastructure [5]. We recall that it provides all standard peer-to-peer functionality such as information sharing, searching and publishing of resources.

Building Blocks. We assume that each peer provides a unique peer identifer (PID). Similar to file sharing networks each peer may publish all resources from its *local content database*, so other peers can discover them by its requests (this also applies to resources downloaded from other peers). All information is wrapped as RDF statements and stored in an RDF repository [1]. Additionally to local meta data (*MKlusch isOrganizerOf CIA2005*) each resource is assigned a topic *(MATES2005 isTypeOf AgentConference)* and hierarchical information about the topics is stored *(AgentConference subTopicOf Conference)*. The topics a peer stores resources for are subsequently referred to as the peers own topics. Note, that our algorithm does not require a shared topic hierarchy, though it is advantageous for it. For successful queries (own queries or those of other peers), which returned at least one match, the *shortcut management* extracts information about answering and forwarding peers to create, update or remove shortcuts in the *local shortcut index*. Contrary to related approaches, such as DHTs, INGA peers only index 'egoistically', i.e. shortcuts on topics they requested themselves. The *routing logic* selects 'most suitable' peers to forward a query to, for all own queries or queries forwarded from remote peers. The selection depends on the knowledge a peer has already acquired for the specific query and the similarity between the query and locally stored shortcuts.

Query and Result Messages. We use a simple query message model which is similar to the structure of a Gnutella query message. Each query message is a quadruple: $QM(q, b, mp, qid)$ where q is a SERQL query (*cf.* footnote 1). We support any SERQL queries, however for routing purposes only the topic information is used. From a query for all *AgentbConferences* organized by *MKlusch*, only *AgentConference* is utilized for routing. b is the bootstrapping capability of the querying peer to allow the creation of bootstrapping shortcuts, mp the message path for each query message containing the unique PIDs of all peers, which have already received the query, to avoid duplicated query messages, and qid a unique query ID to ensure that a peer does not respond to a query it has already answered. Unique query IDs in INGA are computed by using a random number generator that has sufficiently high probability of generating unique numbers. A result message is a tuple: $RM(r, mp, qid)$ where r represents the answer to the query. We just consider results which exactly match the query. Besides the message path mp is copied to the answer message to allow the creation of recommender

---

[1] http://www.openrdf.org/

and content provider shortcuts. We generate simplified queries such as getdata(s,p,o) with s, p, o being either concrete URIs or (for o only) literals. Furthermore, instead of a general RDFS ontology, we assume that we have topic hierarchies, which exploit the transitivity of RDF(S) *subclassOf*.

Semantic Similarity Function. In case the peers in the network share a common topic hierarchy our routing algorithm uses not only exact index hits, but also exploits the semantic similarity between a query and an indexed shortcut. We define the similarity function $sim : q \times sc \rightarrow [0; 1]$ between a query q and a shortcut sc, which are both given by query terms in the same topic hierarchy, as according to [9] as :

$$sim_{Topic}(q, sc) = \begin{cases} e^{-\alpha l} \cdot \frac{e^{\beta h} - e^{-\beta h}}{e^{\beta h} + e^{-\beta h}} & \text{if } q \neq sc \\ 1 & \text{otherwise} \end{cases} \tag{1}$$

where l is the length of the shortest path between q and sc in the graph spanned by the sub topic relation and h is the minimal level in the topic hierarchy of either q or sc. α and β are parameters scaling the contribution of shortest path length l and depth h, respectively. Based on the benchmark data set given in [9], we chose $\alpha = 0.2$ and $\beta = 0.6$ as optimal values.

3   Building and Maintenance of the Index

Each peer is connected to a set of other peers in the network via uni-directional short-cuts. Hence, each peer can locally select all other peers it wants to be linked to. Following the social metaphors in section 1, we generally distinguish between the following types of shortcuts:

3.1   Content Provider and Recommender Shortcuts

Content Provider Layer. The design of the content provider shortcut overlay departs from existing work as published by [13,14] and exploits the simple, yet powerful principle of interest-based locality. When a peer joins the system, it may not have any information about the interest of other peers. It first attempts to receive answers for its queries by exploiting lower layers of the INGA peer network, e.g. by flooding. The lookup returns a set of peers that store documents for the topic of the query. These peers are potential candidates to be added to the content provider shortcut list. Each time the querying peer receives an answer from a remote peer, content provider shortcuts sc to new remote peers are added to the list in the form: *sc(topic, pid, query hits,'c', update)*, where *topic* is the query terms taken from the query message, *pid* is the unique identifier of the answering peer, *query hits* is the number of returned statements, *'c'* is the type of content provider shortcuts and *update* is the time, when the shortcut was created or the last time, when the shortcut was used successful. Subsequent queries of the local peer or of a remote peer are matched against the topic column of the content provider shortcut list. If a peer cannot find suitable shortcuts in the list, it issues a lookup through lower layers, and repeats the process for adding new shortcuts. For an example consider Figure 1(a). Peer 2 discovers shortcuts for the topic */Education/UML* by flooding the default network with a maximum number of hops (TTL) of three hops and creates two content provider shortcuts to peer 3 and peer 5.

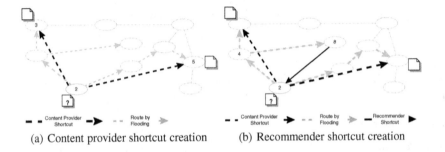

(a) Content provider shortcut creation   (b) Recommender shortcut creation

Fig. 1. Topic specific shortcut creation

Recommender Layer. To foster the learning process of recommender shortcuts, especially for new peers in the network, we consider the incoming queries that are routed through ones peer. A recommender shortcut *sc(topic,pid,query hits maxsim,rp, update)* is created, where *topic* is the set of query terms from the query message. The *PID* for a respective shortcut is extracted from the query message as the PID of the querying peer. Since we will get no information about the number of results retrieved for the query, we set the number of query hits to 1. Finally *r* indicates the type of the shortcut for passive recommender shortcut and *update* is the time, when the shortcut was created or the last time, when the shortcut was used successfully. For an example consider again Figure 1(b). Peer 2 issues the query /Top/Education/UML. Peer 8 creates a shortcut to peer 2 since this query was routed through peer 8.

Content Provider and Recommender Index. We assume that each peer may only store a limited amount of shortcuts, hence only knows a limited set of topic specific neighbors it can route a query to. If the local index size is reached a peer has to decide, which shortcut should be deleted from the index. For each shortcut in the index we compute a rank based on the following types of localities:

Semantic locality. We measure the maximum semantic similarity $maxsim$ between the topic of a shortcut and the topics represented by the local content of a peer according to equation 1. Hence, we retain a shortcut about topic t to a remote peer, if t is close to our own interests.

LRU locality. To adapt to changes in the content and interests we use a LRU replacement policy [1]. Shortcuts that have been used recently receive a higher rank. Each local shortcut is marked with a time stamp when it was created. The time stamp will be updated, if the shortcut will be used successful by the local peer. There is thus an 'oldest' and 'latest' shortcut. The value $update \in [0..1]$ is normalized with difference between the shortcuts time stamp and the 'oldest' time stamp divided by the difference between the 'latest' and the 'oldest'.

Community locality. We measure how close a shortcut leads us to a document. Content provider shortcuts, marked with a c, provide a one hop distance, we set $type = 1$. Recommender shortcuts, marked with a r require at least two hops to reach a peer with relevant documents, we set $type = 0.5$.

We weight the localities and compute the index relevance according to equation 2.

$$relevance = \frac{a * maxsim + b * type + c * update}{a + b + c} \tag{2}$$

Shortcuts with the highest relevance are ranked at the top of the index, while peers with a lower relevance are deleted from the index.

3.2   Bootstrapping Shortcuts

Bootstrapping shortcuts link to peers that have established many shortcuts for different query topics to a lot of remote peers. We determine the bootstrapping capability by analyzing the in-degree and out-degree of a peer. We use the out-degree as a measure of how successful a peer discovers other peers by querying. To weight the out-degree, we measure the amount of distinct sources a peer receives queries from. We use the in-degree as a measure, that such a peer may share prestigious shortcuts with a high availability. By routing a query along bootstrapping shortcuts, we foster the probability to find a matching shortcut for a query and avoid the drawbacks of having to select peers randomly, e.g. by flooding.

Discovery and Update.   Each incoming query that is stored in our index includes the bootstrapping information of the querying peer. While a peer is online it continually updates its content/recommender index based on incoming queries and stores additional bootstrapping shortcuts in the form *sc(pid, bo)*, where *pid* is the PID of the querying peer and *bo* it's bootstrapping capability. Once an initial set of bootstrapping nodes is found, a peer may route its queries to the nodes with the highest *bo* value. One calculates it's *bo* value using equation 3

$$Bo = (1 + |outdegree|) \times (1 + |indegree|) \tag{3}$$

where *out-degree* is the number of distinct remote peers one's knows. To compute an approximation of the *in-degree* without any central server we count the number of distinct peers that send a query via one's peer. To do this from the message path of indexed recommender shortcuts we scrutinize the pen-ultimate peers. The number of distinct pen-ultimate peers denotes one's in degree. To avoid zero values we limited the minimum for both values to one.

3.3   Default Network Shortcuts

When a new peer enters the network, it has not yet stored any specific shortcuts in its index. Default network shortcuts connect each peer p to a set of other peers (p's neighbors) chosen at random, as in typical Gnutella-like networks (e.g. using rendezvous techniques).

4   Dynamic Shortcut Selection

The basic principle of shortcuts consists of dynamically adapting the topology of the P2P network so that the peers that share common interests spontaneously form well-connected semantic communities. To form such semantic communities, for each query

INGA is executed in several steps executed locally and across the network, we already described the steps in [14,10]. The task of the INGA shortcut selection algorithm *Dynamic* is to determine best matching candidates to which a query should be forwarded. We rely on forwarding strategies, depending on the local knowledge for the topic of the query a peer has acquired yet in its index:

- We only forward a query via it's *k best matching* shortcuts.
- We try to select content and recommender shortcuts before selecting bootstrapping and default network shortcuts.
- To avoid overfitting and accommodate a little volatility (especially in the form of new joining peers), queries are also randomly forwarded to some peers.

Algorithm 1. Dynamic

Require: Query q, **int** k, **int** t_{Greedy}
Ensure: $TTL_q < maxTTL$
1: $s \leftarrow TopGreedy(q, Content/RecommenderShortcuts, (k, t_{Greedy}))$
2: **if** $(|s| < k)$ **then**
3:    $s \leftarrow s + TopBoot(BootstrappingShortcuts, (k - |s|))$
4: **end if**
5: $s \leftarrow RandomFill(s, defaultNetworkShortcuts, f, k)$
6: **Return** s.

In step 1 of algorithm *Dynamic* we select k peers from content or recommender shortcuts in subroutine that match the topic of the query with the highest similarity. To avoid forwarding queries along shortcuts with only low similarity we introduce a minimum similarity threshold t_{greedy}. Subroutine *TopGreedy* browses trough the index of all content or recommender shortcuts and identifies the most similar matching shortcuts for a query above t_{greedy}. If two shortcuts have the same similarity, we choose the shortcut with the higher query hits value. The subroutine carefully selects the top-k peers for a query by avoiding different shortcuts with overlapping peers step. If found less then k shortcuts we select the top bootstrapping shortcuts (step 3) in subroutine *TopBoot*. It works similar to *TopGreedy*, but selects the peers with highest bootstrapping capability from the index. It also avoids overlapping peers within the set of selected shortcuts. Finally, in subroutine *RandomFill* we fill the up remaining shortcuts randomly from the default network and return the set of selected shortcuts. The algorithms task is twofold: if the other subroutines fail to discover k peers for a query, it fills up remaining peers until k is reached. The second task of the algorithm is to contribute some randomly chosen peers to the selected set of k peers to avoid overfitting of the selection process as known from simulated annealing techniques. The *Dynamic* algorithm terminates if the query has reached its maximum number of hops.

5   Experimental Evaluation

Open Directory (DMOZ) as Real World Data Set. We base our simulation framework on a data set of the open directory *DMOZ.org*, since it consists of realistic data about the content distribution among persons within a large community. For the topic distribution we select the 1657 topics in the first three levels of the DMOZ hierarchy that have one or more editors assigned to them. We represent one editor by one peer and assume that peers that are interests in a topic also store resources for this topic. We observed that editors are distributed with a heavily tailored Zipf popularity over the topics: 755 topics have 1 editor; 333 have 2 ; 204 have 3 ; . . . ; 44 have 6; . . . ;14 have 10 ; 1 topic has 32 editors. Furthermore some editors are interested in more then one topic. Again we observed a heavily tailored Zipf distribution: 991 editors only have one topic; 295 two; 128 three ; ... one editor 20 and one editor has 22 topics.

Query Distribution. Queries are generated in the experiments by instantiating the blueprint $(*; isTypeOf; topic)$, with topics arbitrarily chosen from the set of topics that had at least one document. We generated 30000 queries, uniformly distributed over the 1657 different topics. We choose a uniform query distribution instead of a ZIPF-distribution, which is typically observed in file sharing networks [12]. This simulates the worst case scenario, where we do not take advantage of often repeated queries for popular topics.

Gnutella Style Network. The simulation is initialized with a network topology which resembles the small world properties of file sharing networks[2]. We simulated 1024 peers. In the simulation, peers were chosen randomly and they were given a randomly selected query to question the remote peers in the network. The peers decide on the basis of their local short cut which remote peers to send the query to. Each peer uses INGA to select up to $pmax = 2$ peers to send the query to. Each query was forwarded until the maximal number of hops $hmax = 6$ was reached.

Volatile Network and Interest Shifts. We implemented the dynamic network model observed for Gnutella networks of [12]: 60% of the peers have a availability of less then 20%, while 20% of the peers are available between 20 and 60% and 20 % are available more then 60%. Hence only a small fraction of peers is available more than half of the simulation time, while the majority of the peers is only online a fraction of the simulation time. Users' interest may change over time, e.g. to account for different search goals. To simulate changing interests, after 15 queries, equal to ca. 15.000 queries over all peers, each peer queries a complete different set of topics.

Evaluation Measures. We measure the search efficiency using the following metrics:

- **Recall** is a standard measure in information retrieval. In our setting, it describes the proportion between all relevant documents in peer network and the retrieved ones.
- **Messages** represent the required search costs per query that can be used to indirectly justify the system scalability.
- **Clustering coefficient** represents the compactness of the network. It captures how many of a node's neighbors are connected to each other. We define the clustering coefficient as

$$C = \frac{1}{|V|} \sum_{v \in V} \frac{|E(\Gamma_v)|}{k_v * (k_v - 1)} \qquad (4)$$

---

[2] We used the Colt library http://nicewww.cern.ch/~hoschek/colt/

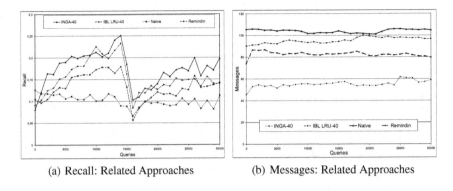

(a) Recall: Related Approaches   (b) Messages: Related Approaches

Fig. 2. Comparison Recall and Message: Dynamic Network 1024 Peers, 6 Hops, k=2

where V denotes the set of peers in the network, k_v denotes the maximum number of shortcuts for a peer v, Γ_v the direct neighbors of a peer and $E(\Gamma_v)$ represents a function that counts the number of links in Γ_v.

- **Average path length** A short average path length denotes a highly directed information flow between two peers in the network. Given two arbitrary selected peers $v_1, v_2 \in V$ and $d_{min}(v_1, v_2)$ the minimum path length between v_1 and v_2, we define the average path length as

$$d = \frac{1}{\binom{|V|}{2}} \sum_{v_1 \neq v_2} d_{min}(v_1, v_2) \tag{5}$$

INGA outperforms in terms of Messages. As a baseline we compare INGA against the strategy of [13](IBL), REMINDIN [14] (all with an index size of 40 entries) and of Gnutella (Naive). Figure 2(a) shows the recall in contrast to the maximum possible recall in a dynamic network. After only 15 queries INGA nearly doubles the recall of the naive approach and drastically outperforms *IBL*. Since INGA and REMINDIN use similar strategies for creating shortcuts both achieve a similar recall. However, after introducing new topics in the network, INGA 's outperforms REMINDIN due to it's optimized index for a dynamic network. Figure 2(b) shows the number of messages. Due to bootstrapping peers, that focus queries to a fraction of peers in the network, INGA outperforms and halves the messages in contrast to a naive approach. In contrast to REMINDIN INGA reduces the number of messages from about 85 to 58 messages.

Tradeoff Between Clustering and Recall. Small-world graphs are defined by comparison with random graphs with the same number of nodes and edges: first, a small-world displays a small average path length, similar to a random graph; second, a small-world has a significantly larger clustering coefficient than a random graph of the same size [6]. To measure the small world characteristics for different index settings we conducted experiments where we only consider the similarity locality (a = 10, b = 0, c = 0), only community locality (with a = 0, b = 10, c = 0), only LRU-locality (a = 0, b = 0, c = 10) and an 'optimal' combination (a = 3, b = 6, c = 1). We discover that the

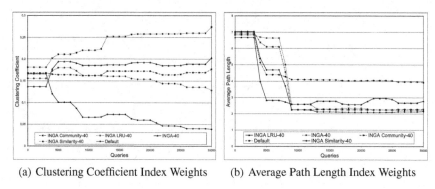

(a) Clustering Coefficient Index Weights   (b) Average Path Length Index Weights

Fig. 3. Index Behavior: Dynamic Network 1024 Peers, 6 Hops, k=2

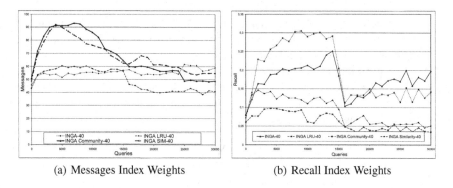

(a) Messages Index Weights   (b) Recall Index Weights

Fig. 4. Index Behavior: Dynamic Network 1024 Peers, 6 Hops, k=2

INGA data-sharing graph displays small-world properties. Figure 3(b) shows, that all index settings reduce the average path length in contrast to the default network. Due to the peer dynamics the default network selects the most stable peers with a path length of four hops while all index settings reduce the path length to 2 hops. However, *INGA LRU-40* stabilizes less than the other approaches. The clustering coefficient increases for most of our index configurations. Only *INGA LRU-40* decreases after a slight increase the clustering coefficient. Hence a LRU strategy alone is not able to create a highly clustered network. However, a high clustering coefficient does not correlate with a high recall: Figure 3(a) shows that the high clustering coefficient of *INGA SIM-40* outperforms while Figure 4(b) shows that the highest recall is achieved through the optimal setting *INGA 40*. Since clustering in the network focusses queries to a small set of peers storing similar shortcuts it reduces the number of randomly discovered peers as well. However, such randomness is crucial in a highly dynamic setting to achieve a high document recall. We therefore recommend the *INGA SIM-40* setting especially for expert finder applications, that use a more static setting and that are optimized towards knowing the right peers in contrast to a high document recall. For applications that prefer a high document recall, we recommend the setting of *INGA 40*.

6   Related Work

First approaches for efficient indexing in P2P architectures were central indices, that have to transmit either meta data about the available content to central indexing peers, like e.g. GlOSS [4] or *Napster*. One of today's main technique for indexing P2P systems are so-called distributed hash tables (DHTs)(see [2] for a survey) that without need of a central index allow to route queries with certain keys to particular peers containing the desired data. While the visualization of keys and objects in the same name space used in structured overlays provides a elegant clean solution to routing within logarithmical bounds it comes at the significant cost of destroying the locality of the content: Content at a user's desktop is co-located with other relevant items, structured overlays destroy this locality meaning that enhanced opportunities for browsing and pre-fetching are lost [7]. Unstructured networks, such as Gnutella, keep this locality, since a query is forwarded to randomly picked neighbors. To bound the number of hops it can travel, each query is tagged with a maximum number of hops (TTL). In addition Gnutella employs a duplicate detection mechanism, so that peers do not forward queries that they have already previously forwarded. To improve the efficiency of Gnutella routing indices local index information are first introduced by [3]. This indexing strategy locally stores information about specific queries and what peers were successfully queried in the past. [13] first considers the semantics of the query to exploit interest-based locality in a static network. They use shortcuts that are generated after each successful query and are used to further requests, hence they are comparable to content provider shortcuts. However their search strategy differs from ours, since they only follow a shortcut if it exact matches a query, else they use a flooding approach. To update the index they use a LRU strategy. REMINDIN [14] used a routing table storing content provider shortcuts and a relaxation based routing strategy. The approach was only designed for a static setting without any index size limitation, an assumptions that is not realistic.

7   Summary and Outlook

The novel design principle of our approach lies in the dynamic adaptation of the network topology, driven by the history of successful or semantically similar queries. This is memorized by using bounded local shortcut indexes storing semantically labelled shortcuts and a dynamic shortcut selection strategy, which forwards queries to a community of peers that are likely to best answer queries. Shortcuts connect peers that share similar interests and thus spontaneously form semantic communities that show typical small world characteristics, e.g. a high clustering coefficient and a low average path length. The clustering of peers within semantical communities drastically improves the overall performance of our algorithm even in a highly volatile setting. In extensive simulations with different index strategies we have shown an trade-off between recall and clustering: Especially in volatile networks leads 'over clustering' to a local optimum which reduces the recall for query. We hope that our findings will find their way into future semantic query routing applications and will help them gaining the ability to deliver high quality search results efficiently.

Acknowledgement. Research reported in this paper has been partially financed by EU in the IST project SEKT (IST-2003-506826). Alexander Löser was generously funded by the German Research Society, Berlin-Brandenburg School in Distributed Information Systems (DFG grant GRK 316/3).

References

1. A. V. Aho, P. J. Denning, and J. D. Ullman. Principles of optimal page replacement. *J. ACM*, 18(1):80–93, 1971.
2. S. Androutsellis-Theotokis and D. Spinellis. A survey of peer-to-peer content distribution technologies. *ACM Comput. Surv.*, 36(4):335–371, 2004.
3. A. Crespo and H. Garcia-Molina. Routing indices for peer-to-peer systems. In *International Conference on Distributed Computing Systems*, july 2002.
4. L. Gravano and H. García-Molina. Generalizing GlOSS to vector-space databases and broker hierarchies. In *International Conference on Very Large Databases, VLDB*, pages 78–89, 1995.
5. P. Haase et al. Bibster - a semantics-based bibliographic peer-to-peer system. In *Proc. of the 3rd International Semantic Web Conference, Japan*. Springer, 2004.
6. A. Iamnitchi, M. Ripeanu, and I. Foster. Small-World File-Sharing Communities. In *23th. IEEE InfoCom HongKong*, 2004.
7. P. J. Keleher, B. Bhattacharjee, and B. D. Silaghi. Are virtualized overlay networks too much of a good thing? In *IPTPS '01: Revised Papers from the First International Workshop on Peer-to-Peer Systems*, pages 225–231. Springer-Verlag, 2002.
8. J. Kleinberg. Navigation in a small world. *Nature*, 406, 2000.
9. Y. Li, Z. Bandar, and D. McLean. An Approach for messuring semantic similarity between words using semantic multiple information sources. In *IEEE Transactions on Knowledge and Data Engineering*, volume 15, 2003.
10. A. Löser, C. Tempich, B. Quilitz, W.-T. Balke, S. Staab, and W. Nejdl. Searching dynamic communities with personal indexes. Technical report, University of Karlsruhe, Institute AIFB, 2005.
11. S. Milgram. The small world problem. *Psychology Today*, 67(1), 1967.
12. S. Saroiu, P. K. Gummadi, and S. D. Gribble. A measurement study of peer-to-peer file sharing systems. *Multimedia Systems*, 9(2), 2003.
13. K. Sripanidkulchai, B. Maggs, and H. Zhang. Efficient Content Location Using Interest Based Locality in Peer-to-Peer System. In *Infocom*. IEEE, 2003.
14. C. Tempich, S. Staab, and A. Wranik. REMINDIN:Semantic Query Routing in Peer-to-Peer Networks based on Social Metaphors. In *Proceedings of the 13th WWW Conference New York*. ACM, 2004.

Programming Cognitive Agents
(Invited Talk)

John-Jules Ch. Meyer

Institute of Information and Computing Sciences,
Utrecht University, The Netherlands

1   Introduction

Although there is a lot of theory around about cognitive agents since the seminal
work by researchers such as Bratman, Cohen & Levesque and Rao & Georgeff
practice of programming 'truly' cognitive agents is still in its infancy. Of course,
several architectures have been proposed and even occasionally been implemented, and there is a prospect of many potential applications of agent-based
systems, but is there a truly systematic way of programming agents with cognitive / mental attitudes such beliefs, desires, intentions, goals, plans, commitments, emotions...? We believe that for this dedicated agent-oriented languages
are needed. A number of these have been developed in the last decade or so. But
programming in them is still hard. Is there a methodology for agent-oriented
programming? Can one structure agent programs better making use of cognitive
notions? And how to verify that an agent program is correct? And how is this
combined with programming *multi*-agent systems and agent societies where coordination of these autonomous agents and more generally social notions such
as norms seem most important? In this paper a number of the issues related
to programming cognitive (multi) agents will be discussed on the basis of work
done in Utrecht around the agent language 3APL.

2   The Philosophical Origins of Cognitive Agents

Although already in older literature, e.g. on philosophical logic, the term 'agent'
is employed, I consider as the start of the present agent-oriented paradigm the
seminal work of the philosopher Michael Bratman [7] who gives a treatment of
the behaviour of a rational (human) agent in terms of mental/cognitive notions
such as beliefs, desires and intentions (BDI). Since then he himself [8] and others
have tried to get a more precise understanding of cognitive notions, either by
trying to formalise these in some logical framework [10,37,26,46] or by devising
architectures for intelligent agents [37,32].

3   Agent-Oriented Software Engineering

Although there is not complete agreement how, it is generally recognised that
by their very nature the design of programs using agents requires new software

T. Eymann et al. (Eds.): MATES 2005, LNAI 3550, pp. 27–34, 2005.

engineering methods, techniques and tools ([47,3]). Some say that we *do* need agent-related concepts (such as BDI) in the analysis and design phase of an agent system [48] but for the implementation we can just use generic high-level programming languages such as JAVA without any in-built agent facilities. To the other extreme, and we are in this camp, some say that it only makes sense to analyse and design in an agent-oriented way if also the implementation is realised using agent concepts ([12], and to a certain extent also [9]).

3.1   Agent-Oriented Programming

In his pioneering paper [44] Shoham introduced the first agent-oriented language in which agent concepts such as beliefs, commitments and commitment rules were employed. Since then there have been proposed a number of programming languages that may be called agent-oriented since they have some typical agent-like features. These include (Concurrent) METATEM [20], Congolog [22] and AgentSpeak(L) [36]. At the moment there are quite a number of agent-oriented languages such as Jason (an interpreter for AgentSpeak), JACK, Jade, Jadex [5], the latter three based on JAVA, and our own 3APL [25]. It is my impression that at present among researchers in the field it is not yet completely clear to what extent these languages must be based on mainstream ones like JAVA and which agent concepts are really adequate or needed for 'true' agent programming. For instance, in the logical frameworks mentioned above one mostly has some notion of declarative goal while in most agent programming languages - if they *have* goals - goals are mostly procedural. We have tried to remedy this situation in 3APL [13] by including both declarative and procedural goals. By doing this it becomes really possible to program agents such that if they have certain declarative goals they may adopt plans for these to achieve them and while executing these plans they may find reasons to revise them. We feel this is truly how an agent should behave.

3.2   Programming Agent Societies: How to Socialise Agents

Of course, for programming multi-agents of agent societies we need more. We need communication between agents, but, more importantly, we need to co-ordinate more or less autonomous agents! For this we can for a part draw on theory and techniques from concurrency and distributed computing, and process algebra in particular. For instance, we can adopt and adapt several communication / synchronisation mechanisms from Communicating Sequential Processes (CSP) and Concurrent Constraint Programming (CCP) to describe agent communication and co-ordination, and employ Structural Operational Semantics (SOS) to specify this in a formal way, as we have done recently in [4].

Another problem related with agent communication, particularly within heterogeneous agent societies, concerns the language (ontology) agents use to reason about their beliefs and communicate with each other. Of course, if agents stem from different sources (designers) and have different tasks they will generally employ different and distinct ontologies (concepts and their representations) for performing their tasks. When communicating it is generally not efficacious to try to transmit their whole ontologies to each other or to translate everything into one giant 'universal' ontology if this would exist anyway. Rather we believe it desirable that agents in their mutual conversation will build a mutual communication vocabulary or ontology which is sufficiently expressive for its purpose but that is as small as possible. In a series of papers [15,16,17] we have tried to come up with such an approach, which we will put to the test in a project on personalised newspaper agents together with IBM.

But there is more: also true social notions such as roles, norms and other deontic concepts come into play here. Typically, when devising an agent society/MAS, we need to specify what the overall goals/task for the MAS is and which norms are to obeyed by the agents in it, typically depending on their role in the system. To be more precise, for developing agent societies the OperA model [18] has been developed consisting of three layers (submodels), viz. the organisational model, the social model, and the interaction model. The idea here is to start out from the organisation of a MAS to be developed by specifying the communication, normative and social structure, and in particular the roles, and the goals and norms associated with these, that should be present in the MAS; then in the social model go on to the specification of the (behaviour of the role enacting) agents that inhabit the MAS, and finally specify exactly what kind of interactions the agents in the MAS are supposed to have with each other, taking into account the roles they play in the system. Furthermore, since in open systems agents may come and go, it is crucial to consider the dynamics of role playing agents. To this end we have looked at the dynamics of roles enacted by agents in MASs [14].

A further interesting notion is that of an *(e-)institution* which is supposed to govern/monitor/enforce such norms on the agents in the MAS [19]. Interesting questions are then how to relate norms with protocols used by the institution, in particular whether following the protocols given provably avoids violation of the norms (cf. [1]. In contrast to what is typically the case when one verifies programs with respect to formal specifications, one here encounters additional interesting but difficult problems of matching rather abstract and perhaps even deliberately vague norms with very concrete actions appearing in the protocols (cf. [24]).

3.3   Semantics, Specification and Verification of Agent Programs

When devising new agent languages with new cognition-inspired notions it is very important to know what these mean exactly. This means that we deem it very important that an agent-oriented language has a formal semantics, either in a denotational or an operational way [2]. A formal semantics not only guides an unambiguous implementation but also renders the possibility to specify and verify programs written in the language in a formal way. Unfortunately, this idea is not yet universally recognised. The first language, Agent0, but also recent languages such as JACK, Jade, and Jadex lack such a semantics. On the other hand, one also see that for languages such as AgentSpeak / Jason and 3APL there are formal semantics. (We ourselves have given a formal semantics of 3APL right from its inception [25], and when devising new constructs for the languages such as declarative goals we always give an operational or denotational semantics to these [13,14,40,43,41,42]). Having established such a semantics one can go further and try and think how the correctness of programs in such a language might be established. To some extent one can re-use old techniques from program correntness such as temporal logic and Hoare's logic, but it is also obvious that these need to be adapted and extended to cater for the new BDI-like constructs available in these languages. For example, in [39] we have looked at the use of dynamic logic for a trimmed-down version of 3APL in order to reason about plan revision in its purest form, which may be viewed as a context-sensitive (and therefore much more complicated!) form of (context-free) recursion. But, although this is a nice theoretical result, there is a lot more to do before this can be used in practice.

4   Getting Even More Cognitive: Beyond BDI?

One might wonder if using BDI-like notions in agent programming is the ultimate use of cognitive-scientific notions. Does it make sense to incorporate even more, such as emotions? Admittedly, at first sight this seems to be ridiculous. Even if it were possible to formalise and implement emotions into agent, what would be the purpose of this? To make agents cry and be unhappy? That would perhaps not only be useless but even also unethical...! However, recent literature points into a direction where emotions or rather emotional states might be very useful for designing agent systems in a still better structured way...

4.1   Emotions in Agent Design

Apart from being an interesting issue for believers in Strong AI, emotions may also serve an engineering purpose. Emotions make sense in describing the behaviour of intelligent agents, and may help structuring the design of agents. From the psychological literature (e.g. [11,33,34]) it is already known that emotions can be viewed as a structuring mechanism. *"Emotional states organize ready repertoires of action"* [33]. This idea as it has been discovered regarding human behaviour may also be directly employed by the designers of artificial agents! First examples of this line of work can be found in [35,45,23]. The general idea is that by distinguishing states that may be called 'emotional' in more or less the same sense as certain states in agents are called mental / BDI-like, one can specify and realise agent behaviour in an even more structured and principled manner than already possible in BDI architectures. For example, it is evident that an agent which in a state of emergency ('panic') has to react to its environment in a different way than when it is in a non-panic state. Also basic emotions such as happiness, sadness, anger and fear have an influence on the agent's way of acting ([33,21,31]). In agent terms this means that the agent's deliberation cycle should take the emotional state into account when selecting plans and goals. Another way to view this is that emotions are complementary to 'rational' attitudes such as BDI (cf. [11]). Emotions may help the agent to choose from the myriad of possibilities. *"Emotions are heuristics"* ([33]). At the moment we are investigating how these ideas can be deployed in the setting of our programming language 3APL [38].

5   The Future of Cognitive Agents

In our opinion the area of cognitive agents will increase further in importance. The reason for this is that in numerous application areas the potential of incorporating 'cognition' or at least cognitive and social notions into systems that are supposed to behave in a more or less intelligent way is recognized by increasingly wider circles. These application areas range from logistic systems like air traffic control to e-business application involving auctions and e-marketplaces, from intelligent service providers on the semantic web, agents playing roles in virtual environments such as games and instruction / training software, multi-agent approaches to grid computing realising high-performance computing for all kinds of computation-intensive applications and intelligent user interfaces realising ambient intelligence in both working and home environments to personal assistants taking the form of true 'companions' helping one with one's professional and leisurely activities. We deem the study of applications extremely important since it is the only way to see whether the great promise of agent technology can really be fulfilled. At the moment we are investigating the use of multi-agent systems in a number of (partly externally funded) projects in areas as diverse as air traffic control [27], multi-expert systems for multi-disciplinary domains (in which multiple expert agents may 'negotiate' their findings [29,30]), mobile phone applications [28], judicial information systems, and we want to extend these to the areas of gaming (with agents as virtual characters) and agent-driven companions for assistance, entertainment and education & training purposes. In [6] Brachman & Lemnios present 'DARPA's New Cognitive Vision', amounting to the expectation that, mainly to overcome flooding of information in the modern information-based society, we need 'cognitive computer systems' that possess cognitive capabilities ('know what they are doing'), can assist humans in an autonomous manner, and 'can respond as robustly to surprise as natural systems can'. The field of multi-agent systems is taken as one of the core technologies, and it is our claim that the matters discussed in this paper should be addressed to make this radiant future possible.

Acknowledgments. I would like to thank my colleagues, former colleagues and students Huib Aldewereld, Robbert-Jan Beun, Frank de Boer, Mehdi Dastani, Jurriaan van Diggelen, Frank Dignum, Virginia Dignum, Rogier van Eijk, Davide Grossi, Koen Hindriks, Wiebe van der Hoek, Joris Hulstijn, Henk-Jan Lebbink, Rick van der Ree, Birna van Riemsdijk, Javier Vázquez-Salceda, Wieke de Vries, and Cilia Witteman for numerous discussions on many of the issues raised in this paper.

References

1. H. Aldewereld, J. Vázquez-Salceda, F. Dignum & J.-J. Ch. Meyer, Verifying Norm Compliancy of Protocols, to appear in Proc. ANI@REM 2005.
2. J.W. de Bakker, *Mathematical Theory of Program Correctness*, Prentice-Hall International, London, 1980.
3. F. Bergenti, M.-P. Gleizes & F. Zambonelli (eds.), Methodologies and Software Engineering for Agent Systems, The Agent-Oriented Software Engineering Handbook, Kluwer, Boston/Dordrecht, 2004.
4. F.S. de Boer, W. de Vries, J.-J. Ch. Meyer, R.M. van Eijk & W. van der Hoek, Process Algebra and Constraint Programming for Modeling Interactions in MAS, to appear in *Applicable Algebra in Engineering, Communication and Computing*, 2005.
5. R.H. Bordini, M. Dastani, J. Dix & A. El Fallah Seghrouchni (eds.), Multi-Agent Programming, Kluwer, Boston/Dordrecht/London, 2005.
6. R. Brachman & Z. Lemnios, DARPA's New Cogitive Systems Vision, http://www.cra.org/CRN/articles/nov02/darpa.html
7. M.E. Bratman, *Intentions, Plans, and Practical Reason*, Harvard University Press, Massachusetts, 1987.
8. M.E. Bratman, D. Israel & M. Pollack, Plans and Resource-Bounded Practical Reasoning, *J. of Computational Intelligence* 4(4), 1988, pp. 349–355.
9. J. Castro, W. Kolp & J. Mylopoulos, Towards Requirements-driven Information Systems Engineering: the TROPOS project, *Information Systems* 27, 2002, pp. 365–389.
10. P.R. Cohen & H.J. Levesque, Intention is Choice with Commitment, *Artificial Intelligence* 42(3), 1990, pp. 213–261.
11. A.R. Damasio, *Descartes' Error: Emotion, Reason, and the Human Brain*, Grosset / Putnam Press, New York, 1994.
12. M. Dastani, J. Hulstijn F. Dignum & J.-J. Ch. Meyer, Issues in Multiagent System Development, in: Proc. 3rd Int. Joint Conf. On Autonomous Agents & Multi Agent Systems (AAMAS 2004) (N.R. Jennings, C. Sierra, L. Sonenberg & M. Tambe, eds.), ACM, New York, 2004, pp. 922-92
13. M. Dastani, M.B. van Riemsdijk, F. Dignum & J.-J. Ch. Meyer, A Programming Language for Cognitive Agents: Goal-Directed 3APL, in: Programming Multi-Agent Systems (Proc. ProMAS 2003) (M. Dastani, J. Dix, & A. El Fallah-Seghrouchni, eds.), LNAI 3067, Springer, Berlin, 2004, pp. 111-130.
14. M. Dastani, M.B. van Riemsdijk, J. Hulstijn, F. Dignum & J.-J. Ch. Meyer, Enacting and Deacting Roles in Agent Programming, in: Agent-Oriented Software Engineering V (AOSE 2004), Revised Selected Papers (J. Odell, P. Giorgini, J.P. Müller, eds.), New York, NY, USA, July 19, 2004, LNCS 3382, Springer, Berlin/Heidelberg, 2005, pp. 189-204.
15. J. van Diggelen, R.J. Beun, F. Dignum, R.M. van Eijk & J.-J. Ch.. Meyer, Optimal Communication Vocabularies and Heterogeneous Ontologies, in: Agent Communication:international Workshop on Agent Communication (AC 2004) (R.M. van Eijk, M.-Ph. Huget & F. Dignum,, eds.), LNAI 3396, Springer, Berlin/Heidelberg, 2005, pp. 76-90.
16. J. van Diggelen, R.J. Beun, F. Dignum, R. van Eijk & J.-J. Ch. Meyer, Communication under Construction: Three Protocols for Lazy Ontology Alignment, accepted for AMKM2005.

17. J. van Diggelen, R.J. Beun, F. Dignum, R. van Eijk & J.-J. Ch. Meyer, Combining Normal Communication with Ontology Allignment, accepted for AC2005.
18. V. Dignum, A Model for Organizational Interaction (Based on Agents, Founded in Logic), Ph.D. Thesis, Utrecht University, Utrecht, 2004.
19. M. Esteva, J. Padget & C. Sierra, Formalizing a Language for Institutions and Norms, in: J.-J. Ch. Meyer & M. Tambe, eds.), *Intelligent Agents VIII*, LNAI 2333, Springer, Berlin, 2001, pp. 348–366.
20. M. Fisher. A Survey of Concurrent METATEM – The language and Its Applications. *Temporal Logic – Proc. of the 1st Int. Conf.* (D.M. Gabbay and H.J. Ohlbach, eds.), LNAI 827, Springer, Berlin, 1994, pp. 480–505.
21. N. Frijda, *The Emotions*, Cambridge University Press, New York, 1987.
22. G. de Giacomo, Y. Lespérance, and H. Levesque. ConGolog, a Concurrent Programming Language Based on the Situation Calculus. *Artificial Intelligence* 121 (1,2), 2000, pp. 109–169.
23. P.J. Gmytrasiewicz & C.L. Lisetti, Emotions and Personality in Agent Design and Modeling, in: *Intelligent Agents VIII* (J.-J. Ch. Meyer & M. Tambe, eds.), LNAI 2333, Spinger, 2002, pp. 21–31.
24. D. Grossi, J.-J. Ch. Meyer & F. Dignum, Modal Logic Investigations in the Semantics of Counts-as, accepted for ICAIL'05, 2005.
25. K.V. Hindriks, F.S. de Boer, W. van der Hoek, and J.-J. Ch. Meyer. Agent Programming in 3APL, *Int. J. of Autonomous Agents and Multi-Agent Systems* 2(4), 1999, pp. 357–401.
26. W. van der Hoek, B. van Linder & J.-J. Ch. Meyer, An Integrated Modal Approach to Rational Agents, in: *Foundations of Rational Agency* (M. Wooldridge & A. Rao, eds.), Applied Logic Series 14, Kluwer, Dordrecht, 1998, pp. 133–168.
27. G. Jonker, J.-J. Ch. Meyer & F. Dignum, A Market Mechanism for Airport Traffic Planning, in: Proc. EUMAS'04 (C. Ghidini, P. Giorgini & W. van der Hoek, eds.), Barcelona, 2004, pp. 365–375
28. F. Koch, J.-J. Ch. Meyer, F. Dignum & I. Rahwan, Programming Deliberative Agents for Mobile Services: The 3APL-M Platform, accepted for ProMAS'05, 2005.
29. H.-J. Lebbink, C. Witteman & J.-J. Ch. Meyer,, A Dialogue Game Approach to Multi- Agent System Programming, in: Proc. 16th Belgium-Netherlands Conf., on Artif. Intell. (BNAIC-2004) (R. Verbrugge, N. Taatgen & L. Schomaker, eds.), Univ. of Groningen, 2004, pp. 251-258.
30. H.-J. Lebbink, C. Witteman & J.-J. Ch. Meyer, A Dialogue Game to Offer an Agreement to Disagree in: Programming Multi-Agent Systems (ProMAS 2004) (R.H. Bordini, M. Dastani, J, Dix & A El Fallah-Seghrouchni, eds.),, LNAI 3346, Springer, Berlin/Heidelberg, 2005, pp. 199-223.
31. J.-J. Ch. Meyer, Reasoning about Emotional Agents, in Proc.16th European Conf. on Artif. Intell. (ECAI 2004) (R. López de Mántaras & L. Saitta, eds.), IOS Press, 2004, pp. 129-133.
32. J.P. Müller. The Design of —Intelligent Agents: A Layered Approach, Springer, Berlin, 1996..
33. K. Oatley & J.M. Jenkins, *Understanding Emotions*, Blackwell Publishing, Malden/Oxford, 1996.
34. A. Ortony, G.L. Clore & A. Collins, *The Cognitive Structure of Emotions*, Cambridge University Press, Cambridge, 1988.
35. R.W. Picard, Does HAL cry digital tears? Emotion and Computers, Chapter 13 of: *HAL's Legacy* (D.G. Stork, ed.), MIT Press, Cambridge MA, 1997.

36. A.S. Rao. AgentSpeak(L): BDI Agents Speak Out in a Logical Computable Language. *Agents Breaking Away* (W. van der Velde and J. Perram, eds.), LNAI 1038, Springer, Berlin, 1996, pp. 42–55.

37. A.S. Rao & M.P. Georgeff, Modeling rational agents within a BDI-architecture, in *Proceedings of the Second International Conference on Principles of Knowledge Representation and Reasoning (KR'91)* (J. Allen, R. Fikes & E. Sandewall, eds.), Morgan Kaufmann, 1991, pp. 473–484.

38. R. van der Ree, Emotions in the Agent Language 3APL (working title), Master's Thesis, Utrecht University, Utrecht, to appear.

39. M.B. van Riemsdijk, F.S. de Boer & J.-J. Ch. Meyer, Dynamic Logic for Plan Revision in Intelligent Agents, in Pre-Proceedings CLIMA V (5th Int. Workshop on Computaional Logic in Multi-Agent Systems) (J. Leite & P. Torroni, eds.), Lisbon, Portugal, September 29-30, 2004, pp. 196-211; to appear in post-proceedings.

40. M.B. van Riemsdijk, M. Dastani, F. Dignum & J.-J. Ch. Meyer, Dynamics of Declarative Goals in Agent Programming, in Proc. DALT 2004 (J. Leite, A. Omicini, P. Torroni & P. Yolum, eds.), AAMAS 2004, New York, 2004, pp. 17-32; to appear in post-proceedings.

41. M. Birna van Riemsdijk, M. Dastani & J.-J. Ch. Meyer, Semantics of Declarative Goals in Agent Programming, accepted for AAMAS'05, 2005.

42. M. Birna van Riemsdijk, M. Dastani & J.-J. Ch. Meyer, Subgoal Semantics in Agent Programming, submitted.

43. M.B. van Riemsdijk, J.-J. Ch. Meyer & F.S. de Boer, Semantics of Plan Revision in Intelligent Agents, in: Ch. Rattray, S. Maharaj & C. Shankland, (eds.), Algebraic Methodology and Software Technology (Proc. AMAST 2004), Stirling, Scotland, LNCS 3116, Springer, Berlin, 2004, pp. 426-442.

44. Y. Shoham. Agent-Oriented Programming. *Artificial Intelligence* 60(1), 1993, pp. 51–92.

45. A. Sloman, 'Damasio, Descartes, Alarms, and Meta-Management', in: *Proc. IEEE Int. Conf. on Systems, Man, and Cybernetics (SMC'98)*, IEEE Computer Society Press, Los Alamitos CA, 1998, pp. 2652–2657.

46. M.J. Wooldridge. *Reasoning about Rational Agents*. MIT Press, Cambridge, MA, 2000.

47. M.J. Wooldridge & P. Ciancarini, Agent-Oriented Software Engineering: The State of the Art, in: P. Ciancarini & M.J. Wooldridge, *Agent-Oriented Software Engineering*, LNCS 1957, Springer, Berlin/Heidelberg, 2001, pp. 1–28.

48. M.J. Wooldridge, N.R. Jennings & D. Kinny, The Gaia Methodology for Agent-Oriented Analysis and Design, *Autonomous Agents and Multi-Agent Systems* 3(3), 2000, pp. 285–312.

Enacting the Distributed Business Workflows Using BPEL4WS on the Multi-agent Platform

Li Guo, Dave Robertson, and Yun-Heh Chen-Burger

CISA, Informatics, The University of Edinburgh, United Kingdom
L.Guo@sms.ed.ac.uk, {dr, Jessicac}@inf.ed.ac.uk

Abstract. This paper describes the development of a distributed multi-agent workflow enactment mechanism using the BPEL4WS[1] specification. It demonstrates that a multi-agent protocol (Lightweight Coordination Calculus (LCC)[8]) can be used to interpret a BPEL4WS specification to enable distributed business workflow[5] using web services[2] composition on the multi-agent platform. The key difference between our system and other existing multi-agent based web services composition systems is that with our approach, a business process model(system requirement) can be adopted directly in the multi-agent system, thus reduce the effort on the validation and verification of the interaction protocol (system specification). This approach also provides us with a lightweight way of re-design of large component based systems.

1 Introduction

Composition of web services has received much interest as a means of supporting Business-To-Business or enterprise application integration. Currently, there are two main approaches for the web services composition: a static workflow technology based approach, for example, BPEL4WS, which is de facto standard for distributed workflow system using web services composition. Using such method, web services are described as activities/atomic activities in a business process model. A workflow engine is used to run the whole business process model, web services thus can be invoked as the business process executes. The basic architecture of such system is shown in figure 1. However,

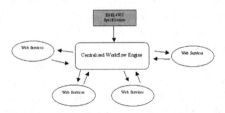

Fig. 1. The infrastructure of conventional workflow based web services composition system

the downside to this approach is that, although the workflow engine can execute these invocations asynchronously (thus generating some degree of parallelism), the process is still centralised, which means it suffers from the single point-of-failure weaknesses

T. Eymann et al. (Eds.): MATES 2005, LNAI 3550, pp. 35–46, 2005.

that plague centralised designs[7] and in some environments, centralisation is not possible, for example, in a peer to peer mobile devices based environment. In addition, the
centralised design may require heavyweight servers. Because all the interactions must
go through the centralised server, if there are huge amounts of transactions taking place
at the same time, the central workflow engine becomes the bottleneck of the whole
system.

An alternative approach is to employ a multi-agent system for web services
coordination[8,10]. With this approach, each agent $\mathcal{A}$ in the multi-agent system is associated with a web service which contains the necessary external behaviours for the
participant (agent). The flow control logic is defined in the multi-agent system protocol which is passed between all the agents together with the messages to tell each
agent what to do next to enable their coordination. The infrastructure of the system is
depicted in figure 2. Although the centralised problem is overcome by using this ap-

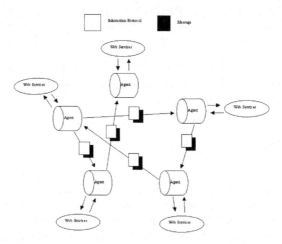

Fig. 2. The infrastructure of MAS based web services composition system

proach, a shortcoming of it is that the interaction protocol (system specification) is at
a very low level of system design. It specifies the message passing that takes place
between different participants at implementation level, mixing both the business and
technical requirements. Therefore, huge effort on the validation and verification is required for the interaction protocol production in order to make sure that the protocol is
strictly consistent with the high level requirements of the business process model.

In this paper, we propose a novel approach, with which a business process model
(BPEL4WS specification) can be used to parameterise a generic multi-agent interaction protocol, thus all the existing BPEL4WS specifications and available tools can
be exploited when we try to enact a distributed business workflow using web services
composition on a multi-agent platform. In section 2, the necessary background introduction to the LCC protocol language and BPEL4WS is given. The infrastructure of our
system is given and explained in section 3. In section 4, we explain in detail how the
agents in the our system coordinate with each other using LCC protocol and BPEL4WS

specification. In section 5, we use a simple example to demonstrate how our approach works. A general discussion on our approach is given in section 6 and in section 7, the conclusion and some possible future work are addressed.

2   Background

2.1   Lightweight Coordination Calculus (LCC)

The Lightweight Coordination Calculus(LCC) is a language for representing coordination between distributed agents. In a multi-agent system the speech acts conveying information between agents are performed only by sending and receiving messages. For example, suppose a dialogue allows an agent a(r1,a1) to send a message m1 to agent a(r2,a2) and agent a(r2,a2) is expected to reply with message m2. Assuming each agent operates sequentially, the sets of possible dialogue sequences we wish to allow for the two agents in the example are as given below, where M1 $\Rightarrow$ A1 denotes a message, M1, send to A1, and M2 $\Leftarrow$ A2 denotes a message, M2, received from A2.

$$a(r1, a1) :: (m1 \Rightarrow a(r2, a2) \, then \, m2 \Leftarrow a(r2, a2))$$
$$a(r2, a2) :: (m1 \Leftarrow a(r1, a1) \, then \, m2 \Rightarrow a(r1, a1))$$

Any agent can change its role according to the definition of the dialogue:

$$a(r1, a1) :: m1 \Rightarrow a(r2, a2) \, then \, a(r3, a1)$$
$$a(r3, ID) :: m2 \Rightarrow a(r4, a3) \, then \, m3 \Leftarrow a(r4, a3)$$

The above clause means that agent a1 takes the role of r1 initially and after sending a message m1 to agent a(r2,a2), it changes its role to r3 and then takes the appropriate behaviours that are defined for a(r3,ID). This capability of LCC is very important for the our work described in this paper.

We refer to this definition of the message passing behavior of the dialogue as the *dialogue framework*. Its complete syntax can be found in [8]. A dialogue framework defines a space of possible dialogues determined by message passing, so the protocols allow constraints to be specified on the circumstances under which messages are sent or received. Two forms of constraints are permitted:

- Constraints under which message, M, is allowed to be sent to agent A. We write M $\Rightarrow$ A $\leftarrow$ C to attach a constraint C to an output message.
- Constraints under which message, M, is allowed to be received to agent A. We write M $\Leftarrow$ A $\leftarrow$ C to attach a constraint C to an input message.

For the earlier example above, to constrain agent a(r1,a1) to send message m1 to agent a(r2,a2) when condition c1 holds in a(r1,a1) we could write: m1 $\Rightarrow$ a(r2,a2) $\leftarrow$ c1.

Agent dialogue may also assume *common knowledge*, either as an inherent part of the dialogue or generated by agents in the course of a dialogue. This knowledge could be expressed in any form, as long as it can be understood by appropriate agents. We recognise the importance of preserving a shared understanding of knowledge between agents but cannot cover this issue in the current paper. As a dialogue protocol is shared among a group of agents it is essential that each agent when presented with a message from that protocol can retrieve the *state* of the dialogue relevant to it and to that message [8].

Pulling all the above elements together, we describe a LCC dialogue protocol as the term:

$$protocol(S, F, K)$$

Where S is the dialogue state; F is the dialogue framework(sets of dialogue clauses); and K is a set of axioms defining common knowledge assumed among the agents.

To enable an distributed workflow agent to confirm a LCC protocol it is necessary to supply it with a way of unpacking any protocol it receives; finding the next moves that it is permitted to take; and updating the state of the protocol to describe the new state of dialogue. There are many ways of doing this but perhaps the most elegant way is by applying rewrite rules (more detailed re-write rules can be found in [8]) to expand the dialogues state. This works as follows[1]:

- An agent receives from some other agents a message with an attached protocol, $\mathcal{P}$, of the form $protocol(S, F, K)$. The message is added to the set of messages currently under consideration by the agent-giving the message set M_i.
- The distributed workagent extracts from $\mathcal{P}$ the dialogue clause, C_i, determining its part of the dialogue.
- Applying the rewrite rules in [8] to give an expression of C_i in terms of protocol $\mathcal{P}$ in response to the set of received messages, M_i, producing: a new dialogue clause C_n; an output message set O_n and remaining unprocess messages M_n (a subset of M_i). These are produced by applying the protocol rewrite rules exhaustively to produce the sequence:

$$\langle C_i \xrightarrow{M_i, M_{i+1}, \mathcal{P}, O_i} C_{i+1}, C_{i+1} \xrightarrow{M_{i+1}, M_{i+2}, \mathcal{P}, O_{i+1}} C_{i+2}, \quad ..., C_{n-1} \xrightarrow{M_{n-1}, M_n, \mathcal{P}, O_n} C_n \rangle$$

- The original clause, C_i, is then replaced in $\mathcal{P}$ by C_n to produce the new protocol, $\mathcal{P}_n$
- The distributed workflow agent can then send the messages in set O_n, each accompanied by a copy of the new protocol $\mathcal{P}_n$.

2.2 Business Process Execution Language for Web Service (BPEL4WS)

The Business Process Execution Language for Web Services (BPEL4WS) is an XML-based language for describing workflow in a distributed environment using web services. With support from IBM and Microsoft, it has become the de facto standard for workflow description. A workflow described in BPEL4WS details the flow of control and any data dependencies among a collection of web services being composed. When enacted, the composition itself becomes available as a meta-web service, eligible for inclusion in other compositions. BPEL4WS requires that all web services be described with available WSDL descriptions. The main BPEL4WS notations are given in figure 3. Due to the industry's increased focus on business process management and acceptance of BPEL4WS, vendors are producing new software tools for workflow design,

---

[1] This part is taken from the paper[8].

The Business Process Execution Language for Web Services (BPEL4WS)

A BPEL4WS workflow description is a structured XML document; as such, a collection of tags defines the BPEL4WS language's vocabulary. Here's a summary of the primary tags and their meanings:

- `<partners>` contains a list of the Web services invoked as part of this workflow;
- `<variables>` contains the variables used in this workflow;
- `<correlationSets>` provides a way to specify precedences and correlations between Web service invocations that cannot be expressed as part of the main workflow;
- `<faultHandlers>` contains exception-handling routines;
- `<compensationHandler>` handles

compensation actions if a transaction rollback occurs; and
- `<eventHandlers>` show how the workflow handles external (asynchronous) events.

Workflow logic is expressed with tags that map to traditional control flow structures:

- `<sequence>` executes the contents in a sequence,
- `<flow>` executes the contents in parallel,
- `<while>` implements a while loop,
- `<switch>` implements a case statement, and
- `<pick>` waits for external event then performs the activity associated with that event.

Within control flow structures, BPEL4WS defines tags that specify what activities to perform. These include the following:

- `<invoke>` invokes a specific Web service,
- `<receive>` receives an invocation message,
- `<reply>` sends a response message, and
- `<assign>` assigns a value, perhaps from a received message, to a variable.

The full BPEL4WS specification describes detailed semantics for the complete set of allowable tags. Additionally, the specification includes an XML Schema for BPEL4WS that can be used to validate syntactic correctness.

Fig. 3. Basic BPEL4WS Syntax[7]

specification, and enactment. An example of one such tool is IBM's BPEL4WS Java Runtime (BPWS4J) platform [6]. Think of the BPWS4J engine as an interpreter for the workflow specification: when the engine receives a workflow description, it enacts the workflow in a centralized manner.

3   A Multi-agent Platform For Distributed Business Workflow Based on BPEL4WS

A BPEL4WS specification contains all the information for running a specified business process model using web services composition, although it was not designed for decentralised multi-agent enactment and, therefore, lacks explicit instructions about how agents should coordinate. Although our multi-agent interaction protocol language (LCC) is more amendable to multi-agent enactment, it requires huge amounts of extra effort in the phases of protocol's verification and validation to ensure that the protocol is strictly consistent with the requirement. As such, the method for performing the BPEL4WS-to-multiagent-enactment is needed. The most straight forward way of doing this is to perform language mapping from BPEL4WS to LCC. Thus, any BPEL4WS specification can be translated to a LCC protocol automatically which is then used by the agents in the multi-agent system. However, an issue that we need to consider is that BPEL4WS is based on the paradigm of imperative programming langauge, while LCC is based on the declarative programming paradigm. Translating a BPEL4WS specification to a LCC protocol is actually the task of translating a imperative programme to a declarative programme, which is not possible in all circumstances.

Therefore, we choose another approach for our work: producing a LCC protocol, which acts as a BPEL4WS interpreter. The BPEL4WS specification and the LCC protocol (BPEL4WS interpreter) are passed together between the agents to enable their coordination. This LCC protocol interpret an BPEL4WS specification so is generic for this style of process model. Based on this idea, a BPEL4WS specification that is defined in any fashion can be interpreted neatly by the LCC protocol when they are passed together in the multi-agent system. The infrastructure of the system based on this approach is given in figure 4. With this infrastructure, the multi-agent interaction protocol, the BPEL4WS specification and the messages are packed and passed together between the agents. Once an agent receives the package, it processes: the incoming message (initiating appropriate behaviors), interaction protocol and BPEL4WS (resolving the next action it needs to take), then it sends out a new package to the next agent to make the coordination continue.

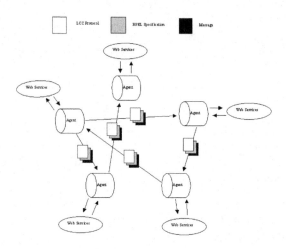

Fig. 4. The infrastructure of our generic MAS platform

4   Agent Coordination Using LCC Protocol and BPEL4WS Specification

4.1   Express BPEL4WS Specification in a Plain String Form

In order to easily interpret the BPEL4WS specification using LCC protocol, we first express the BPEL4WS specification in a plain string form rather than using its original XML syntax directly. For simplicity, only several of the main syntaxes of BPEL4WS model for our work are given below:

$$
\begin{aligned}
Model :=& \{Description, Structure\} \\
Description :=& \ partnerLink \left(\begin{array}{l} name(Constant), parnterLinkType(Constant), \\ myRole(Constant), partnerRole(Constant) \end{array} \right) \\
& |variable(name(Constant), messageType(Constant))|... \\
Structure :=& \ flow([Activity/Structure, Activity/Structure, ...])| \\
& switch([condition(Condition, Activity/Structure), ...])| \\
& while(condition(Condition, Activity/Structure)| \\
& Structure/Activity\ then\ Structure/Activity|...
\end{aligned}
$$

$$Activity := invoke \begin{pmatrix} partnerLink(Constant), portType(Constant), \\ operation(Constant), inputVariable(Constant), \\ outputVariable(Constant), sourceLink(Constant), \\ targetLink(Constant)) \end{pmatrix}$$

$$|receive \begin{pmatrix} partnerLink(Constant), portType(Constant), \\ operation(Constant), variable(Constant), \\ sourceLink(Constant), targetLink(Constant) \end{pmatrix}$$

$$|reply \begin{pmatrix} partnerLink(Constant), portType(Constant), \\ operation(Constant), variable(Constant), \\ sourceLink(Constant), targetLink(Constant) \end{pmatrix}$$

$$|assign \begin{pmatrix} from \begin{pmatrix} expression/opaque/variable(Constant), \\ property(Constant) \end{pmatrix}, \\ to(variable(Constant), property(Constant)), \\ sourceLink(Constant), targetLink(Constant) \end{pmatrix}$$

$$|...$$
$$Condition := Term|Condition \wedge Condition|Condition \vee Condition$$
$$Constant := Term$$

The structure (binary tree) for a BPEL4WS specification that is expressed using the above syntaxes is shown in figure 5.

4.2 Relating the Basic BPEL4WS Activities to LCC Dialogues

The only way for the agents to coordinate with each other in a multi-agent system is through message passing. Therefore, when adopting a BPEL4WS specification in a multi-agent system, the first thing we need to do is to relate the BPEL4WS syntax to message passing. Fortunately, one of the BPEL4WS design principles is to define the interaction (message passing) between two partners through centralised workflow

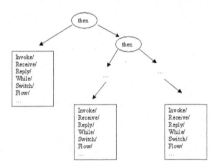

Fig. 5. The structure of the BPEL4WS model in logical form

BPEL4WS Activities	LCC Messages
<receive>	portType: operation: Variable where portType,operation,variable are extracted from the attributes of <receive>
<invoke>	portType: operation: InputVariable then portType: operation: inputVariable: outputVariable
<reply>	Variable

Fig. 6. Translations from BPEL4WS activities to LCC messages

engine. A centralised workflow engine sends and receives messages to/from the participants to enable the interaction by using some basic activities. In our system, each agent acts as a web service proxy. Instead of sending and receiving messages through a centralised server, the messages are taking place directly between participants (agents). Thus, the translation from the BPEL4WS basic activities to LCC dialogues is possible. Space limitations prevent giving the entire translation here, but a segment of it is given below:

4.3   Using LCC Protocol to Interpret the BPEL4WS Specification

In our approach, the LCC protocol is used as an interpreter to tell the agents how to process the BPEL4WS specification attached. The basic idea is: each role defined in the LCC protocol corresponds to a BPEL4WS syntax element. There are five arguments defined for each of the LCC roles:

- $Model$: is a part of BPEL4WS model that is currently processed by the LCC protocol. Because the structure of the BPEL4WS specification is a binary tree, with our approach, the deepest node is always processed first.
- $MList$: stores all the unprocessed parts of a BPEL4WS model and is used to mark the states of the BPEL4WS model's processing. Once a basic BPEL4Ws activity is reached while an agent processes the BPEL4WS model, it starts a new dialogue based on the activity and all of the unprocessed BPEL4WS model stored in $MList$ has to be passed to the next agent.
- $VList$: stores all the concrete values of the variables that are used in workflow enactment. In the centralised environment, all the information about the variables are controlled by the central server, whereas in the distributed environment, all of such information have to be passed around.
- $IDList$: is used to connect a receive activity and its corresponding reply activity.
- $Role$: represents the real participant in the interaction defined in the partnerLink.

The definitions of some of the main LCC roles are given and explained below[2]:

$$a(interpreter(Model, MList, VList, IDList, Role), A_1) ::$$

$$\begin{pmatrix} PortType : Operation : InputVariable \Leftarrow a(invoke(Model, MList, VList, IDList, Role_2), A_2) \\ then \\ \begin{pmatrix} \begin{pmatrix} null \leftarrow Model = ..[\_, partnerLink(\_), portType(\_), operation(\_), inputVariable(\_), \\ \qquad\qquad outputVariable(null), sourceLink(\_), targetLink(\_)] \\ then \\ \begin{pmatrix} null \leftarrow MList = [] \\ or \\ a(interpreter(Head, Rest, VList_1, IDList, Role), A_1) \\ \leftarrow MList = [Head|Rest] \ and \ VList_1 = [InputVariable|VList] \end{pmatrix} \\ or \\ \begin{pmatrix} PortType : Operation : InputVariable : OutputVariable \Rightarrow \\ a(invoke(Model, MList, VList, IDList, Role_2), A_2) \\ \leftarrow Model = ..[\_, partnerLink(\_), portType(\_), operation(\_), inputVariable(\_), \\ \qquad\qquad outputVariable(OutputVariable), sourceLink(\_), targetLink(\_)] \end{pmatrix} \end{pmatrix} \end{pmatrix}$$

$$or\ a(sequence(Model, MList, VList, IDList, Role), A_1) \leftarrow is\_sequence(Model)$$
$$or\ a(flow(Model, MList, VList, IDList, Role), A_1) \leftarrow is_flow(Model)$$
$$or\ a(invoke(Model, MList, VList, IDList, Role), A_1) \leftarrow is\_invoke(Model, Role)$$
$$or\ a(receive(Model, MList, VList, IDList, Role), A_1) \leftarrow is\_receive(Model, Role)$$
$$or\ a(reply(Model, MList, VList, IDList, Role), A_1) \leftarrow is\_reply(Model, Role)$$
$$...$$

---

[2] The full protocol can be found at http://homepages.inf.ed.ac.uk/s0349668/Websites/tools/protocol.inst

$a(interpreter(Model, MList, VList, IDList, Role), ID)$ defined above is used to control the role's changing of the agents. Every agent takes this role first whenever it receives a message associated with the unprocessed BPEL4WS model and then changes to the appropriate role for processing the received BPEL4WS model. Only partial definitions of this role are given here for simplicity.

$$a(sequence(Model, MList, VList, IDList), A_1) ::$$
$$a(interpreter(Model_1, [Model_2|MList], VList, IDList, Role), A_1)$$
$$\leftarrow process\_sequence(Model, Model_1, Model_2)$$

$a(sequence(Model, MList, VList, IDList), A_1)$ corresponds to the BPEL4WS *sequence* activity. Once an agent takes this role, it first gets the first child element $Model_1$ of $Model$, stores the left child elements $Model_2$ in $Mlist$ and then changes its role to $interpreter$ to process $Model_1$. For the other BPEL4WS structure activities, the basic idea is same.

$$a(flow(Model, MList, VList, IDList), A_5) ::$$
$$a(interpreter(Model_1, [NewModel|MList], VList, IDList, Role), A_5)$$
$$\leftarrow process\_flow(Model, Model_1, NewModel)$$

If the role of an agent is $flow$, the agent uses the constraint $process\_flow(Model, Model_1, NewModel)$ to process the BPEL4WS flow activity ($Model$). The function of the constraint is to extract one of the child elements ($Model_1$) of $Model$ and form another flow activity ($NewModel$) using all the left child elements. An assumption we make here is the flow activity has to be processed sequentially in the distributed environment, which is the trade-off of eliminating the centralised server.

$$a(receive(Model, MList, VList, IDList, Role_1), A_1) ::$$
$$VList_2 = [Variable|VList] \text{ and } IDList_1 = [PortType : Operation : Partner : ID|IDList]$$
$$\leftarrow PortType : Operation : Variable \Leftarrow a(Partner, ID)$$
$$then$$
$$\left(\begin{array}{l} \left(\begin{array}{l} a(receive(Model, MList, VList, IDList, Role_1), A_1) \\ \leftarrow \neg check\_receive(Model, PortType, Operation, Variable, Partner) \end{array}\right) \\ or \left(\begin{array}{l} a(interpreter(Head, Rest, VList_2, IDList_1, Role_2), A_1) \\ \leftarrow check\_receive(Model, PortType, Operation, Variable, Partner) \\ and\ MList = [Head|Rest] \end{array}\right) \\ or\ null \leftarrow MList = [] \end{array}\right)$$

When the role of an agent is $receive$, it waits for an incoming message and checks if this message is the appropriate one. A message is a right one if it is sent from the right *partner* of current agent and if it is defined with the right message type. If the message is not what the agent waits for, the agent keeps waiting until it receives the proper one. If the message is the right message, the agent changes its role to $interpreter$ to process the unprocessed BPEL4WS model in $MList$.

$$a(reply(Model, MList, VList, IDList, Role_1), A_1) ::$$
$$Variable1 => a(Partner, ID) \leftarrow \left(\begin{array}{l} process\_reply(Model, Partner, PortType, Operation, Variable) \\ and\ get\_ID(Partner, PortType, Operation, IDList, ID) \\ and\ look\_up(VList, Variable, Variable1) \end{array}\right)$$

An agent sends a message in reply to a message that was received from $a(Partner, ID)$. The $Partner$ and ID is stored in $IDList$ to make sure that the message is sent to the right partner.

$$a(invoke(Model, MList, VList, IDList, Role_1), A_1) ::$$
$$PortType : Operation : InputVariable \Rightarrow a(interpreter(Model, MList, VList, IDList, Role_2), A_2)$$
$$\leftarrow process\_invoke(Model, PortType, Operation, InputVariable, Role_2)$$

$$
\begin{pmatrix}
then \\
\begin{pmatrix}
null \leftarrow Model = ..[\_, partnerLink(\_), portType(\_), operation(\_), inputVariable(\_), \\
\qquad\qquad outputVariable(null), sourceLink(\_), targetLink(\_)] \\
or \\
\begin{pmatrix}
PortType : Operation : InputVariable : OutputVariable \\
\Leftarrow a(interpreter(Model, MList, VList, IDList, Role_2), A_2) \\
then \\
\begin{pmatrix}
null \leftarrow MList = [] \\
or \\
a(interpreter(Head, Rest, VList_3, IDList, Role), A_1) \\
\leftarrow MList = [Head|Rest] \text{ and } VList_1 = [OutputVariable, InputVariable|VList]
\end{pmatrix}
\end{pmatrix}
\end{pmatrix}
\end{pmatrix}
$$

When an agent is of the role *invoke*, it extracts the necessary information: *PortType*, *Operation* and *InputVariable* from the current BPEL4WS invoke activity (*Model*) and sends it out to the next agent that is in the role of *interpreter*) for web service's invocation. If the outputVairable is defined in the current invoke activity, then there will be a response from the message receiver later on. After the sender receives the response, it will changes its role to *interpreter* to continuously process the unprocessed BPEL4WS model.

5   A Simple Case Study

We use a simple example to illustrate how our approach works. The definition for the input BPEL4WS specification is given as follows with all the irrelevant parts ignored:

```
< process name = "loanApprovalProcess" >
  < /variables >
    < variable name = "request" messageType = "CreditInfoMessage"/ >
    < variable name = "approvalInfo" messageType = "approvalMessage"/ >
  < /variables >
  < partnerLinks >
    < partnerLink name = "customer" partnerLinkType = "LinkType" myRole = "approver"/ >
    < partnerLink name = "approver" partnerLinkType = "LinkType" partnerRole = "approver"/ >
  < /partnerLinks >
  < sequence >
    < receive name = "receive" partner = "customer" portType = "approvalPT"
           operation = "approve" variable = "request" >
    < /receive >
    < invoke name = "invokeapprover" partner = "approver" portType = "approvalPT"
           operation = "approve" inputVariable = "request" outputVariable = "approvalInfo" >
    < /invoke >
    < reply name = "reply" partner = "customer" portType = "loanApprovalPT"
           operation = "approve" variable = "approvalInfo" >
    < /reply >
  < /sequence >
< /process >
```

The basic steps for the agents in our system to coordinate using the above BPEL4WS model and LCC protocol are illustrated in figure 7 and are explained below:

- An agent, A_1, receives the BPEL4WS specification, B together with the LCC protocol, P from section 4.2. It takes the role of $a(interpreter(B, [], [], [], \_), A_1)$. It then tries the clauses that are defined in P to find the type of the B by using the constraints $is\_sequence/is\_invoke/...$) to determine the next BPEL4WS operator. For our example, the dominant operator in B is a *sequence* activity. A_1 changes its role to $a(sequence(B, [], [], [], \_), A_1)$.
- A_1 processes B in the role of $a(sequence(B, [], [], [], \_), A_1)$ by using the constraint $process\_sequence(B, B_1, B_2)$ and gets the first element, B_1, of B and the left elements B_2 and then changes its role to $a(interpreter(B_1, [B_2], [], \_), A_1)$ to repeat the first step.

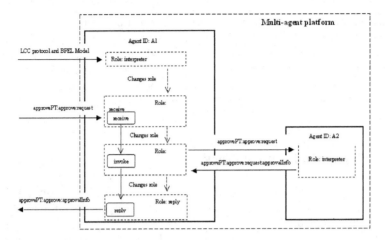

Fig. 7. Agent's coordination for performing the illustrate example

- By repeating the first step, $\mathcal{A}_1$ changes its role to $a(receive(\mathcal{B}_1, [\mathcal{B}_2], [], approver),$ $\mathcal{A}_1)$ and waits for the message $PortType : Operation : request$. Once $\mathcal{A}_1$ receives the message, following the instructions in $\mathcal{P}$, it changes its role to
$a(interpreter(\mathcal{B}_3, [\mathcal{B}_4], [request], [PortType : Operation : Customer : CustomerID], \_), \mathcal{A}_1)$
in which $\mathcal{B}_3$ is the first child element of $\mathcal{B}_2$ and $\mathcal{B}_4$ contains the remaining child elements of $\mathcal{B}_2$.
- By repeating the previous steps, $\mathcal{A}_1$ changes its role to $a(invoke(...), \mathcal{A}_1)$ and sends a appropriate message $\mathcal{M}$ to an agent $\mathcal{A}_2$ together with $\mathcal{P}_1$. $\mathcal{A}_2$ starts processing the $\mathcal{B}_4$ after it receives the $\mathcal{P}_1$ and $\mathcal{M}$. The coordination continues, until the processing of $\mathcal{B}$ is finished.

6 Discussion

Our approach provides an opportunity to build a multi-agent based distributed workflow system starting from a business process model rather than from a interaction protocol, which narrows the gap between the high level requirement and system specification in the development of multi-agent system and connects the business workflow community and multi-agent community. Thus, business users can produce their own business process models that can be used directly in the multi-agent system. Furthermore, since there have been many techniques and tools available for current business process modeling, they can be adopted directly for building the multi-agent system based on our approach.

Notice that the LCC protocol used to interpret BPEL4WS models is independent of any specific message passing infrastructure, although we have described it with respect to a distributed and peer to peer infrastructure, it could equally well be deployed in a more traditional server based style. Different styles of deployment are described in detail in [8]. Furthermore, the protocol can be used prior to deployment in order to predict behaviours and possible errors in interaction[10]. Another advantage is that the workflow engine built using our approach is a real generic server. The only knowledge of it is how to process the LCC protocol and how to invoke the web services but not how to process the particular business process modelling language, which gives us a very efficient and light way for the system re-design and re-implement. Even more general, this approach can be used to adopt any functional requirement, as long as the requirement is operational and can be represented by message passing, on the multi-agent platform.

7   Conclusion and Future Work

In this paper, we have presented a novel technique for constructing distributed business workflows using existing web services composition on a generic multi-agent system platform, which particularly suits the inter-operations among enterprises. By using our approach, a BPEL4WS specification can be used directly for constructing a multi-agent system using web services composition. In such a system, all the real operations are carried by web services that are associated with distributed agents. As mentioned in the discussion section, our approach is not limited to workflow system but can fit any large component based system.

We are currently working on writing the complete LCC protocol for processing the full BPEL4WS syntaxes. We will then be able to test the protocol on a real multi-agent platform to determine various benefits and drawbacks of our approach. After this, the next stage is to solve the business level problem using our approach, such as how to do the transactional control etc.

References

1. *Business Process Execution Lanuage For Web Services specification*, http://www-128.ibm.com/developerworks/library/ws-bpel/.
2. *W3C. Web Services reference*, http://www.w3.org/2002/ws/.
3. *Web Service Definition Language references* http://www.w3.org/TR/wsdl.
4. *MagentA*, http://homepages.inf.ed.ac.uk/cdw/magenta.html.
5. *The Workflow Management Coalition*, http://www.wfmc.org/.
6. *IBM. BPWS4J*, http://www.alphaworks.ibm.com/tech/bpws4j.
7. J.M. Vidal, P. Buhler, and C. Stahl. *Multiagent systems with workflows*. IEEE Internet Computing, 8(1):76-82, January/February 2004.
8. D. Roberston, *A Lightweight Method for Coordination of Agent Oriented Web Services*, Proceedings of AAAI Spring Symposium on Sematic Web Services, 2004.
9. P. A. Buhler, J. M. Vidal, H. Verhagen *Adaptive Workflow = Web Services+Agents*, Proceeding of IEEE International Conference on Web Services 2003.
10. C. D. Walton *Model Checking Multi-Agent Web Services*, Proceeding of AAAI Symposium of Semantic Web Services 2004.
11. P. Buhler and J. M. Vidal. *Enacting BPEL4WS specified workflows with multiagent systems.*In Proceedings of the Workshop on Web Services and Agent-Based Engineering, 2004.

BSCA-P: Privacy Preserving Coalition Formation

Bastian Blankenburg and Matthias Klusch

DFKI - German Research Center for Artificial Intelligence,
Stuhlsatzenhausweg 3, 66123 Saarbrücken, Germany
{blankenb, klusch}@dfki.de

Abstract. In the setting of cooperation of rational web service agents via coalition formation, we devise an algorithm BSCA-P to form recursively bilateral Shapley value stable coalitions. The main focus lies on privacy aspects: we show that the BSCA-P enables the formation of subgame stable and individually rational coalitions while hiding absolute coalition values and payoffs, as well as allowing for anonymous service requests and access.

1 Introduction

Several methods for coalition formation among agents in order to solve task allocation problems have been introduced in the literature (see e.g.[9]). A coalition is defined as a group of agents working together to accomplish complex tasks which cannot (or at a greater cost) be done by single agents. In this context, cooperative game theory provides a well developed and mathematically founded framework to determine which coalitions should be formed and how the respective coalition values should be distributed in an individually rational and stable manner [5] (i.e. no agents has an incentive to break away from its coalition).

In recent years, a number of CF methods which account for different real-world problems have been proposed in the literature. Examples include [2,4] for CF under uncertainty of coalition values, or [11,1] which consider inter-agent trust in CF. The development of privacy preserving CF protocols, however, has not received much attention yet. But it might be unacceptable for an agent that others learn which services are accessed and which utility is achieved. Example applications include health care web service agents, which form coalitions e.g. to automatically handle insurance issues, transportation, hospital and medical personal assignments. But an agent responsible for transportation should probably not need to know which patients are assigned to which doctors. In this paper, we present a protocol which overcomes such privacy issues. More precisely, we present a CF protocol which allows participating agents to

1. hide its (exact) payoff from all but one other agents,
2. hide its individual utility from all other agents,
3. anonymously request and access offered services,

T. Eymann et al. (Eds.): MATES 2005, LNAI 3550, pp. 47–58, 2005.

4. hide the fact that a service from a specific agent has been accessed also from other agents and
5. hide input/output data for services from all agents except the recipient.

The remainder of this paper is organized as follows: in section 2 we introduce our model of web service agents and the coalition game model. In section 3 we show how this model can be exploited to negotiate coalitions while hiding information about coalition values, local worths and payoffs. In section 4 we adopt an anonymous routing protocol to enable anonymous service access and introduce other notions of anonymity. Finally, we propose and discuss the coalition formation protocol BSCA-P in section 5, and conclude in section 6.

2 Coalitions of Web Service Agents

We define a *web service* as any computational process for which all input and output data can be transferred over the internet. If a web service involves the execution of other web services, it is called a *composed web service*. Otherwise, it is called a *primitive web service*. A formal specification of a web service in an appropriate language L is called a *web service description* (L-WSD). Examples for L include WSDL for traditional web services or OWL-S for semantic web services. A message containing an offer to execute a web service ws and an L-WSD of ws is called a *web service advertisement* (L-WSA). A message containing a request for the execution of a web service ws and an L-WSD of ws is called a *web service request* (L-WSR). A comparison of two L-WSDs in order to find out whether an advertised web service and a requested web service match is called a *web service matching* (L-WSM). We then define an *L-web service agent* as an agent which

1. offers any number (including zero) of web services,
2. is able to send L-WSAs for its offered web services,
3. requests any number (including zero) of web services,
4. possesses L-WSDs of its requested web services and
5. is able to perform L-WSMs.

In the following, we consider only sets of web service agents using the same language L, and omit the 'L' in our notation. We also say just 'agent' instead of 'web service agent'. R_a denotes the set of all requests by agent a, and OS_a the set of all offered services by agent a. For simplicity, we assume that each agent only offers primitive web services. The requesting agents might compute compositions of these primitive services. We assume each agent a to have a certain private monetary valuation $w_a(WS)$ for the accomplishment of each service it requests. Finally, the execution of service WS by an agent a has a cost $c_a(WS)$.

We can now model this setting as a *coalition game*. Let $\mathcal{A}$ denote the set of all agents in a given system. We call subsets $C \subseteq \mathcal{A}$ executing services for each other a *coalition*. Let $E_a(C)$ denote the set of all services executed by a, and $R_a(C)$ the set of all services of other members of C which are accessed by a.

Table 1. Offered/requested services in example game

agent a	offers $c_a(.)$		requests $w_a(.)$		agent a	offers $c_a(.)$		requests $w_a(.)$	
a_1	ws_1	1	ws_2	2	a_2	ws_2	1	ws_4	2
	ws_3	2	ws_3	3	a_3	ws_4	1	ws_1	3

Then, a's immediate monetary result (that is, without side-payments) of being a member of C, which we call *local worth* of a in C, is determined by

$$lw_a(C) := \sum_{WS \in R_a(C)} w_a(WS) - \sum_{WS \in E_a(C)} c_a(WS) \qquad (1)$$

Thus, we can define an overall value

$$v(C) := \sum_{a \in C} lw_a(C) \qquad (2)$$

of C, which we call C's *coalition value*. The pair $(\mathcal{A}, v)$ then defines the coalition game. In cooperative game theory, coalitions may not overlap. A *configuration* $(\mathcal{S}, u)$ for a game $(\mathcal{A}, v)$ specifies a *payoff distribution* $u : A \mapsto \mathbb{R}$ for a *coalition structure* $\mathcal{S}$, a partition of A. $u(a), a \in A$ denotes the *payoff* for agent a. u is called *individually rational* iff $\forall a \in A : u(a) \geq v(a)$ and *efficient* iff $\forall C \in \mathcal{S} : \sum_{a \in C} u(a) = v(C)$. We also write $\forall C \subseteq \mathcal{A} : u(C) := \sum_{a_i \in C} u_i$.

In order to implement a payoff distribution u, each agent generally will have to make/receive side-payments. Keeping in mind the local worths we define the total amount of side-payment that a has to receive from other agents in C as

$$sp_u(a, C) := u(a) - lw_a(C) \qquad (3)$$

Of course, $sp_u(a, C)$ can be negative, meaning that a has to make a side-payment of $|sp_u(a, C)|$ to other agents in C. We also write for $C^* \subseteq C$:

$$sp_u(C^*, C) := \sum_{a \in C^*} sp_u(a, C) \qquad (4)$$

If $C^* = C$, we just write $sp_u(C)$.

Corollary 1. *Let $C \in \mathcal{S}$. Then $sp_u(C) = 0$ if an only if u is efficient wrt. $\mathcal{S}$.*

Example 1. Consider a game of three agents: $\mathcal{A} = \{a_1, a_2, a_3\}$. They offer and request services according to table 1. Considering coalition $C_1 = \{a_1, a_2\}$, we have $lw_{a_1}(C_1) = w_{a_1}(ws_2) + w_{a_1}(ws_3) - c_{a_1}(ws_3) = 3$, $lw_{a_2}(C_1) = -c_{a_2}(ws_2) = -1$ and $v(C_1) = 2$.

A solution to a game is given by an individually rational and efficient configuration which satisfies a chosen *stability concept*. Unfortunately, the classical stability concepts are of high computational complexity, i.e. at least exponential. However, we consider only the case where coalitions are built up by a bilateral merging process. We thus utilize a simplified version of the Shapley value[8], the *(recursive) bilateral* Shapley value:

The union C of two disjoint coalitions $C_1, C_2 \subset \mathcal{A} \setminus \emptyset$ is called a *bilateral coalition*. C_1 and C_2 are called subcoalitions of C. A bilateral coalition C is called *recursively bilateral* iff it is the root node of a binary tree denoted T_C for which (a) every non-leaf node is a bilateral coalition and its subcoalitions are its children and (b) every leaf node is a single-agent coalition. We denote the depth of a node C^* in T_C by $d(C^*, T_C)$, i.e.

$$d(C^*, T_C) = \begin{cases} d(C^*, T_C) = 0 & \text{if } C^* = C \\ d(C^*, T_C) = d(C^{**}, T_C) + 1 \text{ otherwise, with } C^{**} \in T_C, C^* \subset C^{**} \end{cases}$$

A coalition structure $\mathcal{S}$ for $(\mathcal{A}, v)$ is called *(recursively) bilateral* if $\forall C \in \mathcal{S}$: C is (recursively) bilateral or $C = a, a \in \mathcal{A}$. The *bilateral Shapley value* $\sigma_b(C, C_i, v), C_i, i \in \{1, 2\}$ in the bilateral coalition C is defined as the Shapley value of C_i in the game $(\{C_1, C_2\}, v)$:

$$\sigma_b(C_i, C, v) = \frac{1}{2}v(C_i) + \frac{1}{2}(v(C) - v(C_k)) \tag{5}$$

with $k \in \{1, 2\}, k \neq i$.

Given a recursively bilateral coalition structure $\mathcal{S}$ for a game $(\mathcal{A}, v)$, a payoff distribution u is called *recursively bilateral Shapley value stable* iff for each $C \in \mathcal{S}$, every non-leaf node C^* in $T_C : u(C_i^*) = \sigma_b(C_i^*, C^*, v_{C^*}), i \in 1, 2$ with $\forall C^{**} \subseteq \mathcal{A}$:

$$v_{C^*}(C^{**}) = \begin{cases} \sigma_b(C_k^p, C^p, v_{C^p}) \text{ if } C^p \in T_C, C^* = C^{**} = C_k^p, \\ \qquad k \in 1, 2 \\ v(C^{**}) \qquad \text{otherwise} \end{cases} \tag{6}$$

In other words, for a merge of two recursively bilateral coalitions, the coalition value is distributed down the coalition tree applying the bilateral Shapley value to the actual payoffs of the respective parent coalitions instead of their coalition values.

Example 2. Consider again the game from example 1 and the bilateral coalition $C_1 = \{a_1\} \cup \{a_2\}$. Since $v(\{a_1\}) = 1$ and $v(\{a_2\}) = 0$, we have $\sigma_b(\{a_1\}, \{a_1\} \cup \{a_2\}, v) = \frac{1}{2} + \frac{1}{2}(2 - 0) = 1.5$ and $\sigma_b(\{a_2\}, \{a_1\} \cup \{a_2\}, v) = \frac{1}{2}(2 - 1) = 0.5$

Now consider a merge of C_1 with $C_2 = \{a_3\}$ ($C = C_1 \cup C_2$). We have $v(C) = 5$ and $v(C_2) = 0$, thus $\sigma_b(C_1, C, v) = 1 + \frac{1}{2}5 = 3.5$ and $\sigma_b(C_2, C, v) = \frac{1}{2}(5 - 2) = 1.5$

For a recursively bilateral Shapley value stable payoff distribution we have to consider v^* with $v^*(\{a_1, a_2\}) = 3.5$ and for all other coalitions $v^*(C) = v(C)$: $u(a_1) = \sigma_b(\{a_1\}, \{a_1\} \cup \{a_2\}, v^*) = \frac{1}{2} + \frac{1}{2}(3.5 - 0) = 2.25$ and $u(a_2) = \sigma_b(\{a_2\}, \{a_1\} \cup \{a_2\}, v^*) = \frac{1}{2}(3.5 - 1) = 1.25$.

3   Hiding Local Worths and Coalition Values

In this section we show that the recursively bilateral Shapley value is well-suited when hiding coalition values and local worths. It is easy to see that (5) can be rewritten as

$$\sigma_b(C_i, C, v) = v(C_i) + \frac{1}{2} \cdot (v(C) - v(C_1) - v(C_2)) \tag{7}$$

with $i \in \{1, 2\}$. Thus, the *additional value*

$$av(C_1, C_2) := v(C_1 \cup C_2) - v(C_1) - v(C_2) \tag{8}$$

produced by forming coalition $C_1 \cup C_2$ is evenly distributed among C_1 and C_2. For recursively bilateral Shapley value stable payoff distributions, this means that each child node in the coalition tree gets half of the additional payoff of its parent node. The share of the total payoff that a node gets is thus directly dependent on its depth in the tree, which is shown by the following lemma.

Lemma 1. *Let $(\mathcal{S}_1, u_1)$ and $(\mathcal{S}_2, u_2)$ configurations for a game $(\mathcal{A}, v)$, with u_1 and u_2 being recursively bilateral Shapley value stable, and $\exists C_1, C_2 \in \mathcal{S}_1 : C = C_1 \cup C_2 \in \mathcal{S}_2$. Then*

$$\forall C^* \in T_C : u_2(C^*) = u_1(C^*) + \frac{av(C_1, C_2)}{2^{d(C^*, T_C)}}$$

Proof. We use induction over $d(C^*, T_C)$: the case $d(C^*, T_C) = 0$ is obvious because of the efficiency of σ_b and the definition of av.

For $d(C^*, T_C) = 1$, we have $C^* = C_i$, $i \in \{1, 2\}$ and $u_2(C_i) = \sigma_b(C_i, C, v) = v(C_i) + \frac{1}{2}av(C)$. Again because of the efficiency of σ_b, $v(C_i) = u_1(C_i)$, and thus $v(C_i) + \frac{1}{2}av(C) = u_1(C_i) + \frac{av(C)}{2^{d(C^*, T_C)}}$.

For $d(C^*, T_C) = k > 1$ and the lemma holds for all C^{**} with $d(C^{**}, T_C) < k$, we have $C^* = C_i^p$, $i \in \{1, 2\}$, $C^p \in T_C$, $d(C_i^p, T_C) = d(C^p, T_C) + 1$ and $u_2(C_i^p) = \sigma_b(C_i^p, C^p, v_{C_i})$ with $v_{C_i^p}(C^p) = u_2(C^p) = u_1(C^p) + \frac{av(C)}{2^{d(C^p, T_C)}}$. Applying 6 and 7, we get

$$u_2(C_i^p) = v(C_i^p) + \frac{1}{2}(u_2(C^p) - v(C_i^p) - v(C_k^p))$$

$$= v(C_i^p) + \frac{1}{2}(u_1(C^p) + \frac{av(C)}{2^{d(C^p, T_C)}} - v(C_i^p) - v(C_k^p))$$

$$= v(C_i^p) + \frac{1}{2}(u_1(C^p) - v(C_i^p) - v(C_k^p)) + \frac{av(C)}{2^{d(C^p, T_C)+1}}$$

$$= u_1(C_i^p) + \frac{av(C)}{2^{d(C_i^p, T_C)}}$$

For the merge of C_1 and C_2 to form $C = C_1 \cup C_2$, we further define the *additional local worth* of agent $a \in C_i$, $i \in \{1, 2\}$:

$$alw_a(C_i, C) := lw_a(C) - lw_a(C_i), \tag{9}$$

and the summarized additional local worth for a subcoalition $C^* \in T_{C_i}$

$$alw(C^*, C_i, C) := \sum_{a \in C^*} (alw_a(C_i, C)) \tag{10}$$

Also, note that

$$av(C_1, C_2) = \sum_{a \in C} lw_a(C) - \sum_{a \in C_1} lw_a(C_1) - \sum_{a \in C_2} lw_a(C_2)$$
$$= alw(C_1, C_1, C) + alw(C_2, C_2, C) \tag{11}$$

The following theorem shows that in order to compute its side-payment when merging coalitions C_1 and C_2, each subcoalition $C^* \in T_{C_i}$ only needs to consider its side-payment for the case without the merge, the additional value $av(C_1, C_2)$ and its additional local worth $alw(C^*, C_i, C)$:

Theorem 1. *Let* $(\mathcal{S}_1, u_1)$ *and* $(\mathcal{S}_2, u_2)$ *configurations for a game* $(\mathcal{A}, v)$, *with* u_1 *and* u_2 *being recursively bilateral Shapley value stable, and* $\exists C_1, C_2 \in \mathcal{S}_1 :$ $C = C_1 \cup C_2 \in \mathcal{S}_2$. *Then* $\forall C^* \in T_{C_i}$, $i \in \{1, 2\}$:

$$sp_{u_2}(C^*, C) = sp_{u_1}(C^*, C_i) + \frac{alw(C_1, C_1, C) + alw(C_2, C_2, C)}{2^{d(C^*, T_C)}} - alw(C^*, C_i, C)$$

Proof. Remember that for any u, $sp_u(C^*, C) = \sum_{a \in C^*} u(a) - lw_a(C) = u(C^*) - \sum_{a \in C^*} lw_a(C)$ (see 4). Because of lemma 1, 9 , 10 and 11, we can rewrite

$$sp_{u_2}(C^*, C) = u_1(C^*) + \frac{av(C_1, C_2)}{2^{d(C^*, T_C)}} - \sum_{a \in C^*} lw_a(C)$$

$$= u_1(C^*) + \frac{av(C_1, C_2)}{2^{d(C^*, T_C)}} - \sum_{a \in C^*} (lw_a(C_i) + alw_a(C_i, C))$$

$$= sp_{u_1}(C^*, C_i) + \frac{av(C_1, C_2)}{2^{d(C^*, T_C)}} - alw(C^*, C_i, C)$$

$$= sp_{u_1}(C^*, C_i) + \frac{alw(C_1, C_1, C) + alw(C_2, C_2, C)}{2^{d(C^*, T_C)}} - alw(C^*, C_i, C)$$

Please note that in the case of $C^* = C_i$, $sp_{u_1}(C^*, C_i) = 0$ because $C_i \in \mathcal{S}_1$ and corollary 1. It is thus clear that in order to obtain recursively bilateral Shapley value stable payoff distributions by repeatedly merging coalitions, subcoalitions have to inform each other only about their additional local worths. Absolute local worths need not to be communicated, and absolute coalition values do not have to be known at all.

The results of this section are employed in the specification of the coalition formation protocol BSCA-P in section 5, but we give an example here:

Example 3. Consider again the situation from example 2. At first $\{a_1\}$ and $\{a_2\}$ merge to form C_1, with $alw_{a_1}(\{a_1\}, C_1) = 3 - 1 = 2$ and $alw_{a_2}(\{a_2\}, C_1) = -1 - 0 = -1$. According to theorem 1 we get

$$sp_u(\{a_1\}) = 0 + \frac{2 + (-1)}{2^1} - 2 = -1.5 \text{ and } sp_u(\{a_2\}) = 0 + \frac{2 + (-1)}{2^1} - (-1) = 1.5$$

Thus, the net amount received by a_1 and a_2 are

$$u(a_1) = lw_{a_1}(C_1) + sp_u(\{a_1\}) = 3 - 1.5 = 1.5 = \sigma_b(\{a_1\}, \{a_1\} \cup \{a_2\}, v)$$
$$u(a_2) = lw_{a_2}(C_1) + sp_u(\{a_2\}) = -1 + 1.5 = 0.5 = \sigma_b(\{a_2\}, \{a_1\} \cup \{a_2\}, v)$$

Second, C_1 merges with $C_2 = \{a_3\}$ to form $C = C_1 \cup C_2$. By looking at the service offers and requests, the agents (and coalition C_1 determine their additional local worths:

$$alw_{a_1}(\{a_1\}, C) = 2 - 3 = -1, alw_{a_2}(\{a_2\}, C) = 1 + 1 = 2,$$
$$alw(C_1, C_1, C) = alw_{a_1}(\{a_1\}, C) + alw_{a_2}(\{a_2\}, C) = 1 \text{ and}$$
$$alw(C_2, C_2, C) = 2 - 0 = 2$$

The additional coalition value is thus

$$av(C_1, C_2) = alw(C_1, C_1, C) + alw(C_2, C_2, C) = 3$$

Applying theorem 1 again, we get for the new payoff distribution u^*

$$sp_{u^*}(C_1) = 0 + \frac{1+2}{2^1} - 1 = 0.5 \text{ and } sp_{u^*}(C_2) = 0 + \frac{1+2}{2^1} - 2 = -0.5.$$

The net payoffs of C_1 and C_2 are of course equal to their resp. bilateral Shapley values:

$$u^*(C_1) = lw_{a_1}(C) + lw_{a_2}(C) + sp_{u^*}(C_1)$$
$$= 2 + 1 + 0.5 = 3.5 = \sigma_b(C_1, C, v) \text{ and}$$
$$u^*(C_2) = lw_{a_3}(C) + sp_{u^*}(C_2) = 2 - 0.5 = 1.5 = \sigma_b(C_2, C, v)$$

For the side-payments within C_1 we again apply theorem 1:

$$sp_{u^*}(\{a_1\}, C) = sp_u(\{a_1\}, C_1) + \frac{1+2}{2^2} - (-1) = -1.5 + 0.75 + 1 = 0.25 \text{ and}$$
$$sp_{u^*}(\{a_2\}, C) = 1.5 + 0.75 - 2 = 0.25$$

4   Anonymous Service Access

In this section, we introduce some anonymity and encryption concepts that enable anonymous and secure web service access.

To achieve this, we use an anonymous communication protocol based on rerouting. In a rerouting protocol, a message is not directly sent to the receiver, but travels over intermediate network nodes, or agents in our case. The specific protocol we utilize is roughly based on onion routing [10]. It was originally defined for HTTP-connections, but we adapt it here for our agent coalition formation setting, by looking only at high-level messages sent between the agents instead of technical details of an underlying protocol. Our focus is to enable the agents to request and access services within their coalition anonymously. We thus also do not bother about problems like possible eavesdropper agents or traffic analysis, as such problems are out of scope of this paper.

The basic idea of the onion routing protocol is to wrap a message in several layers of encryption and reroute it over several rerouting nodes such that no single node is able to determine the sender and receiver of a message. Also,

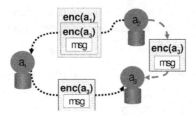

Fig. 1. Two ways of a_2 contacting a_3 via Onion Routing

when one agent contacts another, the nodes over which messages are sent are chosen randomly. Figure 1 illustrates this for a three-agent case. It incorporates a public/private key encryption method, such as the well-known RSA method (originally proposed in [7]). Thus, we extend our agent model such that every agent a is required to possess a private key $privkey_a$ and a matching public key $pubkey_a$ for the chosen encryption method. Further, a needs to be able to execute according encryption/decryption functions. In the following, $enc(pubkey, m)$ denotes a function that encrypts message m using the public key $pubkey$, and $dec(privkey, em)$ denotes the corresponding decryption function for the encrypted message em using the private key $privkey$. To let agent a_1 send an encrypted message m to agent a_2, a_1 encrypts m by executing $enc(pubkey_{a_2}, m)$, sends the result em to a_2 which decrypts it by executing $dec(privkey_{a_2}, em$. Thus, the agents need to perform an initial public key exchange. In the onion protocol, actually only a part of a message is encrypted with the public key method. This part contains a key for a symmetric encryption method, i.e. one that uses the same key for encryption and decryption. The remainder of the message is encrypted with this method. This is done because of performance reasons, since symmetric encryption methods usually are much faster than public key methods. However, we go not into those details here, and consider such optimizations as part of the implementation of the enc and dec functions.

We are now ready to define our anonymous message sending algorithm:

Algorithm 1. *To anonymously send a message m to agent a_2 over i intermediate agents, agent a_1 performs the following:*

1. *Randomly generate an ordered list L with length $i + 1$ of agents, such that $L_j \neq L_{j+1}$, $\forall 1 \leq j < i$, and $L_{i+1} = a_2$, where L_j is the agent at position j in L.*
2. *Set $em_{i+1} := enc(pubkey_{a_2}, m)$.*
3. *For $l = i$ to 1 do:*
   (a) *Set $m^* := (L_{l+1}, em_{l+1})$.*
   (b) *Set $em_l := enc(pubkey_{L_l}, m^*)$.*
4. *Send em_1 to L_1.*

For this to work, each agent also needs to implement an algorithm to handle incoming encrypted messages:

Algorithm 2. *When receiving an encrypted message em, agent a_1 performs:*

1. *Set $m := dec(privkey_{a_1}, em)$*
2. *If m is of the form (a_2, em), $a_2 \in \mathcal{A}$, send em to a_2; else process m like an incoming unencrypted message.*

To measure a degree of anonymity, different notions have been proposed in the literature, such as total or group anonymity, under possibilistic or probabilistic interpretations (see e.g. [6,3]. Here, we will apply the concept of possibilistic *agent k-anonymity*, which requires only that there exists some set of agents K with size k, such that each $a \in K$ is a possible sender. Specifically, this anonymity is measured in the following way. When the two coalitions C_1 and C_2 perform a merge to form $C = C_1 \cup C_2$, they need to compute and inform each other about $alw(C_1, C_1, C)$ and $alw(C_2, C_2, C)$ (see section 3). Because of the definition of the local worths, $alw(C_i, C_i, C) > 0$, $i \in \{1, 2\}$, means that in coalition C_i, more worth is produced by agents getting services executed than costs are produced due to agents executing services. All Agents in C thus can infer that at least one agent $a \in C_i$ accesses a service in C_k, $k \in \{1, 2\}, k \neq i$. We thus obtain the degree of agent k-anonymity for agents in C_i wrt. agents in C_k:

$$aa(C_i, C_k) = |C_i|$$

However, the degree of agent k-anonymity of a wrt. other agents in C_i is in general only $k = 1$. This is because in order to compute $alw(C_i, C_i, C)$, each subcoalition $C^* \in T_{C_i}$ has to compute $alw(C^*, C_i, C)$ first. In particular, agent a has in general to inform some other agent in C_i about $alw(\{a\}, C_i, C)$.

Thus, we also use the concept of *service k-anonymity*, expressing that an agent a accesses any one of k possible services. In the case of agent $a \in C_i$ accessing a service in C_k, the degree of service k-anonymity for a wrt. to the agents in C_i is equal to the total number of services offered by agents in C_k:

$$sa(C_i) = |\bigcup_{a \in C_k} OS_a|$$

In the following, we assume that each agent maintains minimum k-anonymity degrees $aa_{min}(WS) \in \mathbb{N}$ and $sa_{min}(WS) \in \mathbb{N}$ for each service it is interested in requesting. When forming the coalition C, agent $a \in C_i$ then only requests a service WS from an agent in C_k if these minimum degrees are met, i.e. $WS \in R_a(C)$ if

$$aa(C_i, C_k) \geq aa_{min}(WS) \text{ and} \tag{12}$$
$$sa(C_i) \geq sa_{min}(WS) \tag{13}$$

hold.

5   Coalition Formation Protocol BSCA-P

In this section, we finally propose the coalition formation protocol BSCA-P applying the concepts that have been introduced in the previous sections. In the

BSCA-P, each coalition is represented by one agent which is responsible for the communication with other coalitions. To simplify the choice of a representative, we assume there exists an ordering function o defined on the set of all agents. We also assume that service offers, along with the service execution costs, are made public beforehand (e.g., by broadcasting).

Algorithm 3. *For a game $(\mathcal{A}, v)$, $\mathcal{S}_0 := \{\{a\} | a \in \mathcal{A}\}$, $r := 0$ and $\forall C \in \mathcal{S}_0$: $sp_0(C) := 0$. In every coalition $C \in \mathcal{S}_r$, every agent $a \in C$ performs:*

1. *Let $C \in \mathcal{S}_r$, $a \in C$ and $\mathcal{S}^* := \mathcal{S} \setminus C$.*
2. *Communication:*
    (a) *For all $C^* \in \mathcal{S}^*$ do:*
        i. *Determine $R_a(C^*)$ using the sets OS_{a^*} for each $a^* \in C^*$, accounting for costs and ensuring compliance with 12 and 13.*
        ii. *For each service request which is both in $R_a(C)$ and $R_a(C^*)$, keep only the least costly one.*
        iii. *Set $alws_a(C^*) := alw_a(C, C^*)$.*
        iv. *For each bilateral coalition C^a, $C^a \in T_C$, $a \in C^a$, $a = Rep(C_a)$, wait for a message from $Rep(C_i^a)$, $i \in 1, 2, a \notin C_i^a$ containing $alws_{Rep(C)}(C^*)$ and set $alws_a(C^*) := alws_a(C^*) + alws_{Rep(C)}(C^*)$.*
        v. *If $a = Rep(C)$ then send $alws_a(C^*)$ to $Rep(C^*)$; else send $alws_a(C^*)$ to $Rep(C^+)$ with $C^+ \in T_C$, $a = Rep(C_i^+)$, $i \in 1, 2, a \neq Rep(C^+)$.*
    (b) *If $a = Rep(C)$ then receive $alws_{Rep(C^*)}(C)$ and set $alws(C^*) := alws_{Rep(C^*)}(C) + alws_a(C^*)$ for all $C^* \in \mathcal{S}^*$; else go to step 3i.*
3. *Coalition Proposals:*
    (a) *Set $Candidates := \mathcal{S}^*$, $New := \emptyset$ and $Obs := \emptyset$*
    (b) *Determine a coalition $C^+ \in Candidates$ with $\forall C^* \in Candidates$: $alws_a(C^+) \geq alws_a(C^*)$.*
    (c) *Send a proposal to $Rep(C^+)$ to form coalition $C \cup C^+$.*
    (d) *Receive all coalition proposals from other agents.*
    (e) *If no proposal from $Rep(C^+)$ is received and $Candidates \neq \emptyset$, set $Candidates := Candidates \setminus \{C^+\}$ and go to step 3b.*
    (f) *If a proposal from $Rep(C^+)$ is received, then form the coalition $C \cup C^+$:*
        i. *If $o(Rep(C)) < o(Rep(C^+))$ then set $Rep(C \cup C^+) := Rep(C)$; else set $Rep(C \cup C^+) := Rep(C^+)$.*
        ii. *Inform all other $Rep(C^*), C^* \in \mathcal{S}^* \setminus C^+$ and all $a^* \in C$, $a^* \neq a$ about the new coalition and $Rep(C \cup C^+)$*
        iii. *$New := \{C \cup C^+\}$, $Obs := \{C, C^+\}$*
    (g) *Receive all messages about new coalitions. For each new coalition $C_1 \cup C_2$ and $Rep_{C_1 \cup C_2}$, set $Candidates := Candidates \setminus \{C_1, C_2\}$, $New := New \cup \{C_1 \cup C_2\}$ and $Obs := Obs \cup \{C_1, C_2\}$.*
    (h) *Send the sets New and Obs to all other coalition members $a^* \in C$, $a^* \neq a$*
    (i) *If $a \neq Rep(C)$ then receive the sets New and Obs from $Rep(C)$.*
    (j) *Set $r := r + 1$, $\mathcal{S}_r := (\mathcal{S}_{r-1} \setminus Obs) \cup New$.*
    (k) *For each (sub-)coalition $C^* \in T_C$ with $Rep(C^*) = a$, determine $sp_r(C^*)$ according to theorem 1 (using $sp_{r-1}(C^*)$ instead of $sp_u(C^*)$).*
    (l) *If $C_r = C_{r-1}$ then stop; else go to step 2*

Theorem 2. *With $n = |\mathcal{A}|$ and $m := max_{a \in \mathcal{A}}\{|R_a|\}$, the computational complexity of the BSCA-P is in $O(n^3 m^2)$.*

Proof. In any round r, $\mathcal{S}_r \leq n$. The iteration in step 2a is thus done at most n times. In step 2(a)i, for each service in R_a, a has to find an agent in the potential partner coalition which offers this service at the least cost. The conditions 12 and 13 only have to be checked once for each service, for which we assume negligible complexity. Thus, at most nm operations are required in this step. Step 2(a)ii can be done in less than m^2 steps. All other steps within and outside of the iteration in step 2a are of less complexity. Thus, the complexity of one round of the BSCA-P is in $O(n)(O(nm) + O(m^2)) = O(n^2 m^2)$. Since the maximum number of coalition merges is smaller than n (because after at most $n-1$ merges, the grand coalition is formed), the number of rounds is also bound by n. The overall complexity of the BSCA-P is thus $O(n)O(n^2 m^2) = O(n^3 m^2)$.

Theorem 3. *In the BSCA-P, the number of messages sent by an agent is in $O(n^2)$.*

Proof. During each iteration in step 2(a)i, in step 2(a)v a message to the agent's subcoalition representative or to $Rep(C^*)$. Assuming that agents which are representatives of several subcoalitions omit sending messages to themselves, and with at most n iterations in step 2(a)i (see above), the number of messages sent during the iteration is in $O(n)$. The number of messages sent in step 3(f)ii is also in $O(n)$. Thus, with at most n rounds, the overall number of messages sent by an agent in the BSCA-P is in $O(n^2)$

When the protocol is finished and thus coalitions are formed, agents still have to execute the following steps in order to implement the coalitions:

1. Each agent runs algorithm 2 continuously in order to enable anonymous service access.
2. Concurrently, algorithm 1 is executed by the agents requesting services to actually access these services at their providers.
3. All (sub-)coalition representatives execute their respective side-payments sp_r for their (sub-)coalitions. Each representative only makes/receives payments to/from representatives of immediate parent and child coalitions, such that no additional information about payments is gained by any agent.

The last step ensures that only a representative of a two-agent coalition is informed about individual side-payments, and only about two of them: its own, and the other agent of the two-agent coalition. Therefore, only the first partner agent that an agent a coalesces with might ever know a's exact side-payment. However, the individual utilities still remain hidden from all other agents.

6   Conclusions

In this paper, a privacy-preserving coalition formation protocol was proposed. We have shown that in order to form recursively bilateral Shapley value stable coalitions, individual payoffs may be hidden from most agents while individual utilities can be completely hidden, and absolute coalition values need not to be known at all. Also, we showed that within a coalition, services can be accessed by cooperating agents with certain degrees of anonymity. Thus, agents can hide the fact that they access specific services even from agents which are members of the same coalition.

References

1. B. Blankenburg, R.K. Dash, S.D. Ramchurn, M. Klusch, and N.R. Jennings. Trusted kernel-based coalition formation. In *Proc. 4th Int. Conf. on Autonomous Agents and Multi-Agent Systems*, Utrecht, Holland, 2005. to appear.
2. Georgios Chalkiadakis and Craig Boutilier. Bayesian reinforcement learning for coalition formation under uncertainty. In *Proc. 3rd Int. Conference on Autonomous Agents and Multiagent Systems (AAMAS 2004), New York, USA*, New York, USA, 2004. ACM Press.
3. Joseph Halpern and Kevin O'Neill. Anonymity and information hiding in multiagent systems. *Journal of Computer Security*, Special Edition on CSFW 16:75–88, 2003.
4. S. Kraus, O. Shehory, and Gilad Taase. The advantages of compromising in coalition formation with incomplete information. In *Proc. 3rd Int. Conference on Autonomous Agents and Multiagent Systems (AAMAS 2004), New York, USA*, New York, USA, 2004. ACM Press.
5. Martin J. Osborne and Ariel Rubinstein. *A Course in Game Theory*. MIT Press, Cambridge MA, USA, 1994.
6. A. Pfitzmann and M. Köhntopp. Anonymity, unobservability and pseudonymity: a proposal for terminology. In *International Workshop on Designing Privacy Enhancing Technologies*, pages 1–9, New York, 2001. Springer-Verlag.
7. Ronald L. Rivest, Adi Shamir, and Leonard M. Adleman. A method for obtaining digital signatures and public-key cryptosystems. *Commun. ACM*, 26(1):96–99, 1983.
8. L. S. Shapley. A value for n-person games. In H. W. Kuhn and A. W. Tucker, editors, *Contributions to the Theory of Games II*, volume 28 of *Annals of Mathematics Studies*, pages 307–317. Princeton University Press, Princeton, 1953.
9. O. Shehory and S. Kraus. Methods for task allocation via agent coalition formation. *Artificial Intelligence Journal*, 101 (1-2):165–200, May 1998.
10. P F Syverson, D M Goldschlag, and M G Reed. Anonymous connections and onion routing. In *IEEE Symposium on Security and Privacy*, pages 44–54, Oakland, California, 4–7 1997.
11. J. Vassileva, S. Breban, and M. Horsch. Agent reasoning mechanism for long-term coalitions based on decision making and trust. *Computational Intelligence*, 4(18):583–595, 2002.

Towards Service Coalitions: Coordinating the Commitments in a Workflow

Jiangbo Dang and Michael N. Huhns

Department of Computer Science & Engr., University of South Carolina,
Columbia, SC 29208, USA. 1-803-777-3768
{dangj, huhns}@engr.sc.edu

Abstract. Web services are functionalities that can be engaged over the
Internet. A workflow is a set of Web services that are executed by carrying out specified control and data flows among these services to address
some business needs. We believe that commitments among agents can be
used to model a workflow and coordinate several self-interested parties
to execute a workflow. This paper presents a methodology to infer commitments and causal relationships from a workflow by utilizing semantic
descriptions of Web services. We provide an example scenario to show
how commitments of a workflow can be inferred. In addition, we use the
Petri net representation of a workflow to describe our algorithm. With
this technology, agents (service requestors and providers) engaged in a
workflow can negotiate with multiple agents to reach favorable agreements and then coordinate their behaviors through the commitment operations in the context of service-oriented environment, where one or
more self-interested parties can provide services to one or more other
parties.

1 Introduction

In supply chains, e-commerce, and Web services, the participants negotiate contracts and enter into binding agreements with each other by agreeing on functional and quality metrics of the services they request and provide. The functionality of a service is the most important factor, especially for discovering services.
Once discovered, however, services are engaged, composed, and executed by the
participants' negotiating over issues besides QoS (quality of service) metrics to
maximize their profits.

As more complex business operations become candidates for automation, it
is difficult to find one Web service to fulfill a complete business process. The
situation becomes even more complicated when there is no single Web service,
but only a combination of several Web services that can satisfy a business need.
To solve this problem, various standards for coordinating the Web services have
been developed, such as BPEL4WS, OWL-S, and WS-Coordination. We use
OWL-S in our paper since it provides richer semantic descriptions than the
alternatives.

T. Eymann et al. (Eds.): MATES 2005, LNAI 3550, pp. 59–70, 2005.

Semantic Web service technologies, such as OWL-S enable more flexible automation of service discovery and execution and monitoring, and support the composition of more complicated workflows represented as composite services. OWL-S provides a standard language for describing the composition of Web services. Thus we can treat composite services as a process model.

Negotiation is a process by which agents communicate and compromise to reach agreement on matters of mutual interest while maximizing their individual utilities. In a service-oriented environment, it is very likely there are multiple service requestors and providers negotiating simultaneously. Concurrent negotiation is preferred, since it is both time efficient and robust when an agent needs to negotiate with multiple other agents to make a good deal or to request a service involving multiple agents as in a workflow model.

Commitment among agents can be used to model business processes by capturing the interactions among agents. Chopra and Singh [2] proposed a commitment-based formalism to represent multiagent interaction protocols. To be coordinated with other agents in a workflow execution, all participating agents negotiate to reach beneficial contracts and coordinate their commitments to fulfill a business process. The commitments of the agents lend coherence to their interactions over time. For our work, we are interested in inferring commitments and causalities from a business process model and support multiple-issue concurrent negotiation for a workflow among collaborative parties in the future.

2   Background and Related Work

2.1   BPEL4WS, OWL-S, and SWRL

When we choose a representation for Web services, the trade-offs must be made among the expressive power, the rigor, the ease of use, and the computational tractability of a representation [10]. IBM, Microsoft and BEA released BPEL4WS (Business Process Execution Language for Web services) for expressing workflows consisting of Web services. BPEL4WS enables the specification of executable business processes (including Web services) and business process protocols in terms of their execution logic or control flow.

OWL-S is an initiative of the Semantic Web community to facilitate automatic discovery, invocation, composition, interoperation, and monitoring of Web services through their semantic description [4]. OWL-S supports a richer semantic description of Web services by: (1) a profile that describes what the service does, (2) a process model that specifies how the service works in terms of inputs, outputs, preconditions, and result, a.k.a., IOPR, and (3) a grounding that defines how the service is accessed. Both OWL-S and BPEL4WS provide a mechanism for describing a business process model. OWL-S augments the input and output specifications of BPEL4WS with preconditions and results: this enables the side effects of services to be encoded. We can then reason about how services may be composed and infer the commitments and causalities from them.

Semantic Web Rule Language (SWRL) expressions may be used in OWL-S preconditions, process control conditions (such as If-then-Else), and results.

SWRL expressions may also mention process inputs and outputs as variables, thus tying together the two languages. SWRL can make OWL-S more powerful, since it uses the expressive power of rules in a potential emerging standard. In our work, we just use SWRL in a primitive way, as a conjunction of conditions.

2.2   Web Services and Workflow

Semantic Web services, as envisioned by Berners-Lee, are intended to be applied not statically by developers, but dynamically by the services themselves through automatic and autonomous selection, composition, and execution. Web services are standard-based software components that can be accessed over the Internet by other software components [6]. Web services can vary in functionality from simple operations, such as a retrieval of a stock quote, to complex business operations, such as supply chain problems.

Many efforts have been made to automate service composition. In [6], the authors introduced a workflow composer agent to compose Web service workflows by finding and matching the semantic descriptions of Web services. Mandell and McIlraith [7] used a bottom-up approach to integrate Semantic Web technology into automating the dynamic discovery and binding of Web services. Chung et al. [3] presented a Web service framework to support collaborative product commerce. Given a workflow, what issues different participating agents negotiate to reach service agreements and how to coordinate agents to execute a workflow are still challenging problems. In this paper, we focus on how to infer commitments from a workflow and extract issues for collaborative service negotiation.

Given a workflow consisting of several services, service agents negotiate with one another and with resource agents to ensure that global constraints are not violated and that global efficiencies can be achieved. As described in [10], the service agents must be able to engage in negotiation, and they must be describable declaratively, not procedurally, in terms of high level abstractions. As a binary relationship binding two participants, a commitment is a proper abstraction for coordinating different parties of a workflow.

2.3   Negotiation and Commitment

Current standards for Web services do not support multiple-issue negotiations. As a result, several researchers have attempted to merge negotiation from the MAS domain into Web service selection and composition. Petrone [8] proposed a conversation model to enrich the communication and coordination capabilities of Web services by adapting agent-based concepts to the communications among Web services and users.

Multi-linked negotiation describes a situation where one agent needs to negotiate with many other agents about different issues, and the negotiation over one issue influences the negotiation over the other issues. Multi-linked negotiation becomes important in a workflow scenario where a service requestor negotiates with several service providers to reach agreements over a composite service. Zhang et al. [14] presented a mechanism for multi-linked negotiation of task allocation in a cooperative system where a contractee tries to ask another agent to fulfill one of its subtasks that it cannot do itself. Since their protocol does not support concurrent negotiation, it is not possible for a contractee to coordinate among multiple subtasks.

In [13], an approach is proposed to deal with multi-linked negotiation in the context of task allocation. a partial order scheduler is used to find the consistence range for issues in each task and the relationships among them by sorting all issues with their flexibilities and dependencies. In their model, negotiation is viewed as a multidimensional search over multiple issues (time, cost, and the flexibility of the commitment). It is a plan-globally-then-negotiate-separately procedure in which there is no mutual influence among negotiation threads.

Commitments are a key element of the semantics of agent communications [9]. Commitment among agents can be used to model business processes by capturing the interactions among agents. In [11], researchers extract commitments from a set of conversions via Dooley graphs and map Dooley graphs to π-calculus. The formalization of π-calculus helps to derive useful properties and prove soundness of their models. To further apply commitment into Web service, they [12] integrate commitments into service specification by which service providers and requestors exchange commitments instead of messages. Most existing workflow technologies can only apply centralized methods to coordinate and monitor the execution of a workflow through the procedural specifications. In contrast, this paper advances the state of the art in the following ways: Our methodology (1) infers the commitments of service agents involved in a workflow; (2) allows flexible workflow coordination through commitments; (3) makes it possible for service agents to negotiate over issues from the inferred commitments to improve their utilities while optimizing the workflow (4) potentially provides a way to build a flexible and robust workflow by concurrent service negotiation.

The remainder of the paper is organized as follows: Section 3 introduces a motivating workflow scenario and provides its Petri net representation. Section 4 identifies control constructs of a workflow in different representations and describes the algorithm to derive commitments from a workflow. Section 5 discusses further issues related to negotiating a workflow, and Section 6 concludes.

3   A Motivating Scenario

In order to illustrate our methodology, we present a motivating workflow scenario where several parties work together to produce a product. In Figure 1, there are five service agents: *ProductRequestor*, *ProductMaker*, *Analyzer*, *PartsMaker*, and *Driller*. *ProductRequestor* agent A initiates this workflow by sending a product requirement to *ProductMaker* agent B. To meet A's requirement, B designs this product and send its design to the third party *Analyzer* C. C performs some specific tests to ensure this design will meet the requirements. Once the product design is approved, B will generate the requirements for different parts of this product and send them to *PartsMaker* agent D. *PartsMaker* D will design these parts and send the design to C. If C approves the parts design, D will produce the parts for the product. In addition, if the design requires a specific treatment like drilling, a *Driller* agent E will drill the parts. Finally, *ProductMaker B* will polish the parts and assemble the product to finish this workflow.

This workflow is complicated because:

- From the workflow's view, the structure of the workflow is dynamic and uncertain, since it depends on the outputs/results from the antecedent processes. For example, the execution of process *DrillParts* depends on the output from the process *DesignParts*; therefore, we can not know in advance whether *Driller* agent E will be involved.
- From the participant's view, the processes or tasks it needs to perform are also uncertain. It depends on the input of *ReceiveAnalysisRequest* whether the *Analyzer* agent C performs *AnalyzeProductDesign* process or *AnalyzePartDesign* process. Moreover, C has to repeat its processes many times if the outputs from *DesignProduct* or *DesignParts* cannot pass the tests.

Due to the dynamic property of workflow, we believe that commitments and conditional commitments are the proper abstraction to characterize and coordinate collaborative service agents in a workflow.

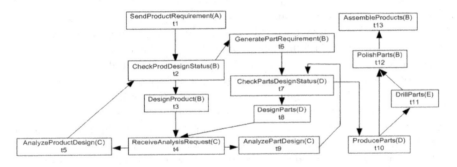

Fig. 1. A *ProduceProduct* Workflow Example

We describe the above workflow as a composite process in an OWL-S file. Its behavior is described in terms of its process model, where the functionality of each subprocess is described by its IOPR. OWL-S adopts two views of processes. First, a process produces a data transformation from a set of inputs to a set of outputs. Second, a process produces a transition in the world from one state to another. This transition is described by the preconditions and results of the process [4]. Inputs and outputs specify the data transformation produced by the process. Inputs specify the information that the process requires for its execution. The inputs are either provided by other processes in the process model or by service clients through message passing. Equivalently, the outputs are either sent to other processes through the data-flow constructs, or to other Web services. The execution of a process may also result in changes of the state of the world. Preconditions specify conditions that should be satisfied for a process to execute correctly. The IOPRs for the *ProduceProduct* example are shown in Table 1.

Table 1. IOPRs of the Processes from the *ProduceProduct* Example

Process	Inputs	Outputs	Preconditions	Results
SendProdRequirement		ProductRequirements		
CheckProdDesignStatus	ProductRequirements AnalysisReport	ProductRequirements		Set Approved
DesignProduct	ProductRequirements	ProductDesign		
GeneratePartsRequirement	ProductDesign	PartRequirements		
PolishParts	Parts	Parts		Polished=true
AssembleProduct	Parts	Products		
ReceiveAnalysisRequest	Design DesignType	Design		
AnalyzeProductDesign	ProductDesign	?Approved AnalysisReport		
AnalyzePartsDesign	PartDesign	?Approved AnalysisReport		
CheckPartDesignStatus	PartsRequirements AnalysisReport	ProductRequirements		Set Approved
DesignParts	PartRequirements	PartDesign		
ProduceParts	PartDesign	Parts ?needDrilled		
DrillParts	Parts	Parts		Drilled=true

Conditions have a pervasive presence in OWL-S. They are used to describe outputs and results that result from the execution of processes. They are also used in the specification of constructs such as if-statements and loops. We use the primitive SWRL rules encoded as XML Literals. These SWRL rules uses rdf:List to represent a conjunction of expressions of true or false values.

In this example, the production of a product would follow the sequential process of receiving a requirement, designing a product or parts, and analyzing product design or parts design, producing a part, drilling if necessary, and polishing and assembling the product. *ReceiveAnalysisRequest* would involve the atomic process of either *AnalyzeProductDesign* or *AnalyzePartsDesign*. Moreover, designing and analyzing would be an iterative process.

Petri nets have been used to model and analyze many kinds of processes, and the colored Petri net extension facilitates the modeling of complex processes where data and time are important factors. Petri nets for workflow modeling provide: (1) a clear and precise formal representation, (2) an intuitive graphical language, (3) full expressiveness with explicitly represented states, and (4) a firm mathematical foundation for property investigation and analysis [1]. To illustrate our algorithm, we transform our example workflow into a colored Petri net. A Petri net $N = (P, T, F)$ consists of a set of transitions T (bars), a set of places P (ellipses), and a flow relation F (arcs) [1]. In a workflow Petri net, a transition represents an atomic process and a place is a passive state. Petri nets are well suited for modeling workflow processes, since there are many available simulation tools for them [1]. Therefore, we can test the Petri nets to determine the soundness and equivalence of workflows and those commitments inferred from a workflow.

A Petri net extended with color, time, and hierarchy is called a high-level Petri net [1]. In this paper we use the first extension to model conditions and relations of processes within a workflow. Other extensions are useful in dealing with time and scale issues of processes, which are beyond the scope of this

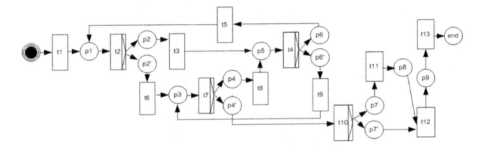

Fig. 2. A *ProduceProduct* Petri Net

paper. In a colored Petri net, each token has a value often referred to as 'color'. Transitions determine the values of the produced tokens on the basis of the values of the consumed tokens, i.e., a transition describes the relation between the values of the 'input tokens' and the values of the 'output tokens'. It is also possible to specify 'preconditions', which take the colors of tokens to be consumed into account. These values match the inputs of a process, the outputs and results of a process, and the preconditions of a process from an OWL-S definition, respectively. Figure 2 shows the Petri net model of our example workflow. The details are discussed in Section 4.

4   Deriving Commitments from a Workflow

4.1   Workflow Control Constructs

Given a workflow, four types of routing are identified by the Workflow Management Coalition (WfMC) in specifying how cases are routed along the processes that need to be executed: sequential, parallel, conditional and iteration. In the process dimension, building blocks such as the AND-split, AND-join, OR-split, OR-join, explicit OR-split, and explicit OR-join are used to model the routing [1].

Sequential routing is used to deal with causal relationships between tasks. Consider t_1 and t_2 from Figure 2. If t_2 is executed after the completion of t_1, then t_1 and t_2 are executed sequentially. Place p_1 represents a result for t_1 and a precondition for t_2. Parallel routing is used in situations where two processes need to be executed, but the order of execution is arbitrary. Considering the two sets of *ProductMaker* and *PartsMaker* in our example, processes after t_1 can be executed in parallel. To model such a parallel routing, two building blocks are used: (1) the AND-split and (2) the AND-join. Conditional routing is used to allow for a routing that may vary between cases. To model a choice between two or more alternatives, the explicit OR-split is used. In Figure 2, t_2 has two output places p_2 and p_2'. The choice between p_2 and p_2' is based on the attribute *Approved*. If *Approved* is true, t_6 will be executed, otherwise t_3 is executed. The iteration routing can be modeled using an explicit OR-split as the iteration of $t_2 - t_3 - t_4 - t_5$ defined in Figure 2. t_2 is a control task that checks the result of t_5. Based on this check, t_3, t_4, t_5 may be executed once more.

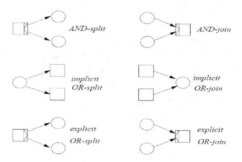

Fig. 3. The Building Blocks for Workflow Modeling [1]

All OWL-S control constructs can be categorized into the discussed four classes of routings or modeled by PN (Petri net) building blocks from Figure 3, e.g., OWL-S Sequence is equal to the PN sequential routing, OWL-S Split and Split-and-Join can be represented by the PN AND-split and AND-join, OWL-S choice is equivalent to the PN explicit OR-split, OWL-S Any-Order can be modeled by the PN parallel routing, OWL-S Condition and If-Then-Else constructs can be represented by the PN conditional routings, OWL-S Iterate, Repeat-While, and Repeat-Until may be modeled by the PN iteration routings.

4.2   Inference Algorithm

In service-oriented environments, the participating agents are distinguished by the services they provide, the services they seek, and the negotiated service agreements to which they commit. The coherent behavior of systems in such an environment is governed by interactions among the agents, and commitments are the proper abstraction to characterize the interactions for monitoring and control of the systems [5].

A service is what an agent performs when it works on and completes a task or process. In this paper, a workflow is represented as a composite service in OWL-S format where each sub-service is described by its IOPR properties. Each sub-service is associated with agents via a process of negotiation. The execution of the workflow is monitored via commitments. A commitment is a well-defined data structure with algebra of operations that have a formal semantics. The agent that is bound to fulfill the commitment is called the debtor of the commitment. The agent that is the beneficiary of the commitment is called the creditor. A commitment has the form $C(a; b; q)$, where a is its creditor, b is its debtor, and q is the condition the debtor will bring about. A conditional commitment $C(a; b; p \rightarrow q)$ denotes that if a condition p is brought about, then the commitment $C(a; b; q)$ will hold. Commitments capture the dependencies among the agents with regard to the workflow and can be inferred by the algorithm 1.

We assume that the data flows and message mappings are well defined in the semantic description. Let $e(v_1, v_2)$ denote an arc from vertex v_1 to vertex v_2. Given a workflow defined as a Petri net $N = (P, T, F)$, we define a directed graph

$N'(V, E)$ where $V = T$ and $e(v_1, v_2) \in E$ if $\exists p$, $e(v_1, p) \in F$ and $e(p, v_2) \in F$. The neighbor nodes of $v \in V$ are stored in $adjacent(v)$ and the color of each vertex $v \in V$ is stored in the variable $color(v)$. We define the start transaction v_0 as the root node of N'.

Since same service agent may execute several atomic processes in one workflow, we need to distinguish between the concepts of agent and role. A role is an abstraction of capabilities used by an agent in dealing with one atomic process. An agent may have several roles, each associated with one commitment. Algorithm 1 produces a set of commitments for service agents. Each commitment is represented as the OWL-S IOPRs, which can be easily transformed into the commitment format we defined in the previous section. These commitments can be used in two ways: coordinating and guiding the negotiations among service agents in a competitive service-oriented environment, and monitoring and controlling the debtor agents to fulfill the workflow by fulfilling their committed tasks. To make this possible, the services have to be defined with a semantic description, and the preconditions/results and inputs/outputs should refer to an ontology. Given IOPRs of the processes defined in Table 1 and the Petri net in Figure 2, let us illustrate Algorithm 1 with our example scenario. For *Driller E* with one process: *DrillParts*.

[DrillParts]
Input: Parts
Output: Parts
Precondition: Completed(ProduceParts) ∧ needDrilled
Result: Drilled

For *ProductMaker B* that owns three atomic processes: *CheckProdDesign-Status*, *DesignProduct*, and *GeneratePartRequirement*.

[CheckProdDesignStatus]
Input: ProductRequirements ∧ AnalysisReport
Output: ProductRequirements ∧ AnalysisReport
Pre-conditions: Completed(SendProdReuqirement)
Result: Set Approved true or false

[DesignProduct]
Input: ProductRequirements
Output: ProductDesign
Pre-conditions: Completed(CheckProdDesignStatus)∧ ¬approved
Result:

[GeneratePartRequirement]
Input: ProductDesign
Output: PartsRequirements
Pre-conditions: Completed(CheckProdDesignStatus)∧ approved
Result:

Algorithm 1. Commitment Inference Algorithm

Notations:

$type(i)$ is the routing block type from vertex i;

$Owner(i)$ is the debtor of the process i;

Q is an empty first-in, first-out queue;

$enqueue(i, Q)$ adds element i into Q;

$dequeue(Q)$ removes and returns the first element from Q;

Initialization:

foreach $v \in V$ **do**
    $color(v) \leftarrow WHITE$
end

$enqueue(v_0, Q)$;

$color(v_0) \leftarrow BLACK$;

Inference:

while $Q \neq \phi$ **do**
    $i = dequeue(Q)$
    foreach $v \in adjacent(i)$ **do**
        if $color(v) = WHITE$ **then**
            $color(v) \leftarrow BLACK$;
            $enqueue(v, Q)$;
        end
    end
    switch $type(i)$ **do**
        case $Sequence$
            for $j, where\ e(i, j) \in E$ **do**
                $precondition(j) = precondition(j) \wedge result(i) \wedge completed(i)$;
            end
            break;
        case $AND - split$
            forall $j, where\ e(i, j) \in E$ **do**
                $precondition(j) = precondition(j) \wedge result(i) \wedge completed(i)$;
            end
            break;
        case $Explicit - OR - split$
            forall $j, where\ e(i, j) \in E$ **do**
                $precondition(j) =$
                $precondition(j) \wedge result(i) \wedge completed(i) \wedge OR - condition(i)$;
            end
            break;
    end
    forall $j, where\ e(i, j) \in E$ **do**
        if $e(i, j) \in E \wedge owner(i) \neq owner(j)$ **then**
            remove e
    end
end

5   Negotiation and Commitments for Workflows

In service-oriented environments, the participating agents negotiate and commit to a service agreement about the execution and completion of a workflow. During the negotiation, the agents communicate and compromise to reach an agreement on matters of mutual interest while maximizing their utilities. The negotiated agreements can be encapsulated as commitment promises [5]. These inferred commitments and relations can be used for collaborative service negotiation. Moreover, we can identify the significant paths or processes and improve the robustness of a workflow by duplicating vital services through negotiations.

In a competitive service-oriented environment, explicit representation of commitments is the proper abstraction to coordinate participating agents in a workflow since: (1) It refers to interagent dependencies through the IOPRs of a task, thus allowing agents to recognize focus points in the revision process where coordination with other agents is needed; and focusing the distributed search this way benefits the efficiency of coordination; (2) An agent first tries to revise task timings that do not involve its commitments during the process of revising its local plan, this heuristic modularizes the revision as much as possible, making it more scalable [5]. Therefore, a centralized workflow execution engine is not necessary for coordinating, monitoring the execution of the workflows, and for verifying the output of the workflow.

ebXML addresses the broad problem of B2B interaction from a workflow perspective. ebXML uses Collaboration Protocol Profiles (CPP) to describe the business processes supported by Web services. A Collaborative Partner Agreement (CPA), an intersection of two CPPs, represents a technical agreement between two or more partners. A business process in ebXML is considered to be a set of business document exchanges between a set of Web services. OWL-S descriptions could be used within ebXML to describe the business processes of interacting Web services. The negotiations and commitments considered in this paper provide a potential representation, semantics, and methodology for establishing the CPA in ebXML.

6   Conclusions

This paper presents a methodology to infer commitments and relations from a workflow by utilizing semantic descriptions of Web services. With a motivating workflow scenario, we provide its semantic descriptions with IOPRs and a Petri net representation. We first identify the control constructs and then describe the algorithm to derive commitments from a workflow.

There are several possible directions for future work. First, this method can be applied to support the negotiation for a composed service with different service agents under constraints such as QoS and dependency issues. Second, we can further explore the power of semantic rule language to describe the relations within a workflow. Third, a process algebra, π-calculus, can be adopted to improve the flexibility of the current commitment model.

References

1. W.M.P. van der Aalst. The Application of Petri Nets to Workflow Management. *The Journal of Circuits, Systems and Computers*, 8(1):21–66, 1998.
2. Amit K. Chopra and Munindar P. Singh. Nonmonotonic commitment machines. In *Proceedings of the International Workshop on Agent Communication Languages and Conversation Policies (ACL)*. Springer, 2003.
3. Moon-Jung Chung, Hong Suk Jung, Woongsup Kim, Ravi Goplannalan, and Hyun Kim. A framework for collaborative product commerce using web services. In *ICWS*, pages 52–60, 2004.
4. The OWL Service Coalition. OWL-S: Semantic Markup for Web Services.
5. Jiangbo Dang, Devendra Shrotri, and Michael N. Huhns. Distributed coordination of an agent society based on obligations and commitments to negotiated agreements. In Paul Scerri, editor, *Challenges in the Coordination of Large-Scale Multiagent Systems*. Springer Verlag, 2005.
6. Mikko Laukkanen and Heikki Helin. Composing workflows of semantic web services. In *Proceedings of the Workshop on Web-Services and Agent-based Engineering*, 2003.
7. Daniel J. Mandell and Sheila A. McIlraith. Adapting bpel4ws for the semantic web: The bottom-up approach to web service interoperation. In *International Semantic Web Conference*, pages 227–241, 2003.
8. G. Petrone. Managing flexible interaction with web services. In *Proc. Workshop on Web Services and Agent-based Engineering (WSABE 2003)*, pages 41–47, Melbourne, Australia, 2003.
9. Munindar P. Singh and Michael N. Huhns. Social abstractions for information agents. In Matthias Klusch, editor, *Intelligent Information Agents*. Kluwer Academic Publishers, 1999.
10. Munindar P. Singh and Michael N. Huhns. *Service-Oriented Computing: Semantics, Processes, Agents*. Wiley, London, UK, 2005.
11. Feng Wan and Munindar P. Singh. Mapping dooley graphs and commitment causality to the pi-calculus. In *AAMAS '04: Proceedings of the Third International Joint Conference on Autonomous Agents and Multiagent Systems*, pages 412–419, Washington, DC, USA, 2004. IEEE Computer Society.
12. Feng Wan and Munindar P. Singh. Enabling persistent web services with commitments. In *Information Technology and Management (ITM)(In Press)*, 2005.
13. Xiaoqin Zhang, Victor Lesser, and Sherief Abdallah. Efficient Management of Multi-Linked Negotiation Based on a Formalized Model. *Autonomous Agents and Multi-Agent Systems*, 2004.
14. XiaoQin Zhang, Victor Lesser, and Rodion Podorozhny. Multi-Dimensional, Multi-Step Negotiation for Task Allocation in a Cooperative System. *Autonomous Agents and MultiAgent Systems*, 2003.

Modeling Minority Games with BDI Agents - A Case Study

Wolfgang Renz and Jan Sudeikat

Multimedia Systems Laboratory,
Hamburg University of Applied Sciences,
Berliner Tor 7, 20099 Hamburg, Germany
Tel. +49-40-42875-8304
{wr, sudeikat}@informatik.haw-hamburg.de

Abstract. Binary decisions are common in our daily lives and often individuals can gain by choosing the minority's side. The socio–economically inspired Minority Game (MG) has been introduced as an exact model of the famous El Farol's Bar Problem, which exhibits complex behavior. In this paper we show that the MG players can be naturally modeled by agents using reactive planning, implemented with a common deliberative programming paradigm, the Belief–Desire–Intention (BDI) model. Our simulation framework is build in Jadex, a forthcoming platform implementing BDI notions. Straightforward implementation of multi–agent simulations is enabled by XML agent descriptions and referenced Java classes. Design of the player agents and simulation results are shown. As a case study, we introduce a new adaptive stochastic MG with dynamically evolving strategies. It exhibits different regimes, reaching from optimal cooperation to destructive behavior, including the emergence of the so called "Schwarzer Peter" game, depending on control parameters. We identify optimization mechanisms like rotation in the working regime as well as metastable behavior.

1   Introduction

Individuals are often faced with difficult decisions. Research has shown that the rationality assumed in economics and classical artificial intelligence – using *deductive reasoning* breaks down under complication. While perfect theoretical solutions can be found in simple scenarios, e.g. null-sum games via minimax-search[1], complicated scenarios make deductive reasoning infeasible for individuals.

Agents get overwhelmed because (1) their *rationality is bounded* and (2) in interactive scenarios agents are often forced to make *assumptions about the future behavior of opponents*, which do not behave rational (see [2] for an enjoyable justification). This leads to ill–defined problems for the individual. When deductive reasoning fails, agents are forced to use *inductive reasoning*. To allow *localized deductions*, simple internal hypothesises about the environment are evaluated and revised continuously.

T. Eymann et al. (Eds.): MATES 2005, LNAI 3550, pp. 71–81, 2005.

A famous setting to examine inductive reasoning is given by the *El Farol Bar Problem* (EFBP) [2]. It is labeled according to a bar in Santa Fe, which is only enjoyable to visit, if it is not too crowded – defined by a certain threshold. Agents are regularly forced to decide, either to *go* there or to *stay home*. In order to do so, they have to anticipate the current amount of customers. Their only source of information is the history of attendings from past evenings. Obviously, this leads to a situation, where inductive reasoning is needed.

A socio–economically inspired, exact formulation of this kind of scenario is given in the so–called *Minority Game* (MG) [3]. An odd number of N players have to make repeatedly binary decisions (e.g. yes or no, 1 or 0). In an economic interpretation, the players can be regarded as consumers deciding to buy from two suppliers. With a memory size of m there are 2^m possible histories and 2^{2^m} possible *strategies* to predict the next choice of the majority.

Each player starts with a randomly generated set of these strategies. They are merely predicting functions and can be described as hash tables, where the key denotes the past history and the associated value is the prediction for the next choice. After every round the agents get informed about the result. Agents in the minority group get rewarded, e.g. by a score increment. In every round the agents compare the actual result with the predictions of all their strategies, in order to rate, which would have lead to proper predictions. Most accurate strategies are used (ties get randomly broken) for future predictions.

This definition of the game does not allow agents to alter their set of strategies, leading to quenched disordered system behavior. Several modifications of the game have been introduced. These range from evolutionary approaches [4],[5] to stochastic simplifications [6]. Despite exhaustive theoretical investigations on the dynamic behavior and possible optimizations of populations (see [7] for an overview), there are still open questions concerning the simultaneous optimization of possibly deliberative behaviors [8]. Also the dynamics of MGs including effective adaption mechanisms have to be further explored. In this paper, we keep strategy space extremely simple and present a new adaptive stochastic MG with its focus on dynamically evolving self–organization and emergent structures.

Complex systems science and statistical physics use *multi–agent based simulations* (MABS) to construct and analyze complex behavior of several individuals [9],[10]. However, the computational models actually used are rarely agent based, in the sense these systems are defined in Multi–Agent Systems (MAS) and Distributed Artificial Intelligence (DAI) research [11]. Coming from the computer science perspective, we argue that the MG can be naturally modeled with BDI agents, allowing reactive planning. The computational models, developed for numerical analysis, can be mapped on this deliberative architecture, designed for general use.

Agent Based Software Engineering (AOSE) is an active research area, which aims to simplify the construction of complex systems by the usage of natural abstractions [12],[13]. A successful abstraction to describe and compute individual agents is the deliberative Belief–Desire–Intention (BDI) model [14]. Methodologies [15],[16] and tools [17] are in active development to support the construction of software systems, using agents as the basic design and programming metaphor.

The above described results in MG simulation lead recently to the definition of *universality* in MAS [18] and have implications for MAS design. Since in the engineering of MAS is not only concerned with system behavior, but also with the performance of individuals, this work examines regimes of behavior in respect to individual gain.

The next Section introduces the BDI architecture and shows how the players in the MG can be naturally modeled as BDI systems. A simplified stochastic version of the MG is presented and analysed in section 3. Finally, section four provides concluding remarks and future directions for research.

2   Modeling a Minority Game with BDI Agents

In general, two kinds of agent architectures can be distinguished. *Reactive* and *deliberative* agents. The first ones react directly upon exterior input (e.g. sensors), while the later ones operate on a symbolic representation of their environment, to achieve intelligent behavior, particularly by means of planning. In opposition to *automatic planning*, i.e. the synthesis of plans from first principles, research has led to agent architectures to allow *reactive planning*, where agents use precompiled plans, developed at design time. E. g. the well known *procedural–reasoning system* [19] has combined this approach with an architecture that allows runtime practical reasoning.

2.1   BDI–Based Agent Models

A successful architecture to develop deliberative agents is the BDI model. Bratman [20] developed a theory of human practical reasoning, which describes rational behavior by the notions *Belief*, *Desire* and *Intention*. Implementations of this model introduced the concrete concepts of *goals* and *plans*, leading to a formal theory and an executable model [14],[21].

Beliefs represent the local information an agent has about both its environment and its internal state. Modeling the structure of the beliefs defines a domain dependent abstraction of environmental entities. It can be seen as the *view–point* of an agent. The goals represent their desires, commonly expressed by certain target states in the beliefs. This concept allows to implement both reactive and pro–active behavior. Reactive mechanisms are modeled by goals or plans which are triggered by the occurrence of certain events, while pro-active behavior is implemented by goals which are not directly triggered. Agents carry out these goals on their own (see [22] for discussion of goals in BDI systems). Finally, plans are the executable means by which agents achieve their goals. In order to reach target states, agents deliberate which plans to execute. A library of plans it available to the individual agent, from which it selects. Single plans are not just a sequence of basic actions, but may also dispatch sub-goals.

2.2   The Jadex Project

The Jadex research project[1] [23],[24], provides the BDI–concepts on top of the well known JADE[2] Agent Platform [25]. A suite of tools facilitate the development, deployment and debugging of Jadex–based MAS. The single agents consist of two parts. First, they are described by the so–called *Agent Description Files* (ADF), which denote the structures of beliefs and goals together with other implementation dependent details in XML syntax. Secondly, the activities agents can perform are coded in plans, these are ordinary Java-classes.

The goals and plans of the single agents can be described as a tree. Some AOSE and Requirements Engineering (RE) methodologies use corresponding trees to model agent behavior (see [26] for an overview). The nodes are goals and plans, which both can dispatch subgoals. The leafs of these trees are plans, since they are the only means to perform activities.

The following case study exemplifies how the reactive planning mechanism can be used to model players in MG–scenarios. The strategies map directly to executable plans, which are used to make a decision for the next vote. Accordingly, the goal hierarchy inside an MG agent expresses the decision process, which leads to the selection of a certain strategy to be applied in the current round. From a Software–Engineering point of view, the use of the Jadex platform is expedient, since it allows convenient adjustment and enhancement of agents. New strategies and goals can be added to the agents incrementally, already existing ones are not effected. Development is eased by the usage of mainstream technologies, namely Java[3] and XML.[4]

3   An Adaptive Stochastic Minority Game with Dynamically Changing Strategies

Here, a new *adaptive stochastic* version of the MG (SMG) with a very simple strategy space is considered, which supports adaptive behavior by introducing rules for time evolving probabilities. A number of papers have shown that some of the interesting behavior of the MG is obtained from simplified SMG's [5],[27],[28]. Our model, in the spirit of models recently discussed [29],[30] displays a dynamical evolution of decision behavior of agents. It generalizes both the simplest SMG [6] and the evolutionary MG (EMG) [4]. Specific behaviors emerge, i. e. alternating or supplier loyal behavior, as the system evolves in time.

3.1   Definition of the MG

The game is round-based and consists of an odd number of N agents and two suppliers. In order to choose one of the suppliers 0 or 1 at each time step, each agent i keeps a probability $p_i(t) \in (0, 1)$ to change the supplier, i.e. it stays with

---

[1] http://vsis-ww.informatik.uni-hamburg.de/projects/jadex

[2] http://jade.tilab.com/

[3] http://java.sun.com/

[4] http://www.w3.org/XML/

the same supplier as in the former step with probability $1 - p_i(t)$. The result of his choice is denoted by $s_i(t) \in \{0, 1\}$. The supplier chosen by the minority of the agents in time step t makes them winners, the majority having chosen the other supplier loose. At the beginning, suppliers $s_i(0)$ are selected randomly and the p_i are chosen uniformly over the interval $[0, 1]$, in our present study. The dynamical evolution consists in the change of the agents probability $p_i(t)$ after each round. After winning, the probability is multiplied by $\lambda_+ > 0$ whereas after loosing it is multiplied by $\lambda_- > 0$ thereby limiting the maximum of the probability to 1.0 in cases of $\lambda_+, \lambda_- > 1$ (see figure 1). Depending on λ_+, λ_- the probability to change the supplier is increased or decreased after winning or loosing, resp. Time evolution is expected to balance agents at mixed strategy or can lead to the extreme cases of *supplier–loyal* strategy $p_i \to 0$ or deterministic *alternating strategy* $p_i = 1.0$. The parameters $\lambda_{+,-}$ span the control space of the emerging adaptive behavior.

3.2   Implementation

Figure 1 gives a brief overview of the simple evolutionary MG. The upper left corner shows the goal hierarchy of the single agents. The call (*msg:request_bid*)

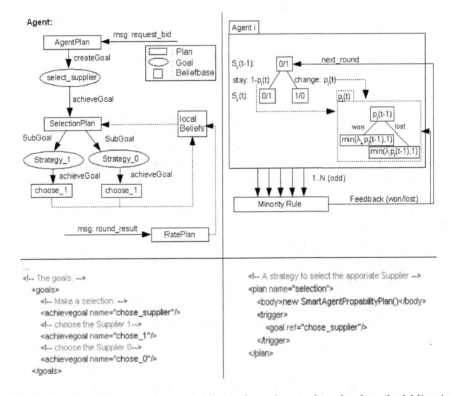

Fig. 1. The Goal hierarchy (upper left), the flow of control in the described Minority Game (upper right) and example XML–code, describing the agents (bottom)

for the next round (i+1) is processed by a plan in each single agent (*AgentPlan*). Upon arrival a new goal (*select_supplier*) is instantiated, which is achieved by a dedicated plan (*SelectionPlan*). There are two possible subgoals, which will either choose supplier 0 or 1. The selectionPlan is responsible to calculate the current probability $p_i(t)$ and to decide the strategy to be used in the current round. Agents get informed about the result of a round by reception of a message (*msg: round_result*). A Plan (*RatePlan*) is responsible to process this message which leads to an update of the local beliefs.

The two XML-snippets in the lower half of Figure 1 were extracted from the according ADF to visualize the internals of the stochastic agents. They show the declaration of the agent's goals (left hand side) and the reference to a Java class (right hand side).

3.3   Simulation Results

Interesting quantities to observe are the difference of the attendance of the two suppliers $A(t) = N_1(t) - N_0(t)$ and its statistical properties, with:

$$A(t) = 2 \sum_{i=0}^{N-1} s_i(t) - N \qquad s_i(t) \in \{0, 1\} \tag{1}$$

The global loss of system according to unbalanced supplier-choices is measured by the long–time average of $\bar{A} = \langle A(t) \rangle_t$, which can become non–zero only in case of non–ergodic freezing, and

$$\sigma^2(t) = A^2(t) - \bar{A}^2 \quad \text{and its long–time average} \quad \overline{\sigma^2} = \langle \sigma^2(t) \rangle_t \tag{2}$$

Furthermore, the success of the individual agent is measured by its score, i.e. the number of rounds won as a function of time. The individual success of the agent population is contained in the score histograms and there statistical properties. Interestingly enough, strict general statements on the relation between global success and individual success have not been given in MGs so far, to our present knowledge [8].

In the following, simulation results and arguments to understand the system behavior are given. An analytical and numerical treatment of the underlying Markov process is to be published in a separate paper.

There are at least *five different regimes of behavior*, the singular fixed–strategies case, two segregation–freezing regimes, one with supplier–loyal the other with deterministic alternating agents, and two regimes where solutions with global cooperations compete with global and individual loss situations. In the *fixed–strategies case* $\lambda_+ = \lambda_- = 1$, all agents keep their initial probabilities p_i and the system evolves in a stationary balanced state $\bar{A} = 0$ with $\overline{\sigma^2} \approx c_{1.0,1.0} N$ (cf. figure 2). The coefficient $c_{1.0,1.0}$ is about a factor of 4 smaller than pure random choice would generate. In comparison, the stochastic MG by [6] would cause an increase proportional N^2 for our conditions, cf. figure 2.

In the *supplier–loyal freezing regime* $\lambda_+, \lambda_- < 1$ time–evolution happens in two stages. In the initial, mixing stage, the minority–supplier changes often and

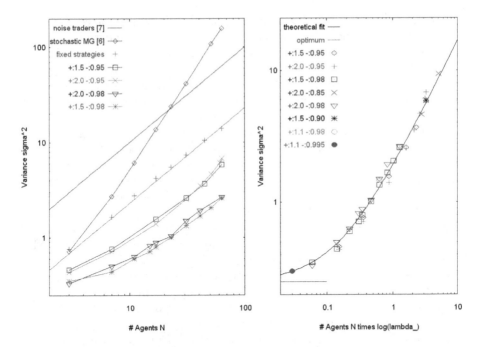

Fig. 2. *Left*: The global loss σ^2 as a function of the number of agents N in the fixed–strategies case $\lambda_+ = \lambda_- = 1$ is about a factor of 4 smaller than random choice (noise traders [7]) would be. If we change our algorithm and let winning agents stay with their supplier with probability one, we obtain the simple stochastic MG by [6], which leads to $O(N^2)$ behavior with our initial distributions. In the working regime, nearly optimal behavior is observed at low N. *Right*: Using a scaling of N with $-\log(\lambda_-)$ inspired by the information–theoretic interpretation of the adaption parameter λ_-, a data collapse is obtained with a crossover from asymptotic optimum at $\lambda_- \to 1$ ("Schwarzer Peter") to asymptotic $O(N)$ at $\lambda_- \neq 1$.

the agents initial probabilities are mixed to some extend, depending on the smaller of the λs, which limits the duration of this initial stage. In the final, freezing stage, $A(t) \to \bar{A} \neq 0$ in general and the minority–supplier is fixed with almost no agent changing side any more, since the $p_i(t)$ become exponentially small.

A similar time–evolution in two stages is observed also in the *deterministic–alternation freezing regime* $\lambda_+, \lambda_- > 1$. The difference is that after the initial mixing stage, the freezing happens according to the fact that all $p_i = 1.0$, and all agents as well as the minority–supplier deterministically alternate.

In both freezing regimes, the agents segregate in two populations, the winners and the losers where the fractions are determined by the ratio of the λs and by the initial distribution of the $p_i(0)$, i.e. a memory effect, which is well-known for freezing phenomena also in the MG. As a consequence, even in both freezing regimes are parameter ranges where the global loss $\bar{A}^2 + \overline{\sigma^2}$ is minimized in $o(1)$. Contrarily, segregation causes the almost constant majority of individual agents to permanently loose in the freezing stage.

Around the half–axis $\lambda_+ > 1, \lambda_- = 1$ an interesting phenomenon occurs, well known as the "Schwarzer Peter" game in german–speaking countries. It means that finally a global optimum solution is obtained with an equal amount of $(n-1)/2$ agents on both sides with $p_i = 1.0$ alternating between the suppliers and there is one agent with $p_j \neq 1.0$. Now, always the group in which the agent j stays is the majority and looses, i.e. pulls the "short straw", the agent j is the "Schwarzer Peter". As soon as we choose λ_- slightly below 1, there are more candidates for the "short straw", so that this role moves around the agents. Then the loss of the single "Schwarzer Peter" is distributed smoothly on all agents. This is kind of a rotation mechanism resolves the segregation observed in the freezing regime and leads to the working regime introduced in the following.

Now we come to discuss the regime $\lambda_+ > 1, \lambda_- < 1$, where winners increase their probability to change the supplier in contrast to loosers, who increase the tendency to stay. As long as λ_- is not too small, an evolution towards mixed strategies is observed and a nice balanced cooperative behavior is observed with both global loss and individual loss even smaller than for the singular fixed–strategies case. This regime can be called the *working regime* of our model. As soon as λ_- is too small, time–evolution again happens in two stages. The beginning stage looks still balanced but a small fraction of agents happen to stick to one supplier because they reach small p_i. Still the minority–supplier changes, and keeps the population homogeneous. This stage can stay for a longer time before the sticky agents segregate and reach size $N/2$. Then, in the final stage the minority–supplier is fixed and an ongoing condensation of the free agents to the majority of non–changing agents occurs, leading to the worst situation, total global and individual loss. This mechanism is reminiscent of nucleation and condensation phenomena at first order phase transitions, including the occurrence of metastability in large systems. Analytical arguments supporting this analogy will be published elsewhere.

Finally, in the regime $\lambda_+ < 1, \lambda_- > 1$ winners increase their tendency to stay whereas losers increase there tendency to change. As long as the product λ_- is not too large, an evolution towards mixed strategies is observed for λ_+ close to 1, which changes to a $\sigma^2 \propto N^2$ for smaller λ_+. These results are similar as those in the fixed–probability model by [6]. If λ_- is large enough, alternating behavior becomes more and more dominant around the half–axis $\lambda_+ = 1, \lambda_- > 1$ where the deterministic–alternation freezing regime sets on.

The rich behavior found in our simple stochastic MG with dynamically changing strategies is of conceptual interest in the understanding of self–organization and cooperation of economic systems. Instead of quenched disorder in the thermal MG model [7], our model contains annealed disorder in the freezing regimes. Furthermore metastability and condensation phenomena can be analyzed by our model, which have not been found in other MG models so far.

In [31] a symbiotic relationship between so–called *producers* and *speculators* has been found. The producers are defined as agents which only apply one strategy in every round, whereas speculators use a set of predictive strategies ($>= 2$). While the producers introduce systematic biases into the market, the speculators remove them, leading to a systematic reduction of fluctuations, thus reducing the losses of the whole population. The agents in our MG form a similar relationship. The selections of loyal agents ($p_i \rightarrow 0$) is predictable, which can be exploited by alternating agents ($p_i = 1.0$). In opposition to [31] the composition of the whole population is not set at design time but adapts itself according to λ_+ and λ_-.

4   Conclusions

In this paper we have presented the MG as an example of how reactive planning can be used to model socio–economic systems with many members who rely on inductive reasoning. We have introduced a new adaptive stochastic MG with dynamically changing strategies which exhibits different regimes including best optimization $\sigma^2 = O(1)$, classical scaling $\sigma^2 \propto N$ and worst case $\sigma^2 \propto N^2$. These regimes evolve adaptively in a self–organized way leading to emergent phenomena like the "Schwarzer Peter" and rotation solutions at the boundary of the working regime. The presented model opens a way to study adaptation mechanisms in MGs with larger stategy space like in the classic MG. Furthermore it is interesting to examine the behavior of our agents in mixtures with agents using differing sets of strategies, e.g. so–called *speculators, producers* and *noise traders* [31,32] or *smart agents* [29].

The presented modeling approach leads to further investigation in economics and computer science. So far the MG has mostly been studied with random boolean strategies or mathematically defined species. We have found new metastable behaviors in our adaptive stochastic MG. It is certainly of large interest to study the conditions under which such metastable behaviors can be obtained in more realistic models. Also in specific application domains the aim of an individual set of strategies is to model the application semantics, relevant for the success of the individual agent [33].

Modeling in BDI notions, as described in this paper, can guide the search for heuristic strategies to be applied in real life scenarios. Currently, AOSE is based on heuristics [34] and methodologies concerning dedicated platforms [16]. A structured approach to identify successful mental attitudes to a given problem will be a useful contribution to AOSE, since it will guide MAS programmers to decide how sophisticated individual agents need to be (recently *universality*, found in reactive MAS has been proposed for this purpose [18]), to solve certain problems.

Acknowledgements

One of us (J.S.) would like to thank the *Distributed Systems and Information Systems* (VSIS) group at Hamburg University, particularly Winfried Lamersdorf, Lars Braubach and Alexander Pokahr for inspiring discussion and encouragement.

References

1. Russell, S.J., Norvig, P.: Artificial Intelligence: A Modern Approach. Number 0-13-103805-2 in Series in Articial Intelligence. Prentice Hall (1995)
2. Arthur, W.B.: Inductive reasoning and bounded rationality. American Economic Review **84** (1994) 406–11 available at http://ideas.repec.org/a/aea/aecrev/v84y1994i2p406-11.html.
3. Challet, D., Zhang, Y.C.: Emergence of cooperation and organization in an evolutionary game. Physica A 246, 407 (1997)
4. Metzler, R., Horn, C.: Evolutionary minority games: the benefits of imitation. In: Physica A329. (2003) 484–498
5. Johnson, N., Hui, P., Jonson, R., Lo, T.: Self-organized segregation within an evolving population. In: Physical Review Letters 82, 3360. (1999)
6. Reents, G., Metzler, R., Kinzel, W.: A stochastic strategy for the minority game. In: Physica A 299. (2001) 253–261
7. Challet, D., Marsili, M., Zhang, Y.C.: Minority Games - Interacting agents in financial markets. Number 0-19-856640-9 in Series: Oxford Finance Series. Oxford University Press (2004)
8. Challet, D.: Competition between adaptive agents: from learning to collective efficiency and back. In: chapter to appear in *Collectives and the design of complex systems*. cond-mat/0210319, Springer (2003)
9. Shalizi, C.R.: Methods and techniques of complex systems science: An overview. Nonlinear Sciences, nlin.AO/0307015 (2003)
10. Parunak, H.V.D., Savit, R., Riolo, R.L.: Agent-based modeling vs. equation-based modeling: A case study and users' guide. In: MABS. (1998)
11. Drogoul, A., Vanbergue, D., Meurisse, T.: Multi-agent based simulation: Where are the agents? In: Proceedings of MABS'02 (Multi-Agent Based Simulation), LNCS, Springer-Verlag (2002)
12. Jennings, N.R.: On agent-based software engineering. Artif. Intell. **117** (2000) 277–296
13. Jennings, N.R.: Building complex, distributed systems: the case for an agent-based approach. Comms. of the ACM **44 (4)** (2001) 35–41
14. Rao, A.S., Georgeff, M.P.: BDI-agents: from theory to practice. In: Proceedings of the First Intl. Conference on Multiagent Systems, San Francisco (1995)
15. Wei, G.: Agent orientation in software engineering. Knowledge Engineering Review **16(4)** (2002) 349–373
16. Sudeikat, J., Braubach, L., Pokahr, A., Lamersdorf, W.: Evaluation of agent - oriented software methodologies - examination of the gap between modeling and platform. In Giorgini, P., Mller, J.P., Odell, J., eds.: Agent-Oriented Software Engineering V, Fifth International Workshop AOSE 2004, Springer Verlag (2004) 126–141
17. Luck, M., Preist, P.M.C.: Agent Technology: Enabling Next Generation Computing. Number ISBN 0854 327886. Agentlink II (2003)
18. Parunak, H.V.D., Brueckner, S., Savit, R.: Universality in multi-agent systems. In: AAMAS '04: Proceedings of the Third International Joint Conference on Autonomous Agents and Multiagent Systems, IEEE Computer Society (2004) 930–937
19. Georgeff, M.P., Lansky, A.L.: Reactive reasoning and planning: an experiment with a mobile robot. In: Proceedings of the 1987 National Conference on Artificial Intelligence (AAAI 87), Seattle, Washington (1987) 677–682

20. M.E.Bratman: Intentions, Plans, and Practical Reason. Harvard Univ. Press. (1987)
21. Rao, A.S.: Agentspeak(l): Bdi agents speak out in a logical computable language. In: MAAMAW '96: Proceedings of the 7th European workshop on Modelling autonomous agents in a multi-agent world : agents breaking away, Springer-Verlag New York, Inc. (1996) 42–55
22. Braubach, L., Pokahr, A., Lamersdorf, W., Moldt, D.: Goal representation for bdi agent systems. In Bordini, R.H., Dastani, M., Dix, J., Fallah-Seghrouchni, A.E., eds.: Second International Workshop on Programming Multiagent Systems: Languages and Tools. (2004) 9–20
23. Braubach, L., Pokahr, A., Lamersdorf, W.: Jadex: A short overview. In: Main Conference Net.ObjectDays 2004. (2004) 195–207
24. Pokahr, A., Braubach, L., Lamersdorf, W.:   Jadex: Implementing a bdi-infrastructure for jade agents. EXP - in search of innovation (Special Issue on JADE) **3** (2003) 76–85
25. Bellifemine, F., Rimassa, G., Poggi, A.: Jade a fipa-compliant agent framework. In: In 4th International Conference on the Practical Applications of Agents and Multi-Agent Systems (PAAM-99), London, UK (1999) 97108
26. van Lamsweerde, A.: Goal-oriented requirements engineering: A guided tour. In Proc. RE01 - Int. Joint Conference on Requirements Engineering (2001)
27. Cavagna, A.: Irrelevance of memory in the minority game. In: Phys. Rev. E 59. (1999)
28. Burgos, E., Ceva, H.: Self organization in a minority game: the role of memory and a probabilistic approach. In: cond-mat/0003179. (2000)
29. Xie, Y., Wang, B.H., Hu, C., Zhou, T.: Global Optimization of Minority Game by Smart Agents. ArXiv Condensed Matter e-prints (2004)
30. Zhong, L.X., Zheng, D.F., Zheng, B., Hui, P.: Effects of contrarians in the minority game. In: cond-mat/0412524. (2004)
31. Challet, D., Marsili, M., Zhang, Y.C.: Modeling market mechanism with minority game. Physica A 276, 284, preprint cond-mat/9909265 (2000)
32. Zhang, Y.C.: Toward a theory of marginally efficient markets. Physica A 269, 30, eprint arXiv:cond-mat/9901243 (1999)
33. Bazzan, A.L., Bordini, R.H., Andrioti, G.K., Vicari, R.M.: Wayward agents in a commuting scenario (personalities in the minority game). In: Proc. of the Fourth Int. Conf. on Multi-Agent Systems (ICMAS'2000), Boston, IEEE Computer Science (2000)
34. Wooldridge, M., Jennings, N.: Software engineering with agents: Pitfalls and pratfalls. In: IEEE Internet Computing. Volume 3. (1999)

A Goal Deliberation Strategy for BDI Agent Systems

Alexander Pokahr, Lars Braubach, and Winfried Lamersdorf

Distributed Systems and Information Systems,
Computer Science Department, University of Hamburg
{pokahr, braubach, lamersd}@informatik.uni-hamburg.de

Abstract. One aspect of rational behavior is that agents can pursue multiple goals in parallel. Current BDI theory and systems do not provide a theoretical or architectural framework for deciding how goals interact and how an agent can decide which goals to pursue. Instead, they assume for simplicity reasons that agents always pursue consistent goal sets. By omitting this important aspect of rationality, the problem of goal deliberation is shifted from the architecture to the agent programming level and needs to be handled by the agent developer in an error-prone ad-hoc manner. In this paper a goal deliberation strategy called Easy Deliberation is proposed allowing agent developers to specify the relationships between goals in an easy and intuitive manner. It is based on established concepts from goal modeling as can be found in agent methodologies like Tropos and requirements engineering techniques like KAOS. The Easy Deliberation strategy has been realized within the Jadex BDI reasoning engine and is further explained by an example application. To fortify the practical usefulness of the approach it is experimentally shown that the computational cost for deliberation is acceptable and only increases polynomially with the number of concurrent goals.

1 Introduction

Goal-directedness is one important characteristic of rational agents, because it allows agents to exhibit pro-active behavior [19] and it is argued that the BDI (belief-desire-intention) model [3] is well suited to describe this kind of agents [16]. Typically, goal-directed agents should be capable of pursuing multiple goals simultaneously. As a consequence the agent's goals can interact positively or negatively with each other [18]. Positive interaction means that one goal contributes to the fulfillment of another one, whereas negative contribution indicates a conflict situation in which one goal hinders the other. Such contribution relationships between goals are commonly used in modeling agent applications, e.g. in the Tropos methodology [7] and in the requirements engineering technique KAOS [10]. Despite their usefulness, most implemented agent systems based on the BDI model do not support any mechanism for handling goal relationships at the architectural level. Hence, the cumbersome task of ensuring that the agent will never process any conflicting goals at the same time is left to the agent developer.

The main aspect of goal deliberation is *"How can an agent deliberate on its (possibly conflicting) goals to decide which ones shall be pursued?"* [5]. Considering this question from an architectural point of view it is of interest how a goal deliberation strategy can be integrated into a BDI infrastructure. Thereby, the agent infrastructure has the

T. Eymann et al. (Eds.): MATES 2005, LNAI 3550, pp. 82–93, 2005.

tasks to activate the strategy at certain points in time and to provide a clearly defined interface by specifying the possible operations for conflict resolution and exploiting positive goal interactions. These operations are constrained by the attitudes supported by the agent architecture. E.g. only when the architecture distinguishes between goals and desires the deliberation process can resort to both concepts.

Tackling the question from a strategy-centric point of view it is necessary to address at least the following issues:

1. *What are the important influence factors that can be used to drive the decision process?* As influence factors all of the agents attitudes such as the active goals or plans can be considered. Additionally, several approaches utilize meta-information about these attitudes such as resource requirements [17,18].
2. *When and how often shall the agent deliberate about its goals?* Generally, the strategy could require that the agent engages in the deliberation process in regular intervals (e.g. time or cycle driven) or on demand (e.g. when a new goal was created) or in a mixture of both.
3. *About what goal set shall the agent deliberate?* The options range from deliberation between just two goals to the consideration of all goals of an agent.

The approach presented in this paper proposes a deliberation strategy called Easy Deliberation which allows for specifying the relationships between goals for conflict detection. At runtime an extended BDI system ensures that the constraints of the concrete deliberation settings, as specified by an agent developer, are respected and only consistent goal sets are pursued at any one time. Main design rationale behind the strategy is the ease of use for agent developers requiring minimal specification overhead.

The remainder of this paper is structured as follows: In Section 2 explicit goal representation as necessary prerequisite for goal deliberation is discussed. Section 3 presents the conceptualization, realization and experimental evaluation of the Easy Deliberation strategy. A brief review of related work is introduced in Section 4. The paper concludes with a summary and an outlook on future work.

2   Explicit Goal Representation

Realizing a goal deliberation strategy has the necessary prerequisite that an agent is aware of its goals at any one time. In classical agent languages such as AgentSpeak(L) [14] and current BDI systems such as JACK [9] or Jason [2] this prerequisite is not fulfilled. The main reason for this shortcoming is that goals are represented in the transient form of events, which causes an agent to only know about its goals at the moment they need to be processed. As a consequence an agent e.g. cannot easily defer the processing of a certain goal, because there is no semantics behind the event representing the agent's intended desire. Hence, in the several papers [5,16] this implicit representation was criticized and different enhancements were proposed.

In this paper we build on the explicit representation of goals as described in [5]. In short, it consists of a generic goal lifecycle (cf. Fig. 1) that exactly describes the states and transition relationships of goals at runtime and forms the basis for different goal types such as perform, achieve, query, maintain. Adopted goals can be in either of the substates *Option, Active* or *Suspended*, whereby only active goals are currently pursued by the agent. Options and suspended goals represent inactive goals, where options are inactive, because the agent explicitly wants them to be, e.g. because an option conflicts with some active goal. In contrast, suspended goals currently must not be pursued, because their context is invalid. They will remain inactive until their context is valid again and they become options.

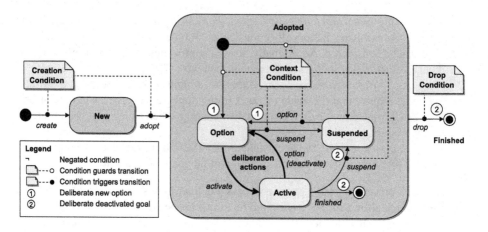

Fig. 1. Goal lifecycle (adapted from [5])

Additionally, some basic properties common to all goal types have been defined. Among those the most important ones are: A creation condition that defines when a new goal instance is created; a context condition that describes when a goal's execution should be suspended (to be resumed when the context is valid again); and a drop condition that defines when a goal instance is removed. At runtime, goal state changes occur, whenever one of the aforementioned conditions triggers or the agent intentionally changes the state, e.g. by exploiting a goal deliberation mechanism for this purpose.

3   The Easy Deliberation Strategy

Integrating a goal deliberation strategy requires that the agent can engage into the deliberation process whenever the strategy demands. Additionally, the operations available to the deliberation mechanism need to be clearly defined (cf. architectural viewpoint in Section 1). As a foundation for the definition of available operations for goal deliberation strategies, the generic goal lifecycle is used (see Fig. 1). For goal deliberation only adopted goals are of relevance as they represent the goals an agent is aware of.

From this lifecycle the operations for *activating* an option and *deactivating* an active goal, i.e. making it an option again, are derived as interface for goal deliberation, i.e. these transitions should be under control of the deliberation strategy (bold transitions in Fig. 1). This set of operations should not be considered as being the only possibility, alternative strategies might incorporate other actions such as *drop*.

3.1 Strategy Conceptualization

The Easy Deliberation strategy is conceived to allow real-time goal deliberation even when an agent pursues a multitude of goals simultaneously. The strategy is based on practical considerations derived from example applications and ideas from goal modeling as can be found in the agent methodology Tropos [7] and the requirements engineering technique KAOS [10], which both propose directed contribution links between goals. According to Section 1, the strategy will be explained by answering the characteristic questions:

1. *What are the important influence factors that can be used to drive the decision process?* The strategy is based only on information about goals, intentionally factoring out the plan level. Two main concepts are used to describe deliberation information within goal type declarations: *cardinalities* and *inhibition arcs*. Cardinalities can be used to constrain the maximum number of active goals of a specific type at runtime, whereas inhibition arcs are used to declare negative contribution relationships between two goals on type level as well as on instance level. On the type level it can be specified that a goal of a given type inhibits goals of the referenced type. For a finer-grained specification instance-level relationships between goals can be defined by attaching constraints to the inhibition links, which determine the goal instances affected by the inhibition. The strategy requires the inhibition links forming a directed acyclic graph to avoid infinite deliberation loops.

2. *When and how often shall the agent deliberate about its goals?* The deliberation process is initiated on demand. In Fig. 1 the triggering state transitions are depicted. Generally two different situations can arise, in which deliberation becomes necessary: First, a goal can become an option either when a new goal is adopted or when the context of a suspended goal becomes valid again. In these cases the deliberation process needs to decide whether the new option can be *activated* and additionally what the consequences of the activation are, i.e. which other active goals need to be *deactivated* to avoid having conflicting goals (*1: Deliberate new option*). Second, an active goal can become inactive when it gets suspended, finished or dropped. In this case, the deliberation has to determine which options have been possibly inhibited by the deactivated goal. For each of these options it needs to be checked whether it can be reactivated (*2: Deliberate deactivated goal*).

3. *About what goal set shall the agent deliberate?* The deliberation process only has to consider a local subset of the agent's goals, derived from the goal that triggered the deliberation with its state transition (see above). For goal types with cardinality, all instances of the goal type have to be considered. In addition, all goals with incoming and outgoing inhibition relationships to the triggering goal have to be taken into account.

In the following both goal deliberation actions will be described more formally. Given that all goals of an agent are in one of the states option, active or other defined by the sets $\Gamma_o, \Gamma_\alpha, \Gamma_\omega$, respectively, the full goal set of an agent is comprised of $\Gamma = \Gamma_o \cup \Gamma_\alpha \cup \Gamma_\omega$ with $\Gamma_o \cap \Gamma_\alpha = \Gamma_o \cap \Gamma_\omega = \Gamma_\alpha \cap \Gamma_\omega = \emptyset$. A goal $\gamma \in \Gamma$ is defined as a tuple $\langle gt, s \rangle$ with gt being the user defined goal template in which creation, context and drop condition among other things are specified and $s \in \{option, active, other\}$

being the actual state of the goal. For simplicity reasons other aspects of concrete goal instances such as parameter values are not considered here.

The *Deliberate new option* action is responsible for activating an option $\gamma_o = \langle gt_o, option \rangle \in \Gamma_o$, if allowed in the current context. Therefore, first it has to be checked, if the goal can be activated by testing cardinality and inhibitions with the predicate $p_{act}(\gamma_o)$ defined as:

$$p_{act}(\gamma_o) : \Gamma_o \to \{true, false\}, p_{act}(\gamma_o) = \forall \gamma \in \Gamma_\alpha (\gamma \nrightarrow \gamma_o) \wedge \mid \Gamma_\eta \mid < f_{card}(gt_o)$$

$$\text{with } \Gamma_\eta = \{\gamma = \langle gt, active \rangle \in \Gamma_\alpha \mid gt = gt_o \wedge \gamma_o \nrightarrow \gamma\}$$

$$\text{and } f_{card}(gt_o) : \Gamma \to \mathbb{N} \text{ (cardinality function)}$$

$$\text{and } \rightarrow \subseteq \Gamma \times \Gamma \text{ (inhibition relation)}$$

The predicate $p_{act}(\gamma_o)$ is to true, when there is no active goal that inhibits goal γ_o, i.e. no pair (γ, γ_o), $\gamma \in \Gamma_\alpha$ is part of the inhibition relation $\rightarrow \subseteq \Gamma \times \Gamma$, and when the number of hindering goals in the set Γ_η is lower than the allowed cardinality of this goal defined by the function $f_{card}(\gamma_o)$. In the set of hindering goals are only those active goals which have the same template as the considered option $gt = gt_o$ and which are not inhibited by the option $\gamma_o \nrightarrow \gamma$ (because these active goals will be subsequently be made to an option). If the goal could be activated it needs to be determined if other currently active goals need to be deactivated. The set of active goals to be deactivated Γ_{inh} is defined as $\Gamma_{inh} = \{\gamma \in \Gamma_\alpha \mid \gamma_o \rightarrow \gamma\}$, which includes all goals the newly activated goal inhibits.

Thus, if an option can be activated the set of adopted goals changes so that the option is made to an active goal and all newly inhibited active goals become options:

$$\Gamma_{new} = \Gamma \setminus \{\gamma_o\} \cup \{\langle gt_o, active \rangle\} \setminus \Gamma_{inh} \cup \Gamma_{opt}$$

$$\text{with } \Gamma_{opt} = \{\langle gt, option \rangle \mid \langle gt, s \rangle \in \Gamma_{inh}\}$$

The *Deliberate deactivated goal* action has to compute for a just deactivated goal $\gamma_o = \langle gt_o, option \rangle \in \Gamma_o$ the set of options Γ_{test} for which it needs to be checked whether they can be reactivated:

$$\Gamma_{test} = \{\gamma \in \Gamma_o \mid gt = gt_o \vee \gamma_o \rightarrow \gamma\} \text{ with } \gamma = \langle gt, option \rangle$$

This set is composed of all options which have the same template as the considered goal $gt = gt_o$, because possibly cardinality allows for another goal of this type being activated. Additionally, all options need to be considered, which were inhibited by the deactivated goal $\gamma_o \rightarrow \gamma$. Note, that this is not the same set as Γ_{inh} because in this case inhibited options instead of active goals are considered. Of course, such goals will only be activated if the deactivated goal was the only inhibitor. As result of performing this action new *Deliberate new option* actions are produced for every option for which the deactivated goal was a *necessary condition* being not activated.

3.2   Realization

The newly conceived deliberation strategy is designed in terms of operations (*Deliberate new option, Deliberate deactivated goal*) which operate on the internal state of the agent. These operations have to be performed at proper times, e.g. when a new goal is adopted or an active goal is suspended or dropped (cf. Fig. 1). Therefore, these operations should not be executed continuously in each interpreter cycle. Instead, they should be activated whenever the need for goal deliberation arises.

To allow such flexible activation of goal deliberation operations a new interpreter architecture is proposed, which does not rely on a fixed interpreter cycle. The basic idea of the architecture is to break up the traditional BDI interpreter cycle [15] into a small set of self-contained meta-actions, which are invoked as needed, rather than being executed in a fixed sequence. The resulting set of meta-actions roughly corresponds to the steps of the original interpreter (see Fig. 2).

```
01  initialize-state();
02  repeat
03      options := option-generator(event-queue);
04      selected-options := deliberate(options);
05      update-intentions(selected-options);
06      execute();
07      get-new-external-events();
08      drop-successful-attitudes();
09      drop-impossible-attitudes();
10  end repeat
```

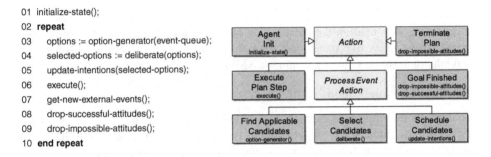

Fig. 2. Abstract interpreter (from [15]) and basic meta actions

The basic mode of operation of the proposed interpreter is depicted in Fig. 3. The interpreter is based on a data structure called *Agenda* where all meta-actions to be processed are collected. The interpreter continuously selects the next entry from the agenda and executes it, thereby changing the internal state of the agent. The execution of an action may further lead to the creation of new actions (*direct effects*), which are inserted into the agenda. Moreover, state changes may cause *side effects*, e.g. when a goal has to be dropped due to a changed belief. These side effects are also inserted to the agenda. More details of this architecture can be found in [11,12].

The presented interpreter architecture has been realized in the Jadex BDI reasoning engine [4,13], which establishes a rational agent layer on top of the JADE platform [1]. In Jadex, an agent type is described within an XML-file that adheres to a BDI metamodel specified in XML schema. In addition, for each plan used by the agent, a plan body has to be implemented in an ordinary Java class.

To integrate the Easy Deliberation strategy into the Jadex system, the basic set of interpreter meta-actions is extended with the newly defined Easy Deliberation actions (*Deliberate new option* and *Deliberate deactivated goal*). The creation of these actions is accomplished through conditions that guard the identified state transitions in the goal

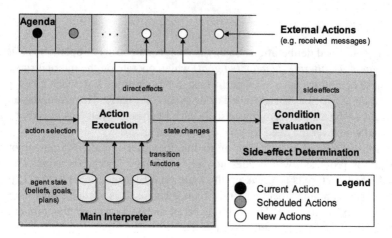

Fig. 3. Interpreter architecture

lifecycle. In order to allow the specification of user-defined deliberation settings in applications the Jadex BDI metamodel has been extended to incorporate the cardinality and inhibition settings directly within the XML agent specifications.

3.3 Example Application

To illustrate the strategy an example application called "cleaner world" is outlined (cf. [5]). The basic idea is that an autonomous robot has at daytime the task to look for waste in some environment and clean up the located pieces by bringing them to a near waste-bin. At night it should stop cleaning and instead patrol around to guard its environment. Additionally, it always has to monitor its battery state and reload it at a charging station when the energy level drops below some threshold. From this scenario the four corresponding top-level goals *PerformLookForWaste*, *PerformPatrol*, *Achieve-CleanupWaste* and *MaintainBatteryLoaded* are derived. Initially, a cleaner possesses a *PerformLookForWaste*, a *PerformPatrol*, and a *MaintainBatteryLoaded* goal, whereas *AchieveCleanupWaste* goals are created for every piece of waste it discovers. To ensure correct operation several constraints must be met and are modeled by specific deliberation settings as described next (cf. Fig. 4):

- Only one *AchieveCleanupWaste* goal must be active at the same time to avoid the cleaner running to different pieces of waste concurrently. Therefore, the cardinality of this goal type is restricted to one.
- The agent must pursue exactly one of the top-level goals at the same time, whereby *MaintainBatteryLoaded* is the most important goal inhibiting all other goals. The *AchieveCleanupWaste* goal inhibits the *PerformLookForWaste* goal to force the agent to clean up known waste before looking for new. These inhibition relationships are introduced at the type-level, i.e. they always apply to all instances of, e.g., *AchieveCleanupWaste* goals. Note, that no deliberation is necessary to decide between *PerformLookForWaste* and *PerformPatrol*, as these goals have different contexts (at daytime vs. at night).

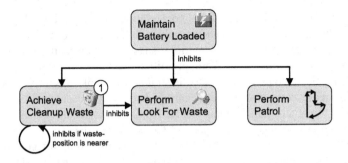

Fig. 4. Constraints between goals of a cleaner agent

```
01 <maintaingoal name="MaintainBatteryLoaded">
02     [omitted parameter and condition specs. for brevity]
03     <deliberation>
04         <inhibits ref="AchieveCleanupWaste"/>
05         <inhibits ref="PerformLookForWaste"/>
06         <inhibits ref="PerformPatrol"/>
07     </deliberation>
08 </maintaingoal>
09
10 <achievegoal name="AchieveCleanupWaste">
11     [omitted parameter and condition specs. for brevity]
12     <deliberation cardinality="1">
13         <inhibits ref="PerformLookForWaste"/>
14         <inhibits ref="AchieveCleanupWaste">
15             $beliefbase.my_location.getDistance($ref.waste.location) >
16             $beliefbase.my_location.getDistance($goal.waste.location)
17         </inhibits>
18     </deliberation>
19 </achievegoal>
```

Fig. 5. Cleaner agent XML fragment

- For improved performance, the cleaner should always clean up the nearest piece of waste first. Hence, an instance-level inhibition arc for the *AchieveCleanupWaste* goal is introduced. An *AchieveCleanupWaste* goal instance inhibits another one, when its waste position is nearer to the agent. Note, that this constraint is not sufficient to replace the cardinality condition introduced earlier, because two or more waste pieces could have exactly the same distance from the cleaner.

The design decisions concerning the deliberation settings of the modeled goals can be directly mapped to the implementation. The extended Jadex XML schema allows deliberation settings to be embedded into the agent's goal specifications (see Fig. 5). The Jadex interpreter then uses these specifications to execute the agent, thereby automatically respecting all modeled dependencies between the goals.

3.4 Evaluation

For agents in dynamic domains, deliberation strategies are only useful, when they provide fast and efficient results, still allowing the agent to quickly react to changes in the environment. The Easy Deliberation strategy was designed to be computationally inexpensive, by only considering bilateral goal relationships. Therefore, the cost for deliberation should increase at most quadratically with the number of concurrent goals of an agent. To verify this analytical expectations, an empirical evaluation was performed.

Figure 6 (a) shows the results from an artificial test case, in which an increasing amount of concurrent goals with instance-level inhibition links has to be processed by an agent. This represents a worst-case scenario, where every present goal competes with any other goal. To obtain generalizable results, Application-specific code is omitted, i.e. no complex actions are performed to achieve the goals. The data we were interested in concerns the pure time for goal deliberation, the remaining time for goal processing (including e.g. plan selection and execution) and the ratio between them. The first thing to note is that the cost of goal processing increases linearly with the number of goals (as shown by the trend function y with regression coefficient R^2). This is due to more plan instances being created, which have to be considered in the plan selection process. Also one can see, that the cost of goal deliberation grows quadratically as expected. Not surprisingly, the ratio between goal processing and deliberation approximates to 100% very fast. With more than 100 concurrent goals, the agent spends 90 percent of its time thinking about which goals to pursue. Nevertheless, the absolute costs of deliberation are low (less than 100 ms even for 500 concurrent goals on a standard desktop PC[1]).

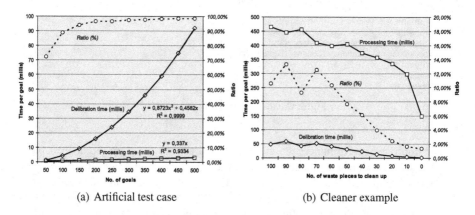

(a) Artificial test case   (b) Cleaner example

Fig. 6. Evaluation results

To collect also data related to practice, a second evaluation was performed in the cleaner example presented above. In this case not only the speed of the reasoning engine was measured, but also the costs incurred by the application. Therefore, in Fig. 6 (b) the time needed for processing a single goal is about 100 times higher, due to the need for computing distances between pieces of waste (for deliberation) and for performing actions like moving the robot around. In this setting the robot starts with 100 cleanup goals which are processing in the order enforced by the deliberation settings. One can see that the deliberation cost decreases faster, as the robot cleans up more and

---

[1] Pentium 4(HT) 3 GHz, 512 MB RAM, WindowsXP, Sun Java 1.4.

more waste. Moreover, in this practical example, the relative time spent for goal deliberation does not exceed 14 percent of the total execution time, although the agent starts with a large number of goals (100). Even though a generalization of these results for other application domains cannot easily be drawn, this example is an indication for the overhead incurred by using explicit goal deliberation being acceptable, when used in the right context.

3.5 Discussion

The Easy Deliberation strategy has been used in several example applications and is sufficiently expressive for a wide variety of settings. Nevertheless, due to its simplicity it exhibits several conceptual limitations:

- The strategy does only consider bilateral relationships. Hence, it is impossible to specify e.g. that two goals together are more important than another single goal.
- Conflicts between subgoals cannot always be resolved optimally, e.g. when a conflict between subgoals could be resolved by replacing one of the subgoals with another non-conflicting subgoal [16].
- Conflicts at plan level are not considered, which means that inconsistencies between plans e.g. because of access to conflicting resources are not detected.
- Positive interactions between goals are not considered, which means that the strategy cannot identify and exploit potentially common subgoals.

Although some of these limitations indicate that the strategy cannot be applied universally to all kinds of problems, it is a straight-forward and easily understandable mechanism, due to reusing ideas from modeling approaches. The reason for choosing inhibition links instead of using utility values is that it allows to adopt a local view and frees the agent developer from establishing a global ordering between all goals. Our practical experiences have shown that the explicit declaration of goal deliberation information makes agent specifications simpler and more readable because concerns are clearly separated. The overhead in many practical settings is low, because a typical application consists of several different agents each deliberating only about small sets of related goals. Moreover, empirical evaluations reveal that the strategy only incurs low computational costs in general.

4   Related Work

The topic of goal deliberation within a single agent has not attracted much attention in the BDI agent community yet. One reason for this deficiency is that most implemented systems do not explicitly support goals and desires. Instead, these systems use a transient representation of goals as a type of event rendering the consideration about goals impossible [16]. In the area of planning agents a considerable amount of work has been devoted to plan scheduling. Main objectives of plan scheduling concern avoiding conflicts in plan execution and exploiting common steps via plan merging [6,8]. These approaches are different in that they require agents to have complete plans and do not support real-time decision control about goals and plans [17].

Our work concerning the Easy Deliberation strategy is similar to the work of Than-garajah et al., who propose strategies for detecting and resolving conflicts [17] as well as for exploiting positive goal interaction [18]. The influence factors of the conflict res-olution strategy from [17] are annotated meta-data to plans and goals called "interaction summaries" containing information about their effects, pre- and in-conditions. This in-formation is used at runtime to defer the adoption of possibly conflicting goals resp. the execution of plans. Compared to Easy Deliberation, the strategy greatly differs in the amount and the kind of deliberation data used and the resulting behavior. Our approach is designed to manage with minimal deliberation information based on agent modeling techniques providing an easy usable mechanism. In contrast, Thangarajah et al. require more detailed information that in return allows for handling conflicts also at plan level. Furthermore, besides ensuring that only conflict free goals are pursued, our strategy also respects the intended order of processing and is suitable for all goal types due to the underlying generic goal lifecycle.

5   Conclusion and Outlook

This paper motivates the need for goal deliberation strategies. To release the agent de-veloper from the burden of ensuring that an agent always pursues consistent goal sets, an agent needs explicit information allowing it to deliberate about its goals, and au-tonomously select an appropriate goal set based on the current situation. In this paper the requirements for goal deliberation are discussed and a set of characteristic questions for conceiving a specific goal deliberation strategy is proposed.

The Easy Deliberation strategy is developed based on concepts from agent modeling techniques. It is designed to be intuitive to use with little specification effort and enables an agent to deliberate about its goals by activating and deactivating certain goals. The realization introduces two strategy specific meta-actions that are added to the underly-ing BDI interpreter architecture, by determining their activation points. During agent execution, the strategy enforces that only conflict free goals are pursued, additionally respecting the relative order of goal importance. Practical experiences with different applications indicate that the strategy considerably simplifies agent development and only incurs a low computational overhead.

Future work is devoted to the further investigation of deliberation strategies. We intend to experiment with alternative strategies, e.g. based on the work of Thangara-jah et al. for comparing the effectiveness of different approaches in typical application domains. Especially, it is interesting to evaluate the advantages of detecting also plan conflicts and possibly extend the Easy Deliberation strategy in this respect.

References

1. F. Bellifemine, G. Caire, and G. Rimassa. JADE: The JADE platform for mobile MAS applications. In *Net.ObjectDays 2004: AgentExpo*, 2004.
2. R. Bordini and J. Hübner. *Jason User Guide*, 2004.
3. M. Bratman. *Intention, Plans, and Practical Reason*. Harvard University Press, Cambridge, Massachusetts, 1987.

4. L. Braubach, A. Pokahr, and W. Lamersdorf. Jadex: A BDI Agent System Combining Middleware and Reasoning. In M. Klusch R. Unland, M. Calisti, editor, *Software Agent-Based Applications, Platforms and Development Kits*. Birkhäuser, 2005.
5. L. Braubach, A. Pokahr, D. Moldt, and W. Lamersdorf. Goal Representation for BDI Agent Systems. In *Proceedings of the Second Workshop on Programming Multiagent Systems (ProMAS04)*, 2004.
6. B. Clement and E. Durfee. Identifying and resolving conflicts among agents with hierarchical plans. In *AAAI Workshop on Negotiation*, 1999.
7. F. Giunchiglia, J. Mylopoulos, and A. Perini. The Tropos Software Development Methodology: Processes, Models and Diagrams. In *Proc. of 1st Int. Joint Conf. on Autonomous Agents and Multiagent Systems (AAMAS'02)*, 2002.
8. J. Horty and M. Pollack. Evaluating new options in the context of existing plans. *Artificial Intelligence*, 127(2):199–220, 2001.
9. N. Howden, R. Rönnquist, A. Hodgson, and A. Lucas. JACK Intelligent Agents-Summary of an Agent Infrastructure. In *Proc.of the 5th ACM Int.Conf. on Autonomous Agents*, 2001.
10. E. Letier and A. van Lamsweerde. Deriving operational software specifications from system goals. *SIGSOFT Softw. Eng. Notes*, 27(6):119–128, 2002.
11. A. Pokahr, L. Braubach, and W. Lamersdorf. A BDI Architecture for Goal Deliberation. In *Proceedings of the Fourth International Joint Conference on Autonomous Agents and Multiagent Systems (AAMAS'05)*, 2005.
12. A. Pokahr, L. Braubach, and W. Lamersdorf. A Flexible BDI Architecture Supporting Extensibility. In *The 2005 IEEE/WIC/ACM International Conference on Intelligent Agent Technology (IAT-2005)*, 2005.
13. A. Pokahr, L. Braubach, and W. Lamersdorf. Jadex: A BDI Reasoning Engine. In J. Dix R. Bordini, M. Dastani and A. Seghrouchni, editors, *Multi-Agent Programming*. Kluwer, 2005.
14. A. Rao. AgentSpeak(L): BDI Agents Speak Out in a Logical Computable Language. In R. van Hoe, editor, *Seventh European Workshop on Modelling Autonomous Agents in a Multi-Agent World*, Eindhoven, The Netherlands, 1996.
15. A. Rao and M. Georgeff. BDI Agents: from theory to practice. In *Proc. of the 1st Int. Conf. on MAS (ICMAS'95)*, 1995.
16. J. Thangarajah, L. Padgham, and J. Harland. Representation and Reasoning for Goals in BDI Agents. In *Proc. of the 25th Australasian Computer Science Conf. (ACSC2002)*, 2002.
17. J. Thangarajah, L. Padgham, and M. Winikoff. Detecting and Avoiding Interference Between Goals in Intelligent Agents. In *Proc. of the 18th Int. Joint Conf. on AI (IJCAI 2003)*, 2003.
18. J. Thangarajah, L. Padgham, and M. Winikoff. Detecting and Exploiting Positive Goal Interaction in Intelligent Agents. In *Proc. of in the 2nd Int. Joint Conference on Autonomous Agents and Multiagent Systems (AAMAS 2003)*, 2003.
19. M. Wooldridge and N. Jennings. Intelligent Agents: Theory and Practice. *The Knowledge Engineering Review*, 10(2):115–152, 1995.

Estimating Utility-Functions for Negotiating Agents: Using Conjoint Analysis as an Alternative Approach to Expected Utility Measurement

Marc Becker, Hans Czap, Malte Poppensieker, and Alexander Stotz

Department of Business Information Systems I,
University of Trier,
54296 Trier, Germany
{marc.becker, hans.czap, malte.poppensieker,
stot4101}@uni-trier.de

Abstract. Utility-based software agents are especially suited to represent human principals in recurring automatic negotiation applications. In order to work efficiently, utility-based agents need to obtain models of the relevant part of the principal's preference structure – represented by utility functions. So far agent theory usually applies expected utility measurement. It has, as we will show, certain shortcomings in real life applications. As an alternative, we suggest an approach based on con-joint analysis, which is a well-understood procedure widely used in marketing research and psychology, but gets only small recognition in agent theory. It offers a user-friendly way to derive quantitative utility values for multi-attribute alternatives from the principal's preferences. In this paper, we introduce the technique in detail along with some extensions and improvements suited for agent applications. Additionally a learning algorithm is derived, keeping track of changes of the principal's preference structure and adjusting measurement errors.[1]

1 Introduction

Negotiating software agents are discussed for basically two kinds of applications. First, they can be applied in studying and evaluating the theoretic models of game theory and economics. Second, negotiating software agents can be used for real life problem solving. Examples of this range from negotiating network traffic to solving complex equilibrium problems. One area of special interest is using software agents as proxies for their human users (principals) in recurring situations where choices between different alternatives have to be made. Most of the time, those alternatives are characterized by multiple attributes.[2]

In this paper, we adopt the idea of utility functions to serve as the connection between human principal and artificial agent. This requires a valid method for measuring that part of a human's utility function that is relevant for the fulfilment of a given task and communicating it to the decision component of the artificial agent.

---

[1] The German National Research Foundation [DFG] has supported this paper as part of their priority research program "Multi-agent Systems and their Business Applications".

[2] An application example for this – using utility based agents for automated operating room scheduling – is described in [7].

T. Eymann et al. (Eds.): MATES 2005, LNAI 3550, pp. 94–105, 2005.
© Springer-Verlag Berlin Heidelberg 2005

For this, we give an introduction to general utility theory in chapter 2. It is shown, that while Expected-Utility-Theory (EU-Theory) still forms the backbone of game theoretic modeling, it is not very well suited for agent applications. Therefore, we propose using Conjoint-Analysis (CA), a technique which proved to be useful in marketing analysis and which aims at providing a simple way for the assessment of utility functions. In chapter 3 a general overview to CA is given, while in chapters 4 and 5 the basics of conjoint-analytical utility measurement are detailed.

Because using utility functions in agents cannot be based on a static one-time utility evaluation, a learning mechanism must be established that accounts for the inter-temporal validity of measurement. A still experimental learning mechanism that integrates completely with negotiating agents and conjoint analytical utility measurement is introduced in chapter 6. The concepts detailed in chapters 4 to 6 are implemented in the LACAM-Software tool that is available at our homepage.[3]

2 Preferences and the Utility-Function

Basically, utility is understood as a measure of a person's wellbeing. This concept dates back to the eighteenth and nineteenth century and relies on the work of British utilitarian philosophers and economists. In their view the concept of wellbeing relates directly to happiness, i.e. they tried to explain a person's behaviour as his[4] attempt to maximize his wellbeing and happiness all at once [16].

Facing the difficulties of measuring a utility function, modern economists try to explain people's behaviour in terms of preferences, i.e. ordinal comparisons of different events. In so far, the utility function of a person becomes a convenient mathematical representation of his preferences, which is only valid on an ordinal scale of measurement.

An ordinal approach suffices for the study of individual decision making where a single individual has to adapt optimally to a given situation, which cannot be altered by this individual himself. This results in a simple maximization problem, which is not sufficient for many real life problems though. Real economic and social problems have many elements in common with the maximization problem, but they usually differ in one essential element: if two or more persons have to negotiate with each other, the possible results for each individual not only depend on his own actions but on those of all others as well. This leads to a situation in which all participants try to maximize their individual utility functions, of which they do not control all variables.[5] Solving negotiation problems implies that concessions and compromises have to be made by every participant. This requires more knowledge than the information

---

[3] In the final chapter, further information and download-links regarding the *LACAM*-Software are provided.

[4] In this paper, we usually use male forms when referring to people. Of course, everything applies to female persons respectively.

[5] In economic modelling, this problem is usually countered by the standard model of 'perfect competition'. By assuming a considerable great (ideally infinite) number of participants - and introducing a bunch of further strict constraints - the influence of each individual participant on market prices becomes negligible, which reduces market decision making back to determining the optimal quantity adaptation, a problem that can again been solved by standard maximizing approaches.

transferred in preference rankings. The individuals need not only to know which alternative they prefer, they must although have a notion about how much they prefer one alternative to another, i.e. they must know the strength of their preferences.

To solve this problem, von Neumann and Morgenstern used an axiomatic approach to prove the existence and the measurability of cardinal utility functions, based on the Bernoulli-Principle. They showed that by introducing probabilities and lotteries to the system of ordinal preference measurement, enough information is generated for deriving interval scaled utility functions valid up to linear transformations [23].

Given an individual with a complete preference structure, i.e. the individual can tell for any two events, which he prefers or if he is indifferent between them, EU-Theory assumes that the individual cannot only compare alternative events but combinations of events and stated probabilities.

Let the individual choose the best (E_b) and the worst event (E_w) from the set of possible events. All other events in the individual's preference ordering are situated in between E_b and E_w ($E_b \geq E_1, E_2 \ldots E_n \geq E_w$). For determining the EU of event n (EU (E_n)), the individual has to decide (hypothetically) between E_n and a lottery (L) in which E_b happens with a probability p and E_w happens with the probability $1-p$, i.e. the individual must state the probability p at which he is indifferent between the sure event E_n and the lottery (L). The indifference probability will then be recorded as EU (E_n).

In practise, this is usually done by first setting $p = 0$. In this situation, the individual will prefer E_n to L. Now p is gradually raised until it reaches the probability p^* at which the individual becomes indifferent between E_n and L. EU (E_n) then equals the stated probability p^*. By repeating these steps for every decision-relevant event, a cardinal utility function for the individual is derived [15].

It is important to note, that the shown approach to utility theory aims mainly at proving the existence of cardinal utility, thus only demonstrating a theoretical approach to its measurement. It is not intended to develop a reliable empirical method of utility measurement.

This is sufficient for using EU in academic reasoning, as it frees theoretical models from the limits of approaches based on ordinal preference. Despite of this, it is not suitable for most real-world applications, as will be shown below.

The first defect of the EU-approach is that expected utility differs from both the classical notion (the numerical representation of wellbeing) and the modern notion (the numerical representation of the strength of preferences) of utility. EU mixes the individual's strength of preferences inseparably with the individual's attitude towards risk. This remains uncritical for applications regarding a risky environment, the usual subject of theoretical analysis. In reality though, decisions are most often made not under risk but under uncertainty. While decision making under risk specifies situations, in which each action leads to a set of possible specific outcomes, each outcome occurring with a known probability, under uncertainty the probabilities of these outcomes are completely unknown or even not meaningful. The risk centred approach to utility and decision making of EU is simply not applicable in these situations.

The differences between risk and uncertainty lead directly to the second defect of EU. It assumes that people are able to compare different probabilities, because they are trained to it from constantly making risky decisions in real life. Actually, they are only trained to make decisions in uncertain situations, which require using heuristics, best practises or feelings [8]. Even trained decision theorists regularly show irrational decision behaviour in experiments about EU-measurement as is shown by the Allais-Paradox [2].

Due to the fact that most people are regularly untrained in evaluating probabilities, statements like "if the probability of the good outcome is raised by 1%, then I am indifferent between the sure and the risky option", do not seem to be more reliable then a direct rating approach, in which individuals are asked to directly assign utility values to concrete events.

Software agents that act as their principals' representatives need a utility function that emulates the principal's preference structure as exactly as possible. Utility functions based on EU cannot achieve this, because of the defects shown above. Given the deficits of EU and the requirements of agent applications, we propose using CA as an alternative method of utility measurement that bases on a measurement procedure resembling real life decision making.

3 Conjoint Analysis as an Alternative Approach to Utility Measurement

In comparison to EU, CA offers an approach to utility measurement that has considerably lower cognitive demands on the principal. Instead of enhancing preference information by introducing lotteries and choice experiments, which adds a great deal of complexity to the measurement procedure, CA aims at statistically revealing additional information hidden in ordinal preference statements. This increases the effort for designing measurement interviews, but leads to significant reductions in complexity on the side of the respondent. In fact, he is only required to create a preference ranking over some presented events.

The foundations of CA were laid out in a seminal paper by Luce and Tukey in 1964 [17]. During the last decades, CA has been successfully applied by psychologists and marketing researchers to a number of different problems, but was somewhat neglected in the decision sciences [9].

In CA, decision situations are described in the form of events. Every event is characterized by a number of attributes, each attribute being made up of certain levels. By decomposing the principal's ordinal preference evaluation (ranking) of the events, CA assigns each of these levels a cardinal utility value, called part-worth-utility (short: part-worth). Relying on the fact, that through the ordering of multi-attributive objects (or events) more information than a simple ordinal ranking is generated, the relative importance of each attribute level can be calculated and expressed as part-worth. This is done by analyzing the occurrence of the different attribute levels within the ranking. Combining the part-worths by means of an additive utility function an interval scaled total utility function – sufficient for agent negotiation applications – is generated.

Applying CA to agent applications can be done in three consecutive steps that will be detailed below:

First, the application specific survey design must be created. In this step the foundations of valid measurement are laid. Using CA as an interface between principal and agent, easiness of handling in combination with good validity of measurement is required.

Second, the actual conjoint interview consisting of preference measurement and data analysis is conducted [3].

In addition to traditional CA, in agent applications a third step has to be included. Because using utility functions in agents cannot be based on a static one-time utility evaluation, a learning mechanism must be established that accounts for the inter-temporal validity of measurement. Its main assignments consist of fixing measurement errors and adjusting to over-time changes in the principal's preference structure.

3.1 Setting Up the Survey

As stated earlier, CA demands some effort in constructing the survey; especially the correct determination of attributes and attribute levels for the specific application is crucial. In order to generate valid results, there are some constraints on the selection of attributes and attribute levels:

- All attributes relevant for the principal's decision have to be considered.
- The attributes must be independent of each other.
- There must be a compensatory relation between the attributes.

Though these constraints might appear to be very strict, most domains can be modelled according to them.

The events that have been characterized in that way have to be presented to and evaluated by the principal. An event presented to the principal is called a *stimulus*. There are three different approaches for deriving the stimuli:

- full profile design,
- random design,
- systematic design.

In the full profile design, all possible events are presented. Because the amount of possible events grows exponentially with the number of attributes, it can be overwhelming for any principal to rate all of them, even with only a small number of attributes and levels. In order to make CA practically useful for agent applications, a method is required for reducing the quantity of stimuli, while still maintaining a good quality of the resulting utility function.

In a random design, a certain number of stimuli are chosen without respect to the distribution of the different attribute levels in the sample. It can be used to estimate the utility over all events statistically. An advantage of this approach is that the size of the sample can be chosen arbitrarily. Still, as a major drawback, some attribute levels might not appear sufficiently often in the sample to allow an estimation of utility values with sufficient validity.

The systematic approach usually finds a better set of stimuli than the random design limiting the number of stimuli while still representing the set of all possible events as close as possible. A systematic design can be used to guarantee uncorrelated estimation of all part-worths [12].

Addelman has shown that the condition of "orthogonal frequencies" is sufficient to achieve this goal. It requires every attribute level to appear with all levels of the other attributes in proportional frequency to their number of appearances in the whole sample. Addelman calls designs that hold this condition *Orthogonal Main-Effect Plans (OMEPs)* and also suggests a method to construct them [1].

Unfortunately, this method requires some human intuition and is not appropriate to be used with computer systems. Therefore an algorithm based on suggestions by Jacroux is introduced here. His method guarantees to compute a minimal OMEP; that is the design of smallest sample size that still allows uncorrelated estimation of part-worths. The number of events in this design depends on the structure of attributes and levels in each specific case [10].

The algorithm starts off by constructing a set of *Mutually Orthogonal Latin Squares (MOLS)*. A Latin Square of size *n* is a tableau of *n* rows and *n* columns which are filled with *n* distinct symbols in a way that every symbol appears only once in each row and in each column respectively. Two Latin Squares of the same size are *orthogonal*, if superimposed on each other every ordered pair of symbols appears exactly once. In a set of MOLS, every pair of squares is mutually orthogonal. For a given size *n* there exist *n-1* MOLS if *n* is a prime or a power of a prime. To construct such a set of MOLS, Galois fields are used [19].

To create a sample for a symmetrical design (i.e. each attribute has the same number of levels) for *n+1* attributes each having *n* levels, all MOLS of size *n* are superimposed on each other and row and column symbols are added to each cell. Jacroux has shown that a minimal OMEP has $N = \overline{s_1 s_2}$ elements, if $\overline{s_1}$ and $\overline{s_2}$ satisfy

$$\overline{s_1 s_2} = \min_{x \geq s_1, y \geq s_2} xy < 2s_1 s_2, s_3\{lcm(x, y)\} \leq xy$$

where:

s_i = number of levels of attribute i with $s_n \geq s_{n+1}$ for all n.

lcm(x,y) = least common multiplier of x and y.

With this information, the algorithm constructs a symmetrical design for $\overline{s_2}$ levels using MOLS, which needs to be adjusted in case of an asymmetrical design (i.e. the attributes each have different numbers of levels) [10]. Additional levels for the first attribute can be introduced by partially duplicating the sample, changing the levels of only the first attribute. Other attributes that have too many levels are collapsed using a n-to-1 relation. For instance, the scheme

$$0 \rightarrow 0$$
$$1 \rightarrow 1$$
$$2 \rightarrow 0$$

can be used to collapse a three level attribute to a two level attribute. The resulting design is a minimal OMEP, which is presented to the principal in order to be ranked. Addelman has proven that using such corresponding schemes does not affect the condition of orthogonal frequencies, thus allowing uncorrelated estimation of all part-worths [1].

Unfortunately, there are a few combinations of attributes and levels this approach cannot provide an OMEP for. One way to deal with these few cases would be to fall back to a random sample implying all the problems for the validity of the results as mentioned above. Instead, it seems more reasonable to alter the setup of the experiment in order to use a number of attributes and attribute levels the algorithm can handle.

3.2 Interview and Analysis

Having decided on the set of stimuli the next step is the analysis of the principal's preference structure. Therefore, the principal has to evaluate the stimuli. An intuitive method for evaluation is the ranking method. It requires that the principal assigns a rank to each stimulus according to his preferences.

Using CA in the context of agent systems, which relieve the principal from coordination tasks, implies that the interaction with the principal should be as intuitive and easy as possible. We propose the following approach:

A limited number of stimuli is presented to the principal at once and has to be brought into the right order. Every additional stimulus is inserted into the existing order by pair wise choice, i.e. the principal repeatedly decides between the new stimulus and an already sorted stimulus just by stating his preference between the two alternatives.

After the ranking is finished, the part-worths for the different attribute levels are calculated based on the order[6] of the stimuli revealed by the principal. Assuming an additive utility function, the principal's total utility for a multi-attributive event E_0 is represented by the sum of its part-worths [12]:

$$U(E_0) = \sum_{j=1}^{J} \sum_{m=1}^{M_j} \beta_{jm} * x_{jm}$$

where:

$U(E_0)$ = Total utility of the event E_0

β_{jm} = Part worth utility of level m of attribute j

$$x_{jm} = \begin{cases} 1 \text{ if level } m \text{ of attribute } j \text{ occurs in } E_0 \\ 0 \text{ else} \end{cases}$$

Assuming that the distance between the ranks revealed by the principal is equidistant, the rank order can be interpreted metrically. Estimating the part-worths can now simply be done by an ordinary least square regression.[7]

The part-worths (β_{jm}) of the attribute levels are calculated by subtracting the base utility ($\bar{p}$) from the average empirical rank ($\bar{p}_{jm}$) of an attribute level: $\beta_{jm} = \bar{p}_{jm} - \bar{p}$

The term base utility refers to the average rank of all stimuli:

$$\bar{p} = \frac{\sum_{i=1}^{N} p_i}{N}$$

where:

p_i = Rank of stimulus i

N = Number of stimuli

The average empirical rank of an attribute level is denoted as the average rank of all stimuli containing a certain attribute level:

---

[6] Notice that the rank number is reversed. That means that the highest rank is assigned to the most preferred stimulus.

[7] Actually, this is the 'quick and dirty method' for deriving part-worths, that is used by most commercial conjoint applications like SPSS, and which assumes equidistance between the ranks revealed by the principal. More correct is the application of non-metric algorithms like MONANOVA [13], [14], LINMAP [22] or PREFMAP [5], which lead to slightly better results at the cost of greater complexity [6]. In the LACAM-Software presented below, MONANOVA is implemented as an addition to the OLS-Regression.

$$\overline{p}_{jm} = \frac{\sum\limits_{i=1}^{N} p_i * b_{ijm}}{\sum\limits_{i=1}^{N} b_{ijm}}$$

where:

$\overline{p}_{jm}$ = Average empirical rank of the attribute

j with the level m

$$b_{ijm} = \begin{cases} 1 \text{ if level } m \text{ of attribute } j \text{ occurs in the stimulus } i \\ 0 \text{ else} \end{cases}$$

Given the part-worths of the different attribute levels the total utility of any event can easily be calculated according to the additive utility function [3].

The found part-worths represent the principal's preference structure as close as possible. With the help of those part-worths, the total utility of every possible event can be calculated. Therefore, they can be used as the basis for agent negotiation processes. Unfortunately the principal's preference structure is likely not to be stable over time. In order not to confront the principal with the whole conjoint interview again, there is a need to develop an alternative that requires less involvement of the principal.

4 Learning

Considering the fact that individual preferences may change over time, a utility function that was determined once by CA cannot be regarded as statically valid for ever. Instead, an agent system that is supposed to be in use for a longer period must be able to dynamically adjust to changes within the principal's preferences. That is, it needs to detect if the agents utility function still represents the principals preferences correctly and adjust it in case it does not.

To accomplish this task, user interaction is required. As, obviously, intelligent agents are supposed to make their principals' lives easier, too much interaction is not beneficial. Research has shown that while most users are willing to give some short feedback about the quality of the agent's work, they consider a longer procedure as frustrating and annoying [20]. Keeping that in mind, we have designed a procedure for permanently monitoring the quality of the agent's utility model, while reducing communication with the principal to a minimum.

4.1 Learning Process

The learning process proposed in this chapter is based on the main idea that in order to facilitate easy communication, the principal only needs to respond to a single question after selected negotiations done by the agent. For this, he must evaluate the actual result of the negotiation (E_r) together with the next possible alternative the agent would have been able to reach (E_a). Note that the latter was not preferred by the agent because its total utility is considered lower than the utility of E_r in its model. The principal must now state if the agent's behaviour was correct, taking into account these two outcomes. In case it was, the system acted accurately, and there is no need to change the utility function. Otherwise, there must be an inaccuracy in the utility model, or the user would not have disapproved the agent's decision.

Here exists a typical Credit-Assignment-Problem, where it is not evident which of the part-worths to assign the blame for the wrong decision [21]. Therefore, the algorithm regards all part-worths relevant for E_r or E_a as equally responsible for the wrong decision. That means that in order to correct the model, the part-worths of all attribute levels that occur in E_r will be lowered by a constant factor. Respectively, the values involved in E_a will be raised.

Consider the recent part-worths β_{jm} as determined with the metric solution or MONANOVA. Analyzing the events E_r and E_a a set of 'change values' β_{jm} is determined, with:

$$\gamma_{jm} = \begin{cases} -1, \text{ if level } m \text{ of attribute } j \text{ occurs in } E_r \text{ and not in } E_a \\ 1, \text{ if level } m \text{ of attribute } j \text{ occurs in } E_a \text{ and not in } E_r \\ 0, \text{ else} \end{cases}$$

The corrected part-worths β_{jm}' are then calculated as:

$$\beta_{jm}' = \beta_{jm} + w \cdot \beta_{jm}$$

The factor w is included as a weight that is used to account for the distance between E_r and E_a. If the total utility of the two events differs greatly, w must be chosen higher than in a case with a small gap. Specifically, we set it in such a way that the total utility of E_r and E_a will match, if they are calculated basing on the new part-worths β_{jm}'. To do this, the linear equation of total utility – as presented in chapter 3 - is solved for w. Over time, with this method, the calculated part-worths converge asymptotically against the values that correctly represent the principal's preferences.

By using the weight w, the set of corrected part-worths β_{jm}' can be calculated. Figure 2 illustrates how this procedure influences the ranking of objects. In the new model, the total utility values for the result of the negotiation and the next possible outcome are now equal. Note that other objects might also change their position in the ranking as their total utility is affected by the change of part-worths.

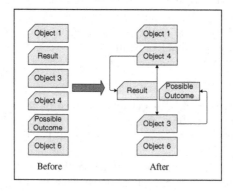

Fig. 1. Improved ranking after applying new part-worths

4.2 Gradual Learning

Psychology scholars distinguish two different forms of attitude change towards certain issues: Conditioning is associating the issue with a positive or negative mood created by another factor and thus changing the opinion towards it [18]. Persuasion is general communication that aims at altering decisions [4]. Both of these two forms are usually considered persistent.

Still, psychological research has shown that a great deal of a person's recorded attitudes depends on the mood the person is actually in. Of course, these discrepancies are tightly coupled with the mood and will diminish when it changes.

A learning algorithm must therefore try to recognize permanent changes of preference structure caused by either conditioning or persuasion but should be invariant to temporal changes caused by certain moods. In order to accomplish this, a function for assessing the consistency of a perceived change in preferences with the user behavior in the past is needed. This consistency can be identified by performing a trend analysis over historically recorded part-worths. A high similarity between the part-worths β_{jm}', as calculated in chapter 4.1, and the trend-induced values suggest a permanent preference change; while a high difference implies mood-based behavior.

A trend analysis can be done by calculating a linear trend function for each part-worth, using OLS-Regression. The trend function can then be used for estimating trend-induced part-worths $\hat{\beta}_{jm}$ valid for the current point of time. The resulting value is then compared with β_{jm}' and the weight w adjusted, depending on the distance between the two values:

$$w' = \begin{cases} w \cdot (1 - \dfrac{|\,\hat{\beta}_{jm} - \beta_{jm}'\,|}{0.2}), & \text{if } |\,\hat{\beta}_{jm} - \beta_{jm}'\,| < 0.2 \\ 0, & \text{else} \end{cases}$$

Based on this, the new set of part-worths β_{jm}'' can be calculated as:

$$\beta_{jm}'' = \beta_{jm} + w' \cdot \gamma_{jm}$$

By regularly updating the agent's utility function with these adapted part-worths a constant operation of an agent system can be maintained.

5 Conclusion

In this paper, we dealt with a central problem of agent theory; that is how to align the actions of an agent to a principal's preference structure. Especially we focused on a situation where recurring decisions have to be made between different multi-attributive alternatives. We suggested using a utility-based decision component in such a case, which leads to the problem of determining the principal's utility function. Expected Utility measurement as the standard approach to accomplish this has certain deficits. Although it has played an important role in game and decision theory, we consider it as impractical for agent applications. We have therefore described conjoint analysis as a more practicable method for determining human utility functions. Our examination also provided a method to reduce the number of stimuli that have to be evaluated by the principal making CA more easily applicable for real life situations.

While CA has been evaluated thoroughly in many studies and approved functional, our learning algorithm still undergoes empirically evaluation and development. To apply our ideas in practice, we developed a specialized conjoint analysis tool for agent applications (*LACAM – Learning Agents and Conjoint Analytical Methods*), as part of our Policy-Agents Hospital-Scheduling MAS. Designed as a self-contained system component *LACAM* can be easily adapted to existing utility-based agent systems. Readers are encouraged to download and evaluate it at our project homepage: http://www.wi.uni-trier.de/forschung/projekte/projekte/Agenten.htm. A more extensive (German) documentation [11] of the software tool is available on this page as well. We also extended the software with the presented learning algorithm that is still experimental. Further development and testing will take place during the course of the project. Any remarks regarding the software tool and especially the learning component are very welcome.

References

[1] Addelman, S.: Orthogonal Main-Effect Plans for Asymmetrical Factorial Experiments, in: Technometrics, Vol. 4(1), 1962, pp. 21-46.

[2] Allais, M.: Le Comportement de l'Homme Rationnel devant le Risque: critique des Postulats et Axiomes de l'Ecole Américaine, in: Econometrica, Vol. 21, 1953, pp. 503-546.

[3] Backhaus, K.; Erichson, B.; Plinke, W.; Weiber, R.: Multivariate Analysemethoden – Eine anwendungsorientierte Einführung, Berlin 2000.

[4] Brembeck, W.; Howell, W.: Persuasion – A Means of Social Influence, 2nd Ed., Englewood Cliffs, NJ 1976.

[5] Caroll, J.D.: Individual Differences and Multidimensional Scaling, in: R.N. Sheppard; A.K. Romney; S.B. Nerlove (Hrsg.), Multidimensional Scaling: Theory and Applications in the Behavioral Sciences, Vol. 1, 1972, pp. 105-155.

[6] Chattin, P.; Wittink, D. R.: Further Beyond Conjoint Measurement: Towards a Comparison of Methods, in Perrault, W. D. (ed): Advances in Consumer Research, Chicago 1977.

[7] Czap, H.; Becker, M.: Multi-Agent Systems and Microeconomic Theory: A Negotiation Approach to solve Scheduling Problems in High Dynamic Environments, in Proceedings of 36th Annual Hawaii International Conference on System Sciences (CD-Rom), Hawaii 2003.

[8] Gingerenzer, G.; Selten, R. (eds.): Bounded Rationality: The Adaptive Toolbox, Cambridge 2001.

[9] Green, P. E.; Krieger, A.M.; Wind, Y.: Thirty Years of Conjoint Analysis: Reflections and Prospects, in: Inter-faces, Vol. 31/3, 2001, pp. 56-73.

[10] Jacroux, M.: A Note on the Determination and Construction of Minimal Orthogonal Main-Effect Plans, in: Technometrics, Vol. 34(1), 1992, pp.92-96.

[11] Kessler, M.; Poppensieker, M.; Porten, M.; Stotz, A.; Zub, D.: Lernende Agenten & conjoint-analytische Verfahren - Entwicklung einer Conjoint-Analyse-Software zur Verwendung in FIPA-konformen Multiagentensystemen, Studienprojekt am Lehrstuhl für Wirtschaftsinformatik I der Universität Trier, Trier 2004.

[12] Klein, M.: Die Conjoint-Analyse: Eine Einführung in das Verfahren mit einem Ausblick auf mögliche sozialwissenschaftliche Anwendungen, in: ZA-Information No. 50, 2002, pp. 7-45.

[13] Kruskal, J.B.: Analysis of Factorial Experiments by Estimating Monotone Transformation of Data, in: Journal of the Royal Statistical Society, Series B, Vol. 27, 1965, pp. 251 -263.

[14] Kruskal, J.B.: Nonmetric Multidimensional Scaling: A Numerical Approach, in: Psychometrika, Vol. 29/2, 1964, pp. 1-27.

[15] Laux, H.: Entscheidungstheorie, Berlin et al 2003.

[16] Luce, R. D.; Raiffa, H.: Games and Decisions – Introduction and Critical Survey, New York 1957.

[17] Luce, R. D.; Tukey, J. W.: Simultaneous Conjoint Measurement: A New Type of Fundamental Measurement, in: Journal of Mathematical Psychology, Vol. 1, 1964, pp. 1-27.

[18] Oskamp, S.: Attitudes and Opinions, 2nd Ed., Englewood Cliffs, NJ 1991.

[19] Raghavarao, D.: Constructions and Combinatorial Problems in Design of Experiments, New York 1971.

[20] Schiaffino, S.; Amandi, A.: User – interface agent interaction: personalization issues, in: International Journal of Human-Computer Studies, Vol. 60, 2004, pp. 129-148.

[21] Sen, S.; Weiss, G.: Learning in Multiagent Systems, in: Weiss, G. (ed.): Multiagent Systems – A Modern Approach to Distributed Artificial Intelligence, Cambridge 1999.

[22] Srinivasan, V.; Shocker, A.D.: Estimating the Weight for Multiple Attributes in a Composite Criterion Using Pairwise Judgements, in: Psychometrika, No. 38/ 1973, pp. 473-493.

[23] Von Neumann, J.; Morgenstern O.: Theory of Games and Economic Behavior, Princeton 1942.

Reconciling Agent Ontologies for Web Service Applications

Jingshan Huang, Rosa Laura Zavala Gutiérrez, Benito Mendoza García,
and Michael N. Huhns

Computer Science and Engineering Department,
University of South Carolina,
Columbia, SC 29208, USA
{huang27, zavalagu, mendoza2, huhns}@engr.sc.edu

Abstract. Because there is still no agreed-upon global ontology, Web services supplied by different providers typically have individual and unique semantics, described by independently developed ontologies. The seamless connection of these distributed Web services for business-to-business applications depends heavily on reconciling the disparate semantics, possibly by integrating the ontologies. In this paper, we describe an approach to reconcile ontologies from distributed Web services. Our approach is totally automated, and features the following: i) alignment of the ontologies is performed without previous agreement on the semantics of the terminology in each ontology; ii) both linguistic and contextual features are considered; iii) the use of WordNet for linguistic analysis; iv) integration of heuristic knowledge for contextual analysis; and v) inference of new relationships by applying several rules based on domain-independent relationships and property lists. Experiments have been carried out to show the promising results of our system.

1 Introduction

Web service applications, such as supply-chain purchase orders and automated order enactment, have been shown to offer great potential value to businesses. Initial on-line automation activities were tightly coupled in the sense that business partners predefined the terms of their interaction using standards such as EDI and XML [12]. Recently, the emergence of Web services has led the software industry into a service-oriented approach to software development. Service-oriented computing is a loosely coupled methodology, based on the use of standard protocols (UDDI for discovery, WSDL for description, BPEL4WS for coordination, and SOAP for communication). The use of Web services provides greater flexibility with respect to the interoperability, reuse, and development of applications in a distributed environment.

Although there can be some value in accessing a single Web service through a semantically well-founded interface, a greater value is clearly derived through enabling a flexible composition of services, which will not only create new services, but also potentially add value to preexisting ones [1]. Therefore, the seamless connection of distributed Web services becomes increasingly critical. However, due to the lack of an agreed-upon global ontology, Web services from different providers

T. Eymann et al. (Eds.): MATES 2005, LNAI 3550, pp. 106–117, 2005.

typically have heterogeneous semantics. Agents that automatically reconcile ontologies, and thereby understand and integrate the information from different sources, would greatly facilitate Web service-based application interoperability.

It is impractical to have a unique and global ontology that includes every concept that is or might be included as part of the Web. However, it is reasonable that there might be ontologies for specific domains and sub-domains of the Web, and even for individual Web pages. It is clear, then, that the challenge is to be able to align and use different ontologies.

In this paper, we describe **PUZZLE**, a system that implements an approach to construct a merged ontology from distributed and independently designed ontologies. We also explain the potential application of our system in Web service-based transactions. We assume that: 1) we are dealing with Web services for similar domains; 2) ontological representations have been derived from Web service documentations, e.g., WSDL and SOAP specifications; and 3) agents are willing to communicate with each other to reach consensus among ontologies.

In [2] the main technique for semantic mapping between two ontology concepts relies on simple string and substring matching. We extend that work to incorporate: further linguistic analysis; contextual analysis based on the properties of the concepts in the ontology and the relationships among these concepts; extended use of WordNet [10] to include the search of not only synonyms but also antonyms, plurals, hypernyms, and hyponyms; use of the Java WordNet Library API [9] for performing run-time access to the dictionary, instead of having to initialize the synonym set a priori; integration of heuristic knowledge into the contextual analysis phase; and reasoning rules based on the domain-independent relationships *subclass*, *superclass*, *equivalentclass*, *sibling*, and each ontology concept's property list to infer new relationships among concepts. Existing research efforts incorporate some of these features, but none has investigated them in combination.

The rest of the paper is organized as follows. Section 2 briefly discusses related work in ontology matching. An overview of the **PUZZLE** system is given in Section 3. Section 4 describes the details of our system. Section 5 reports the experiments conducted and analyzes the results, and Section 6 concludes.

2 Related Work

A lot of research work has been carried out in ontology matching. There are two approaches to ontology matching [7]: instance-based and schema-based. All of the systems mentioned below belong to the latter, except for GLUE [8].

GLUE introduces well-founded notions of semantic similarity, applies multiple machine learning strategies, and can find not only one-to-one mappings, but also complex mappings. However, it depends heavily on the availability of instance data. Therefore, it is not practical for cases where there is an insignificant number of instances or no instances at all.

In [3], a method is investigated for agents to develop local consensus ontologies to help in communications within a multiagent system of B2B agents. This work shows the potential brought by local consensus ontologies in improving how agents conduct B2B Web service discovery and composition. It also explores the influence of a lexical database in ontology merging. However, it does not take into consideration the properties of ontology concepts.

Cupid [5] combines linguistic and structural schema matching techniques, as well as the help of a precompiled dictionary. But it can only work with a tree-structured ontology instead of a more general graph-structured one. As a result, there are many limitations to its application, because a tree cannot represent multiple-inheritance, an important characteristic in ontologies.

For HELIOS [11], WordNet is used as a thesaurus for synonyms, hyponyms, hypernyms, and meronyms. However the thesaurus has to be initialized for each domain for which it is used. If additional knowledge or a different domain is needed, then the user has to input the respective terminology interactively.

S-Match [4] is a modular system into which individual components can be plugged and unplugged. The core of the system is the computation of relations. Five possible relations are defined between nodes: equivalence, more general, less general, mismatch, and overlapping. Giunchiglia et al. claim that S-Match outperforms Cupid, COMA, and SF in measurements of precision, recall, overall, and F-measure. However, as Cupid does, S-Match uses a tree-structured ontology.

3 Overview of Our Solution

The goal of our work is to construct a consensus ontology from numerous independently designed ontologies. The main idea of our approach is that any pair of ontologies, $G1$ and $G2$, can be related indirectly through a semantic bridge consisting of other previously unrelated ontologies, even when there is no direct relationship between $G1$ and $G2$. The metaphor is that a small ontology is like a piece of jigsaw puzzle. It is difficult to relate two random pieces of a jigsaw puzzle until they are constrained by other puzzle pieces. Furthermore, for the semantic bridge between a given pair of ontologies $G1$ and $G2$, the more ontologies the semantic bridge comprises, the better the semantic match between $G1$ and $G2$.

In order to construct a consensus ontology from a number of ontologies, we take two ontologies and merge them into a new one, and then we iteratively merge the resultant ontology with each additional one. We will explain next our method for merging two ontologies.

We represent an ontology using a directed acyclic graph. In order to merge two ontologies, G_1 and G_2, we try to relocate each concept (node) from one ontology into the other one. We adopt a breadth-first order to traverse G_1 and pick up a concept C as the target to be relocated into G_2. Consequently, C's parent set $Parent(C)$ in the original graph G_1 has already been relocated into the suitable place(s) in the destination graph G_2 before the relocation of C itself.

Firstly, we address the issue of the *relocation value* of a target concept C against any other concept C'. A relocation value is a value from 0 to 1, reflecting the likelihood of correctly relocating a concept. As equation 1 below indicates, a relocation value is calculated as the weighted sum of the values from linguistic matching and contextual matching.

$$relocation\ value = w_{linguistic} * v_{linguistic} + w_{contextual} * v_{contextual}. \tag{1}$$

When trying to match concepts, we consider both linguistic and contextual features. The meaning of an ontology concept is determined by its name and its relationship with other concept(s). In this paper, we assume that the linguistic factors contribute 70 percent and the contextual factors contribute 30 percent in concept matching. That is, $w_{linguistic}$ is set to 0.7 and $w_{contextual}$ is set to 0.3 in equation 1. The former is greater than the latter, because in our experiments, the input ontologies have less contextual information. Therefore, we do not want the contextual factors to dominate in the matching process. Notice that these weight values can always be customized according to different application requirements.

We claim that there are five mutually exclusive relationships between any two concepts (see details in Section 4.2.2). From all the candidate concepts in the destination graph G, we build a list of candidate concepts for each type of relationship of C (see details in Section 4.1). Within each list, we calculate the relocation value of C against each concept in that list, and then choose the one producing the highest value. After we finish processing all candidate lists, we have sufficient information to be able to relocate C.

4 Details of the PUZZLE System

The following pseudocode describes the top level procedure of our algorithm.

```
PUZZLE Algorithm - merge(G₁, G₂)
   Input: Ontology G₁ and G₂
   Output: Merged ontology G₂
   begin
      new location of G₁'s root = G₂'s root
      for each node C (except for the root) in G₁
            Parent(C) = C's parent set in G₁
            for each member pᵢ in Parent(C)
               pⱼ = new location of pᵢ in G₂
                     relocate(C, pⱼ)
            end for
      end for
   end
```

4.1 Linguistic Matching

The linguistic factor reflects how the ontology designer wants to encode the meaning of a concept by choosing a preferable name for it. **PUZZLE** uses both string and substring matching techniques when performing linguistic feature matching. Furthermore, we integrate WordNet by using the JWNL API in our system. In this way, we are able to obtain the synonyms, antonyms, hyponyms, and hypernyms of an English word, which has been shown to increase the accuracy of linguistic matching dramatically. In addition, WordNet performs some preprocessing, e.g., the transformation of a noun from plural form to singular form.

We claim that for any pair of ontology concepts C and C', their names N_C and $N_{C'}$ have the following mutually exclusive relationships, in terms of their linguistic features.

- *anti-match*: N_C is a antonym of $N_{C'}$, with the matching value $v_{\text{linguistic}} = 0$;
- *exact-match*: either N_C and $N_{C'}$ have an exact string matching, or they are the synonyms of each other, with the matching value $v_{\text{linguistic}} = 1$;
- *sub-match*: N_C is either a postfix or a hypernym of $N_{C'}$, with the matching value $v_{\text{linguistic}} = 1$;
- *super-match*: $N_{C'}$ is either a postfix or a hyponym of N_C, with the matching value $v_{\text{linguistic}} = 1$;
- *leading-match*: the leading substrings from N_C and $N_{C'}$ match with each other, with the matching value $v_{\text{linguistic}}$ equaling the length of the common leading substring divided by the length of the longer string. For example, "active" and "actor" have a common leading substring "act", resulting in a *leading-match* value of 3/6;
- *other*: the matching value $v_{\text{linguistic}} = 0$.

When relocating C, we perform the linguistic matching between C and all the candidate concepts. For each candidate concept C', if an *exact-match* or a *leading-match* is found, we put C' into C's candidate *equivalentclass* list; if a *sub-match* is found, we put C' into C's candidate *subclass* list; and if a *super-match* is found, we put C' into C's candidate *superclass* list. Then we continue the contextual matching between C and each concept in the three candidate lists to make the final decision.

4.2 Contextual Matching

The context of an ontology concept C consists of two parts, its property list and its relationship(s) with other concept(s). Notice that the latter is not explicitly expressed in any formula. Instead, we integrate the relationship factor into our system by the three reasoning rules specified in Section 4.3.

4.2.1 Property List Matching

Considering the property lists, $P(C)$ and $P(C')$, of a pair of concepts C and C' being matched, our goal is to calculate the similarity value $v_{\text{contextual}}$ between them.

$$v_{\text{contextual}} = w_{\text{required}} * v_{\text{required}} + w_{\text{non-required}} * v_{\text{non-required}}. \tag{2}$$

v_{required} and $v_{\text{non-required}}$ are the similarity values calculated for the *required* property list and *non-required* property list respectively. w_{required} and $w_{\text{non-required}}$ are the weights assigned to each list. In this paper, we choose 0.7 and 0.3 for w_{required} and $w_{\text{non-required}}$. v_{required} and $v_{\text{non-required}}$ are calculated by the same procedure.

Suppose the number of properties in two property lists (either *required* or *non-required* ones), P_1 and P_2, is n_1 and n_2 respectively. Without loss of generality, we assume that $n_1 \leq n_2$. There are three different matching models between two properties.

1. *total-match*
   - The linguistic matching of the property names results in either an *exact-match*, or a *leading-match* with $v_{\text{linguistic}} \geq 0.9$; and
   - The data types match exactly.

Let v_1 = number of properties with a *total-match*, and $f_1 = v_1/n_1$. Here f_1 is a *correcting* factor embodying the integration of heuristic knowledge. We claim that between two property lists, the more pairs of properties being regarded as *total-match*, the more likely that the remaining pairs of properties will also hit a match as long as the linguistic match between their names is above a certain threshold value. For example, assume that both P_1 and P_2 have ten properties. If there are already nine pairs with a *total-match*, and furthermore, if we find out that the names in the remaining pair of properties are very similar, then it is much more likely that this pair will also have a match, as opposed to the case where only one or two out of ten pairs have a *total-match*.

2. *name-match*
    -   The linguistic matching of the property names results in either an *exact-match*, or a *leading-match* with $v_{linguistic} \geq 0.9$; but
    -   The data types do not match.

    Let v_2 = number of properties with a *name-match*, and $f_2 = (v_1 + v_2)/n_1$. Similarly to f_1, f_2 also serves as a *correcting* factor.

3. *datatype-match*
    Only the data types match. Let v_3 = number of properties with a *datatype-match*.

After we find all the possible matching models in the above order, we can calculate the similarity value v between the property lists as

$$v = (v_1 * w_1 + v_2 * (w_2 + w_2' * f_1) + v_3 * (w_3 + w_3' * f_2))/n_1 . \tag{3}$$

where:

-   the value range of v is from 0 to 1;
-   w_i (i from 1 to 3) is the weight assigned to each matching model. We use 1.0 for *total-match*, 0.8 for *name-match*, and 0.2 for *datatype-match*;
-   w_i'(i from 2 to 3) is the *correcting* weight assigned to the matching models of *name-match* and *datatype-match*. We use 0.2 and 0.1 respectively;

4.2.2 Relationships Among Concepts

Given any two ontology concepts, we can have the following five mutually exclusive relationships between them:

-   *subclass*, denoted by $\subseteq$
-   *superclass*, denoted by $\supseteq$
-   *equivalentclass*, denoted by $\equiv$
-   *sibling*, denoted by $\approx$ and
-   *other*, denoted by $\neq$

OWL Full provides eleven relationship axioms [6]: *subClassOf, equivalentClass, disjointWith, sameIndividualAs, differentFrom, subPropertyOf, equivalentProperty, inverseOf, transitiveProperty, functionalProperty,* and *inverseFunctionalProperty*. The first three axioms will be used as follows.

The *subClassOf* axiom will represent *subclass-superclass* relationship. The *equivalentClass* axiom will be used for specifying the *equivalentclass* relationship. As for *sibling* relationship, there is no direct support from OWL axioms. However, the *disjointWith* axiom is a good choice, given the condition that each ontology is reasonably designed. That is, we make an assumption that under a same parent class, all the siblings within the same level will be disjoint with each other. Otherwise, a new *superclass* should be added for those siblings with intersection.

4.3 Reasoning Rules

PUZZLE uses three domain-independent rules, each regarding the relationship among ontology concepts, to incorporate the reasoning into our system. These rules are applied to concepts from different ontologies. Therefore, we refer to them as *inter-ontology reasoning*.

Suppose we have three ontologies A, B, and C, each of which is designed according to the OWL Full specification. Furthermore, let $n(A)$, $n(B)$, and $n(C)$ be the sets of concepts in A, B, and C respectively, with $n_i(A)$, $n_j(B)$, and $n_k(C)$ be the individual concept for each set (*i* from 1 to $|n(A)|$, *j* from 1 to $|n(B)|$, and *k* from 1 to $|n(C)|$), and $P(n_i(A))$, $P(n_j(B))$, and $P(n_k(C))$ be the property list for each individual concept.

Consider the property lists $P(n_i(A))$ and $P(n_j(B))$, let s_i and s_j be the set size of these two lists. There are four mutually exclusive possibilities for the relationship between $P(n_i(A))$ and $P(n_j(B))$:

- $P(n_i(A))$ and $P(n_j(B))$ are consistent with each other if and only if
  - i.   *Either* $s_i = s_j$ *or* $|s_i - s_j|/(s_i + s_j) \leq 0.1$, and
  - ii. $v_{contextual} \geq 0.9$

  We denote the corresponding concepts $n_i(A)$ and $n_j(B)$ by $n_i(A) \xleftrightarrow{\ p\ } n_j(B)$;
- $P(n_i(A))$ is a subset of $P(n_j(B))$ if and only if
  - i. $s_i \leq s_j$, and
  - ii. $v_{contextual} \geq 0.9$

  We denote the corresponding concepts $n_i(A)$ and $n_j(B)$ by $n_i(A) \xrightarrow{\ p\ } n_j(B)$;
- $P(n_i(A))$ is a superset of $P(n_j(B))$ if and only if
  - i. $s_i \geq s_j$, and
  - ii. $v_{contextual} \geq 0.9$

  We denote the corresponding concepts $n_i(A)$ and $n_j(B)$ by $n_i(A) \xleftarrow{\ p\ } n_j(B)$;
- Other.

Rules 1 and 2 consider two ontologies, A and B.

[Rule 1]. This rule is straightforward, claiming that the *superclass/subclass* relationship of a class is transferable to its equivalent class(es).
-   Preconditions:
    $n_i(A) \equiv n_k(B)$ and $(n_i(A) \subseteq n_j(A)$ or $n_i(A) \supseteq n_j(A))$
-   Conclusion:
    $n_k(B) \subseteq n_j(A)$ or $n_k(B) \supseteq n_j(A)$

[Rule 2]. If two classes share the same parent(s), then their relationship is one of: *equivalentclass*, *superclass*, *subclass*, and *sibling*. For example, if we know that two classes have similar names and similar property lists, we still cannot conclude that they must be equivalent to each other, considering the possibility of the existence of badly designed ontologies. However, if we also know that these two classes have the same parent(s), then the probability of them being equivalent will dramatically increase.
-   Preconditions:
    $n_{i1}(A) \supseteq n_{i2}(A)$ and $n_{k1}(B) \supseteq n_{k2}(B)$ and
    $n_{i1}(A) \equiv n_{k1}(B)$ and

1. $n_{i2}(A) \xleftrightarrow{P} n_{k2}(B)$ and (the names of $n_{i2}(A)$ and $n_{k2}(B)$ have either an *exact-match*, or a *leading-match* with $v_{\text{linguistic}} \geq 0.65$)

2. $n_{i2}(A) \xrightarrow{P} n_{k2}(B)$ and the name of $n_{k2}(B)$ is a *sub-match* of the name of $n_{i2}(A)$

3. $n_{i2}(A) \xleftarrow{P} n_{k2}(B)$ and the name of $n_{k2}(B)$ is a *super-match* of the name of $n_{i2}(A)$

4. None of above three holds

- Conclusion:
1. $n_{i2}(A) \equiv n_{k2}(B)$
2. $n_{i2}(A) \supseteq n_{k2}(B)$
3. $n_{i2}(A) \subseteq n_{k2}(B)$
4. $n_{i2}(A) \approx n_{k2}(B)$

Rule 3 considers three ontologies, A, B, and C.

[Rule 3]. If two classes have no direct relationships between them, we consider a third one to see if it can provide a semantic bridge between the original two. In theory, the more ontologies the semantic bridge comprises, the more likely we can succeed in discovering the hidden relationships that are not obvious originally.

- Preconditions:
  $n_{i1}(A) \equiv n_{j1}(C)$ and $n_{j2}(C) \equiv n_{k2}(B)$ and
  $n_{k1}(B) \subseteq n_{k2}(B)$ and $n_{j1}(C) \subseteq n_{j2}(C)$ and

1. $n_{i1}(A) \xleftrightarrow{P} n_{k1}(B)$ and (the names of $n_{i1}(A)$ and $n_{k1}(B)$ have either an *exact-match*, or a *leading-match* with $v_{\text{linguistic}} \geq 0.65$)

2. $n_{i1}(A) \xrightarrow{P} n_{k1}(B)$ and the name of $n_{k1}(B)$ is a *sub-match* of the name of $n_{i1}(A)$

3. $n_{i1}(A) \xleftarrow{P} n_{k1}(B)$ and the name of $n_{k1}(B)$ is a *super-match* of the name of $n_{i1}(A)$

4. None of the above three holds

- Conclusion:
1. $n_{i1}(A) \equiv n_{k1}(B)$
2. $n_{i1}(A) \supseteq n_{k1}(B)$
3. $n_{i1}(A) \subseteq n_{k1}(B)$
4. $n_{i1}(A) \approx n_{k1}(B)$

5   Experiments and Discussion of Our Results

First, we envision the following example application of **PUZZLE** in Web service-based transactions. In the domain of real estate, there might be many reasons why different agencies would like to communicate with each other. Consider the case where a real estate agent did not initially find any housing matching a client's requirements. It would be helpful if that agent directly connected to other agents and found something for the client, instead of sending the client away to find another agent. The ability of an agent to reach other potential suppliers would lead to better service, less work for the client, and ultimately happier clients. Another situation is that several agencies might want to put together a unified interface to users, so that all of them together offer a wider range of options to clients. In order to carry out communications among agencies without the need to agree on predefined data interchange formats, the agencies can benefit from automated ontology matching abilities as provided by **PUZZLE**.

In this section, we describe a set of experiments we conducted, whose purpose was to determine whether or not **PUZZLE** generates a consensus ontology. We evaluate **PUZZLE** in terms of precision, recall, and merging convergence.

5.1 Experimental Setup

● Test ontologies

Three sets of ontologies in three different domains, i.e., "Building", "Human", and "Sports" were used for evaluating the performance of the **PUZZLE** system. They were constructed by graduate students in computer science and engineering at our university. There are 16 ontologies for the domain of "Building", having between 10 and 15 concepts with 19 to 38 properties and 31 to 49 relationships among the concepts. For the other 2 domains, no property was defined for any concept. We have 54 ontologies for the domain of "Human", with between 7 and 28 concepts; and 23 ontologies for the domain of "Sports", with between 4 and 22 concepts.

5.2 Experimental Results and Analysis

Our experiments simulate having a set of agents, each of which has a local ontology and is willing to communicate with the other agents. They try to reconcile their local ontologies to form a consensus one.

5.2.1 Evaluation of the Resultant Ontology

To decide whether a consensus ontology is obtained, we asked two ontology experts to carry out a manual mapping and we compared their results with ours. Both *precision* and *recall* measurements are applied in the evaluation during the process of

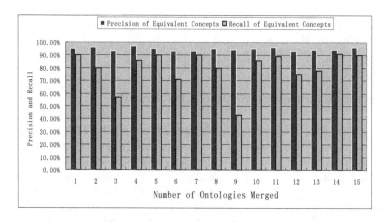

Fig. 1. Precision and Recall Measurements of Resultant Ontology for "Building"

merging ontologies one at a time. The evaluation result is shown in Figure 1. Due to the space limit, we only show the result for "Building" domain and omit the other two. Notice that this result is not statistically valid but indicative. Both measurements reflect a promising result, especially for "Building" domain. For "Human" and "Sports" domain, the results are not as good as that of "Building" domain. The reason is straightforward. Although in Section 3 we mention that our experiment ontologies

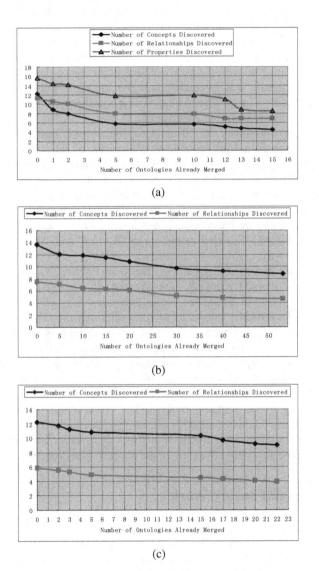

Fig. 2. (a) Merging Convergence Experiment for "Building". (b) Merging Convergence Experiment for "Human". (c) Merging Convergence Experiment for "Sports".

have less contextual information than linguistic one, we claim that contextual factor does play an important role in determining the mapping among ontology concepts. That is the reason we chose ontologies of both with and without properties in the experiment. The result verifies our claim.

5.2.2 Analysis of Merging Convergence

One hypothesis is that as each additional ontology is merged into a consensus one, there should be fewer new items (concept, relationship, or property) added to the consensus. To test this hypothesis, the following experiment has been conducted. We calculated the number of newly discovered information at certain points during the merging process. For different domain, the testing points chosen are different. For example, in "Building" domain we picked up the points when the first, second, fifth, tenth, twelfth, thirteenth, and fifteenth ontologies were merged. For the other two domains, please refer to figure 2-b and 2-c, which together with figure 2-a, show the results of this hypothesis-verifying experiment.

Out of the 16 ontologies in "Building" domain we had available for our experiments, we considered all possible combinations of the order by which they could be merged, in order to remove any bias that might be introduced by the presence of unusual ontology samples. This is a huge number; for example, there are 1680 combinations when the second ontology is to be merged, and 25000 for the fifth one. It is impossible to try all these orders. Our solution is that if the population size is less than or equal to 30 we try all possible orders; otherwise we randomly choose a sample space of size 30. The experiment data in "Human" and "Sports" domains was treated in the same way.

A monotonically decreasing pattern is shown in Figure 2-a. As the number of ontologies already merged increases, the number of concepts, relationships, and properties learned from additional ontologies decreases. We believe that the number of new items will eventually converge to zero, although the sixteen ontologies we have available for this experiment are not enough to verify this belief. In figure 2-b and 2-c, the similar monotonically decreasing pattern is found. However, the converge tendency is not so obvious, comparing to that in figure 2-a. In "Building" domain, when the last ontology was being merged, the number of newly discovered concepts is around 37% of that number when the 0th ontology being merged, i.e., at the very beginning of the merging process. The corresponding percentages in the "Human" and "Sports" domains are 65% and 74%, respectively. This is again due to a lack of property information. In fact, sometimes it is even difficult for ontology experts to determine a potential mapping in the absence of a property list.

6 Conclusion and Future Work

Ontology matching is a critical operation in the Semantic Web, especially for business-to-business applications. In this paper, we presented the **PUZZLE** system, a schema-based approach combined with inter-ontology reasoning, which learns to reconcile ontologies for applications within a single domain. This completely automated matching is carried out at the schema level, without a previous agreement over the different terminology semantics. **PUZZLE** considers both linguistic and contextual features of an ontology concept, integrates heuristic knowledge with several matching techniques, and incorporates the reasoning among ontologies. A set of experiments showed a promising result from this system.

Future work includes: adopting machine learning techniques to make agents more intelligent; considering other relationships, such as *partOf, hasPart, causeOf*, and *hasCause*; integrating the OWL Validator into our system; and testing our method against other well-known ones in ontology matching, by using more general ontology libraries.

References

1. Singh, M. P., and Huhns, M. N.: Service-Oriented Computing Semantics, Processes, Agents. 1st edn. Wiley (2005)
2. Stephens, L., Gangam, A., and Huhns, M. N.: Constructing Consensus Ontologies for the Semantic Web: A Conceptual Approach. In: World Wide Web Journal, Vol. 7, No. 4. Kluwer Academic Publishers (2004) 421 – 442
3. Williams, A., Padmanabhan, A., and Blake, M. B.: Local Consensus Ontologies for B2B-Oriented Service Composition. In: Proceedings of the Second International Joint Conference on Autonomous Agents and Multiagent Systems. ACM Press (2003) 647 – 654
4. Giunchiglia, F., Shvaiko, P., and Yatskevich, M.: S-Match: an algorithm and an implementation of semantic matching. In: Proceedings of the 1st European Semantic Web Symposium, Vol. 3053. Springer-Verlag (2004) 61 – 75
5. Madhavan, J., Bernstein, P. A., and Rahm, E.: Generic Schema Matching with Cupid. In: Proceedings of the 27th VLDB Conference. Springer-Verlag (2001)
6. W3C: OWL Web Ontology Language Reference. http://www.w3.org/TR/owl-ref (2004)
7. Rahm, E., and Bernstein, P. A.: A survey of approaches to automatic schema matching. In: The VLDB Journal, Vol. 10. Springer-Verlag (2001) 334 – 350
8. Doan, A., Madhavan, J., Dhamankar, R., Domingos, P., and Halevy, A.: Learning to match ontologies on the Semantic Web. In: The VLDB Journal, Vol. 12. Springer-Verlag (2003) 303 – 319
9. JWNL: Java WordNet Library – JWNL 1.3. http://sourceforge.net/projects/jwordnet/ (2003)
10. Miller, A. G.: WordNet: A Lexical Database for English. In: Communications of the ACM, Vol. 38, No. 11. ACM Press (1995) 39 – 41
11. Castano, S., Ferrara, A., Montanelli, S., and Racca, G.: Matching Techniques for Resource Discovery in Distributed Systems Using Heterogeneous Ontology Descriptions. In: Proceedings of the International Conference on Information Technology: Coding and Computing (ITCC04), Vol. 1. IEEE Computer Society Press (2004) 360 – 366
12. Zavala Gutiérrez, R. L. and Huhns, M. N.: On Building Robust Web Service-Based Applications. In: Extending Web Services Technologies: The Use of Multi-Agent Approaches. Kluwer Academic Publishing (2004)

An Agent-Based Knowledge Acquisition Platform

David Sánchez, David Isern, and Antonio Moreno

University Rovira i Virgili (URV),
Department of Computer Science and Mathematics (DEIM),
Av. Països Catalans, 26. 43007 Tarragona, Catalonia, Spain
{david.sanchez, david.isern, antonio.moreno}@urv.net

Abstract. Accessing up-to-date information in a fast and easy way implies the necessity of information management tools to explore and analyse the huge number of available electronic resources. The Web offers a large amount of valuable information, but its human-oriented representation and its size makes extremely difficult any kind of computer-based processing. In this paper, a combination of distributed AI and information extraction techniques is proposed to tackle this problem. In particular, we have designed a *multiagent system* that composes ontologies from *taxonomies* of terms. Moreover, the obtained ontology is used to represent, in a structured way, the currently available web resources. The paper analyses the application of this approach in some examples in the medical domain.

1 Introduction

Researchers typically assess the evolution of their discipline by reading scientific journals, attending conferences or, quite often, by hearsay. On the other side, the Web offers a way for fast data access and information exchange that could represent a great help but, unfortunately, it is impossible to analyse manually due to the huge amount of available resources and their weak structure.

These electronic repositories are usually accessed by means of keyword-based search engines (e.g. Google, Altavista) allowing a user to retrieve information by stating a combination of words that have to appear in the retrieved documents. This type of search usually suffers from two problems derived from the nature of the query and the lack of structure in the documents: a) the difficulty to set the most appropriate and restrictive search query, and b) the tedious evaluation of the huge amount of potential resources obtained. Moreover, while search engines provide support for the automatic retrieval of information, the tasks of extracting and structuring relevant information and its further processing remain to be done by the human user. In this sense, a methodology for representing the web resources in a structured way depending on the main topics of a desired domain can be a great help for any researcher. Thus, the important point is to find a way of creating and representing the domain's knowledge structure efficiently. Here is where ontologies [4] become indispensable.

In general, ontologies allow organizing and centralizing knowledge in a formal, machine, and human understandable way, making themselves an essential component to many knowledge-intensive services like the Semantic Web [3], knowledge man-

T. Eymann et al. (Eds.): MATES 2005, LNAI 3550, pp. 118–129, 2005.

agement, and electronic commerce. However, they are traditionally built entirely by hand, capturing the knowledge in a static way. This knowledge is usually evolvable (especially in technological domains) and an ontology maintenance process is required to keep the ontological knowledge up-to-date. A computer-based ontology construction process becomes a very important deal for information engineers, especially with highly dynamic domains like the Web. The building process has been described by several authors [6, 10] by five main steps: *i*) identification of concepts and instances, *ii*) word sense disambiguation, *iii*) taxonomic construction, *iv*) identification of non taxonomic relations, and *v*) ontology population.

However, the processing of a huge repository like the Web is a very time consuming task. In order to handle this problem, the agent paradigm is a promising technology for information retrieval. *Multiagent systems* provide some advantages with respect to traditional systems such as scalability, flexibility and autonomy [18] and they are very suitable for implementing dynamic and distributed systems. Several projects applying MAS to information retrieval and knowledge acquisition such as [7, 13] indicates that agents can provide domain independence and flexibility to this type of systems. Although agents could operate in a completely autonomous way, in our case the supervision of a human expert is recommended to limit the search only to the knowledge areas that are really interesting for the desired domain, maximizing the throughput of the learning process.

So, in this paper we present *a combination of new AI methodologies to extract knowledge from the Web to build semi-automatically an ontology of concepts and web resources for a given domain, through a distributed agent-based platform.*

The rest of the paper is organized as follow. Section 2 introduces the methodology used to obtain taxonomies of terms, discover instances and propose non-taxonomical relations. Section 3 describes the agent-based platform used to compose a final ontology from individual taxonomies of terms, under the supervision of a human expert. Section 4 explains the way of representing the results and discusses the evaluation against other information retrieval systems in relation to *precision* and *recall*. The final section contains the conclusions and proposes lines of future work.

2 Taxonomy Creation from Unstructured Documents

The basis of the proposed ontology construction process is the intensive use of a methodology [16] for constructing taxonomies of terms and web resources that are relevant for a domain. The most important characteristic of the method is that the whole process is performed automatically and autonomously directly from the Web.

The algorithm is based on analysing a large number of web sites in order to find important concepts for a domain by studying the neighbourhood of an initial keyword that characterizes the desired searched domain. Concretely, in the English language, the immediate anterior word for a keyword is frequently classifying it (expressing a semantic specialization of the meaning), whereas the immediate posterior one represents the domain where it is applied [8]. So, on the one hand, the previous word for a specific key*word* is used for obtaining the taxonomical hierarchy of terms (e.g. *breast cancer* will be a subclass of *cancer*). The process is repeated recursively in order to create deeper-level subclasses (e.g. *metastatic breast cancer* is a subclass of *breast cancer*). On the other hand, the *posterior word* for the specific *keyword* is used to categorise the web resources, considered as a tag that expresses the context in where the searched domain is applied (e.g. *colorectal cancer research* will be a domain of application of *colorectal cancer* covered on a specific web document). Moreover, particular examples (i.e. proper names) for a discovered concept are found based on the way that they are represented in the text, considering them as *instances* in the defined hierarchy. In both cases, the most representative web sites for each class or instance are also retrieved and categorised according to the specific topic covered. Finally, a *polysemy detection algorithm* is performed in order to disambiguate polysemic domains. This algorithm performs a clusterisation of the discovered subclasses, in order to group the most similar ones, detecting automatically different sets of terms that correspond with different word senses.

Fig. 1. Examples of classes, instances and URLs discovered for the *lung cancer* domain

The result of the process is a hierarchical and categorized organization of the available resources according to the *classes* –concepts- and *instances* -particular examples-discovered for the given domain (see Fig. 1 for an example of the obtained hierarchy for the *lung cancer* domain).

In order to detect and extract relevant information from the Web, the method relies on a search engine for searching and accessing the available web resources. It constructs dynamically the appropriate search queries for the search engine, obtaining the most adequate corpus of web resources at each time. Moreover, the search engine is also used for checking the relevance of the extracted terms and evaluating the strength of the taxonomical relationships between them through a statistical analysis based on the number of estimated results available in the Web.

As an additional step, the methodology analyses and extracts the sentences from where concepts of the taxonomy are extracted. This knowledge could be very useful in a latter stage of the ontology construction process to obtain more complex relations like non-taxonomical ones. Concretely, analysing the subject and the object of a sentence we can infer a new relationship between them according to the verb (which can express a taxonomical or non taxonomical relationship). Some authors such as [9] have been used that approach successfully for ontology learning.

In order to ease a future evaluation of the discovered set of sentences, the analyser applies several syntactic processing tools to obtain a simplified but meaningful view of the original sentence. Then it uses several *Natural Language Processing* tools to analyse the sentence syntactically and select only those ones that express knowledge in a simplified way, excluding ambiguous syntactical constructions like conditionals or futures (some examples of selected sentences can be found in Table 1). Sentences that accomplish a set of simplicity rules like the described ones are typically called *text nuggets,* and they are commonly used for different knowledge acquisition and information extraction tasks [14].

As will be shown in section 3, the additional knowledge acquired by the analysis of those sentences will be used by the proposed agent-based platform (with the supervision of a human expert) in order to discover non-taxonomical relationships, expand the analysis and build a final ontology for the domain.

3   Distributed Ontology Building Process

Once an initial taxonomy of terms that are relevant for the domain is obtained through the described methodology we can use the discovered knowledge to find more complex relationships and performs further analysis. Concretely, using the extracted sentences for particular discovered terms, we can find other concepts that are related to the domain with a certain relationship (in many cases, a non-taxonomical one). With that new concept, a new taxonomical analysis in the same way as has been described can be performed, obtaining a complex network of knowledge with the rich semantics that ontologies require. In this case, some of the previously obtained knowledge (e.g. the concept from which this one has been obtained) can be added to the queries performed in order to restrict and contextualize the search, obtain the most suitable resources and, in consequence, improve the throughput of the learning process.

However, the described process for creating taxonomies is a very time consuming task, especially when dealing with such a general and enormous repository as the Web. Concretely, accessing and downloading web documents online overheads the execution and affects seriously on the system's performance. So, if we plan to perform several taxonomical analysis iteratively, they may suppose a computational cost that is hard to be assumed by a centralized approach.

However, as several tasks of the learning process can be performed concurrently (e.g. construct different taxonomies, evaluate text nuggets, cluster terms, etc.) a distributed approach can promise a great improvement over a centralised one. However, as the execution requirements are very dynamic as they are defined by the knowledge acquired at execution time, coordination, flexibility and dynamicity are fundamental. In order to handle this problem, the agent paradigm is a promising technology for information retrieval [18].

Therefore, we present a supervised agent-based platform for building ontologies from the combination of taxonomies of several interrelated terms that are selected into a semiautomatic way.

3.1 Multiagent System Architecture

The system is composed of several autonomous entities (agents) that could be deployed around a network. Each agent can be considered as an execution unit that follows a particularly modeled behavior and interacts (communicates) with other ones, coordinating their execution for achieving a common goal. The inter-agent communication allows them to share partial results and coordinate their efforts in order to construct the final ontology. Concretely, there are three kinds of agents in the MAS:

a) *User Agent* (UA): allows the human expert to interact with the system. Through this agent, she can configure, initialize and control the construction process in order to obtain an ontology that fits with her interests.

b) *Internet Agent* (IA): It implements the taxonomy construction methodology described in section 2. For a specific initial query, it performs the web search process and returns the result. The coordinated action of several IAs with specific queries allows obtaining a set of partial results (taxonomies) that can be joined and interrelated adequately in order to build the final ontology. As this construction process is very time consuming, it is important that these agents could execute concurrently (or in parallel using a computer network) and co-ordinately in order to achieve the highest efficiency. They are highly reusable components as they are initialized and finished dynamically depending on the ontology construction's requirements.

c) *Coordinator Agent* (CA): it coordinates the ontology construction process by receiving orders from the user and creating, configuring and finalising the appropriated IAs to explore web domains. Partial results obtained from the execution of each IA are received and composed to create the final ontology. Note that although the ontology construction is centralised by this agent, its work load in relation to the IAs (even with several machines available) is quite reduced.

3.2 Ontology Construction Steps

The system is composed of several types of agents that coordinate their work to model and solve the ontology construction process in an efficient and scalable way. Moreover, the supervision of a human expert is required to drive the search towards the knowledge areas in which she is interested, retrieving the highest amount of useful knowledge with the maximum efficiency. As shown in Fig. 2, the steps of the process are:

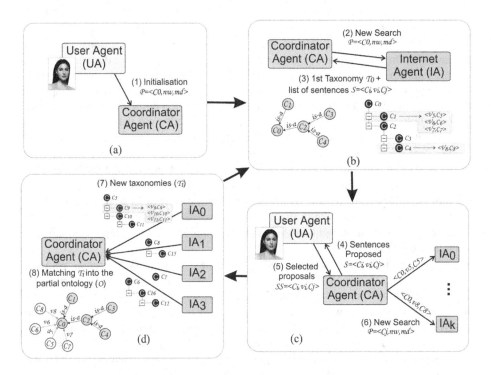

Fig. 2. Steps of the agent-based ontology building process

- The process begins when the user introduces through the UA (see Fig. 2a) the initial parameters of the search: the concept that represents the domain in which she is interested, number of web sites to evaluate and maximum depth of each hierarchy (C_0, nw and md respectively). The UA sends this information to the CA that will start to construct the associated ontology.

- Then, as it is shown in Fig. 2b, the CA creates and initializes the first IA that starts building the taxonomy that corresponds with the initial concept by creating the initial search query. This IA executes the methodology described in section 2 and returns the following results: the taxonomy T_0 associated with the initial concept, a set of related web pages for each concept and instance found, and a set of relevant sentences (S) involving the discovered concepts in the form *Subject (C_i)* + *Verb (V_i)* + *[Preposition]* + *Object (C_j)*. Either the *Subject* or the *Object* must contain a concept included in the taxonomy; the other will be a new term. Both are related with the relationship specified by the verb (which can be taxonomical or non-taxonomical) and will be used to retrieve new knowledge for the domain. Examples of sentences for the *cancer* domain are listed in Table 1.

- At this point the CA includes T_0 in the ontology (only composed of the initial concept) and sends the set of sentences to the UA. Then the human expert must consider which of these proposals are correct and/or interesting for her interests in order to continue the search. So, the user selects a subset of sentences (SS) to be evaluated (see Fig. 2c), sending them to the CA. Concretely, each one expresses a relationship between a concept (C_i) that is included in the current partial ontology and a new one (C_j) that defines another domain to be explored; the relation between them will be labelled with the verb V_i (optionally a prepositional verb). For instance, for the discovered concept *breast cancer* for the *cancer* domain, the term *radiotherapy* could be found in a proposed sentence with the verb *receives*, representing a non-taxonomical relation in the ontology. It is also possible to specify which of those concepts and relations will be expanded through new web searches (e.g. *polyp*) and which ones will be included directly into the ontology without evaluation as they represent simple facts (e.g. *hair loss*, *smokers*).

- For each new concept (C_j) extracted from each selected sentence in SS that should be evaluated and has not been considered yet, the CA creates and initializes a set of IAs to build several taxonomies associated to those concepts. In order to maintain the initial context, the CA attaches the root concept (C_0) to all queries specified for each IA, as shown in Fig. 2c. Future improvements can consider also C_i or other previously acquired knowledge for the domain as a bootstrap for contextualizing new searches.

- Again, the IAs builds taxonomies for each new concept concurrently with the specific execution conditions, and finally they send a new set of results (terms, relationships, web resources, instances, etc) to the CA.

- The CA joins the new taxonomies obtained (T_j) by the IAs into the global ontology, by relating the new concepts with the existing ones through the relationships specified by the verbs of the sentences from which they were extracted. Note that the direction of the relation will depend on the role of each concept into the original sentence (subject or object). This is a very critical process in order to obtain a coherent and useful representation of the knowledge. As will be described in the final section, several questions that are not fully developed at this moment regarding the joining of partial results and the processing of verb labels in a semantic way should be considered carefully.

- In addition to the taxonomies, new sentences sets are received by the CA that will send them to the UA to perform a new user-centred evaluation. The process will be repeated while the user selects new interesting terms to be evaluated.

At the end of the process, the CA will store the final ontology composed of several *is-a* taxonomies interrelated with verb-labelled relationships. This knowledge does not give a complete view of the full domain and all its relationships, but it offers a representation of the knowledge in which the user is interested over a specific domain (e.g. *treatments* and *symptoms* of certain types of *cancers*).

4 Case Study: *Cancer* Domain

For illustrative purposes, in this section we will show the results obtained for a medical domain such as *cancer*, and how it could be useful for a medical researcher to extract or structure this specific knowledge from the Web.

The ontology building process begins with a concept given by the user, in this case, the term *cancer*. As a result of this first search, a taxonomy for that term containing several concepts related to *cancer* is obtained in a tree-based way. For instance, at the first level of the taxonomy, different kinds of *cancer* are identified (e.g *lung cancer, colorectal cancer, breast cancer*). Recursively, these concepts can contain different subclasses such as *metastatic, metachronous* or *nonpolyposis*, in the case of *colorectal cancer*. In addition to this hierarchy, a list of sentences that can contain non taxonomic relations are presented to the user (see examples in Table 1).

Table 1. Examples of sentences obtained from web sites. **Bold** represents the user's choice.

Concept	Sentences
breast cancer	**[breast_cancer][receives][radiotherapy]**
	[the pill][protects][against][breast_cancer]
	[most breast_cancers][are][ductal carcinomas]
colon cancer	**[colon_cancers][start][as][polyps]**
colorectal cancer	**[most colorectal_cancers][begin][as][a polyp]**
	[all colorectal_cancer patients][require][a colostomy]
	[most colorectal_cancers][start][in][the glandular cells]
lung cancer	**[lung_cancer][causes][paraneoplastic syndromes]**
	[spiral_scans][find][lung_cancer]
	[lung_cancer][tend to develop][in][smokers]
	[asbestos exposure][increases][lung_cancer risk]
	[lung_cancer treatment][depends][on][tumor size]
cervical cancer	**[cervicography or colposcopy][screening][for][cervical_cancer]**
skin cancer	[ozone depletion][increases][skin_cancer risk]
	[fair-skinned people][develop][skin_cancers]
cranial radiotherapy	**[cranial_radiotherapy][causes][hair loss]**
beam radiotherapy	[external beam_radiotherapy][include][x-ray therapy]
hyperplastic polyp	**[hyperplastic_polyps][occur][in][normal gastric mucosa]**
	[colorectal hyperplastic_polyps][are][benign lesions]

The user can select the ones that she considers correct and covers a desired related topic (marked in **bold**). For instance if she is interested in treatment and prevention for *breast cancer* she could select the first two sentences of the list that are related to *radiotherapy* and *the pill* respectively. In this case, *radiotherapy* is evaluated for obtaining a new taxonomy and *the pill* is considered as a simple fact. All those partial results are joined creating a final complete ontology as shown in Fig. 3.

It is important to note that each concept of the final ontology stores valuable web information for the domain, like the categorized list of available web sites and a set of instances that represent proper names like healthcare organizations or institutions (see some examples for the *lung cancer* class in Fig.1).

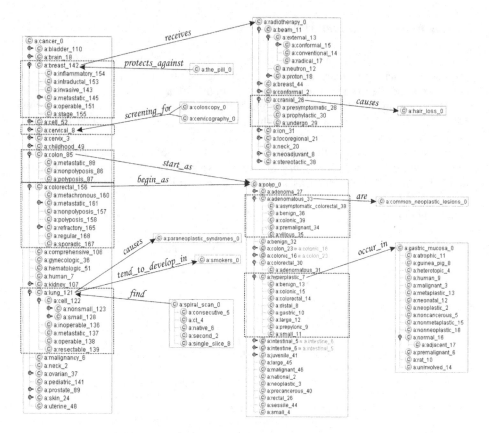

Fig. 3. Part of the ontology obtained for the *cancer* domain

5   Ontology Representation and Evaluation

The final ontology composed of the CA is stored in the standard representation language OWL: a semantic markup language for publishing and sharing ontologies on the Web [3]. It is supported by many ontology visualizers and editors, like Protégé, allowing the user to explore, understand, analyse or even modify the ontology easily.

Concerning the evaluation of ontologies, it is recognized to be an open problem [5]. Regarding our proposal, the evaluation is a task that, at this moment, is a matter of current research. However, some evaluations have been performed manually and others are planned to be performed automatically comparing the results against other methodologies or available semantic repositories such as WordNet.

In our case, as the non-taxonomical relations have been selected by a human expert, we have centred the evaluation in the automatically obtained taxonomies. Their evaluation is performed manually at this moment. Whenever it is possible, a representative human made classification is taken as the ideal model of taxonomy to achieve (*Gold Standard*). Then, several tests for that domain are performed with different sizes of search. For each one, we apply the standard measures *recall* and *precision* (see an example of evaluation for the *Cancer* domain in Fig. 4). As a measure of comparison of the quality of the obtained results against similar available systems, we have evaluated *precision* and *recall* against hand-made web directory services and taxonomical search engines (a detailed evaluation of those system can be found in [17]). For the first case, we have used Yahoo, as it can be considered the most popular human-made directory-based search engine. For the second case, we have selected the taxonomical search engine Clusty as it seems to be the one that provides best and more complete results from the available ones and AlltheWeb as it provides high quality query refinements involving domain related terms. This comparison can also give us an idea of the potential improvement of our structuring and representation of web resources (as shown in section 2) in relation to the results presented by currently available web search engines.

Some conclusions from the evaluation of the results for several domains are:

- The performance of the candidate selection procedure is high as the number of mistakes (incorrectly selected and rejected items) is maintained around 15-20%.
- The growth of the number of discovered concepts (and in consequence the *recall*) follows a logarithmic distribution in relation to the size of the search due to the redundancy of information and the relevancy-based sorting of web sites presented by the search engine. Moreover, when a certain point in which a considerable amount of concepts has been discovered is reached, precision tends to decrease due the growth of false candidates. As a consequence, analysing a large amount of web sites does not imply obtaining better results than with a more reduced corpus due to, among other reasons, the ranking algorithms of the web search engines that potentially present the most relevant and useful web sites in first place.
- Comparing the performance to Yahoo, we see that although its *precision* is the highest, as it has been made by humans, the number of results (*recall*) is quite limited. In relation to the automatic search tools, Clusty and AlltheWeb, the first one tends to return more results (*recall*) but with low *precision* whereas the second one offers an inverse situation. In both cases, the performance (*recall-precision* compromise) is easily surpassed by our proposal.

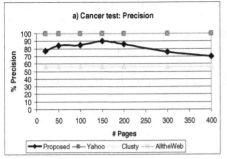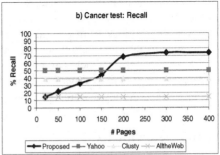

Fig. 4. Evaluation of results for the *Cancer* taxonomy

6   Conclusions

Some authors have been working on ontology learning from different kinds of structured information sources (like data bases or knowledge bases [12]). However, taking into consideration the amount of resources available easily on the Internet, we believe that ontology creation from unstructured documents like web sites is an important line of research. In this sense, many authors [1, 2, 11] are putting their efforts on processing natural language texts. In most cases, an ontology of basic relations (WordNet) is used like a semantic repository. Moreover, in most cases, a relevant corpus of documents carefully selected is used as a starting point. In consequence, these approaches have problems with very concrete domains, or dynamic environments like the Web.

In contrast, our proposal does not start from any kind of predefined knowledge, like WordNet and, in consequence, it can be applied over domains that are not typically considered in semantic repositories as, for example, *Biosensors* [15]. Moreover, the supervision of a human expert that allows driving the search only to the desired areas of knowledge, and the distributed execution based on agents, improve the efficiency and the throughput. These facts result in a scalable and suitable method for acquiring knowledge from a huge and dynamic repository as the Web. The final ontology and the structured list of web sites can be a great help for many knowledge intensive tasks as the Semantic Web [3] and for improving the accessing of web resources in relation to the currently available web search engines.

As future lines of research, some topics can be proposed:

- In the current version, the number of potential sentences returned for human evaluation could be quite high. To assist the user in this task, we plan to perform a filtering process to obtain only the most common or relevant sentences or those whose verbs could be the most important or frequent for the searched domain.
- A detailed study on the casuistry of the taxonomy joining process should be considered carefully in order to detect implicit relationships from redundant or equivalent concepts among the obtained taxonomies.
- Regarding to the discovered verb labelled relationships, in order to obtain an easily usable and interoperable knowledge base, verb expressions should be simplified (e.g. the verbal form *"is usually included into"* expresses a *"part of"* type relationship). In this sense, some basic relationship types can be considered for this task (e.g. *is-a, part-of, related-to, similar-to, cause/effect, result*, etc).
- Several executions from the same domain and parameters in different moments can give us different ontologies, maintaining the results up-to-date. A study about the changes between them can tell us how a domain evolves.
- As mentioned before, ways for automate or at least easing the evaluation of every step of the ontology learning process will be studied.

Acknowledgements

The work has been supported by *Departament d'Universitats, Recerca i Societat de la Informació* of Catalonia.

References

1. Alfonseca E. and Manandhar S.: An unsupervised method for general named entity recognition and automated concept discovery. In Proceedings of the 1st International Conference on General WordNet, Mysore, India, 2002.
2. Ansa O., Hovy E., Aguirre E., Martínez D.: Enriching very large ontologies using the WWW. In Proceedings of of the Ontology Learning Workshop of the European Conference of AI (ECAI-00), Berlin, Germany, 2000.
3. Berners-lee T., Hendler, J., Lassila O.: The semantic web. Scientific American (284):5, pp.34-43. 2001.
4. Fensel D.: Ontologies: A Silver Bullet for Knowledge Management and Electronic Commerce. Springer-Verlag, 2001.
5. Fensel D. and Gómez-Pérez, A.: A Survey on Ontological Tools. Deliverable 1.3. OntoWeb: Ontology-based Information Exchange Management, 2000.
6. Fernández-López M., Gómez-Pérez A., Juristo N.: METHONTOLOGY: From Ontological Art Towards Ontological Engineering. In Proceedings of Spring Symposium on Ontological Engineering of AAAI. Stanford University. USA, 1997.
7. Gibbins N., Harris S. and Shadbolt N.: Agent-based semantic web services. Journal of Web Semantics: Science, Services and Agents on the World Wide Web, (1):2, pp 141-154, 2003.
8. Grefenstette G.: SQLET: Short Query Linguistic Expansion Techniques: Palliating One-Word Queries by Providing Intermediate Structure to Text. In Proceedings of: Information Extraction: A Multidisciplinary Approach to an Emerging Information Technology. RIAO'97. LNAI 1299, pp. 97-114. Montreal, Quebec, Canada, 1997.
9. Kavalec, M., Maedche, A. and Skátek, V.: Discovery of Lexical Entries for Non-taxonomic Relations in Ontology Learning. In: Proceedings of SOFSEM 2004: Theory and Practice of Computer Science, LNCS 2932, pp. 249-256. Merin, Czech Republic, 2004.
10. Lamparter S., Ehrig M., Tempich C.: Knowledge Extraction from Classification Schemas. In Proceedings of CoopIS/DOA/ODBASE 2004, LNCS 3290, pp. 618-636, Larnaca, Cyprus, 2004.
11. Maedche A., Staab S.: Discovering conceptual relations from text. In Proceedings of ECAI 2000. IOS Press, Berlin, Germany, 2000.
12. Manzano-Macho D., Gómez-Pérez A.: A Survey of Ontology Learning Methods and Techniques. Deliverable 1.5. OntoWeb: Ontology-based Information Exchange Management, 2000. Available at www.ontoweb.org.
13. Moreno A., Riaño D., Isern D., Bocio J., Sánchez D., Jiménez L.: Knowledge Explotation from the Web. In Proceedings of 5th International Conference on Practical Aspects of Knowledge Management (PAKM 2004). LNAI 3336. Viena, Austria, 2004.
14. Paşca, M.: Finding Instance Names and Alternative Glosses on the Web: In Proceedings of Computational Linguistics and Intelligent Text Processing: 6th International Conference, (CICLing 2005), LNCS 3406, pp.280-292. Mexico City, Mexico, 2005.
15. Sánchez, D. and Moreno, A.: Creating ontologies from Web documents. Recent Advances in Artificial Intelligence Research and Development. IOS Press, vol. 113, pp.11-18. 2004.
16. Sánchez, D. and Moreno, A.: Automatic Generation of Taxonomies from the WWW. In: Proceedings of the 5th International Conference on Practical Aspects of Knowledge Management. LNAI 3336, pp. 208-219. Vienna, Austria, 2004.
17. Yeol Yoo, S. and Hoffmann, A.: A New Approach for Concept-Based Web Search. In Proceedings of AI 2003: Advances in Artificial Intelligence: 16th Australian Conference on AI, LNAI 2903, pp. 65–76. Perth, Australia, 2003.
18. Wooldridge, M.: An Introduction to multiagent systems. John Wiley and Sons, Ltd., West Sussex, England, 2002.

An Agent Architecture for Ensuring Quality of Service by Dynamic Capability Certification

Thorsten Scholz, Ingo J. Timm, and Rainer Spittel

University of Bremen, Center for Computing Technologies (TZI)
{scholz, i.timm, rasp}@tzi.de

Abstract. Agents and web services encapsulate key functionalities and therefore offer a high degree of flexibility and scalability. Semantic web services integrate explicit service descriptions with formal semantics allowing for reasoning on service discovery, chaining, and application. The key challenge here is the identification of *appropriate* services, which is supported by research on semantic web services. However, problems with assessing quality of service just start to begin when services have been discovered. In this paper, we will propose an agent-based approach for third-party quality of service certification enabling reliable distributed problem solving which is evaluated prototypically.

1 Introduction

Nowadays web services have been established as de-facto standard for interface design and implementation in large-scale applications, e.g., business information systems. They encapsulate key functionalities and therefore offer a high degree of flexibility and scalability. However these interfaces use implicit semantics for capability description and thus prevent reasoning about the offered services. In context of the semantic web, semantic web services (e.g. [Solanki et al. 2004], [Mika et al. 2004]) integrate explicit service descriptions with formal semantics allowing for enhanced reasoning on service discovery, service chaining, and service application. Especially the approach of dynamic service chaining based on sophisticated inferences, e.g., AI-planning, is a promising approach for solving a broad variety of problems. This approach is comparable to team formation in multiagent research, e.g., *model of cooperation* [Wooldridge 2000]. Analogously, the process of service chaining can be decomposed into four steps: Identification, service-chain formation, application planning, and application execution. In current research, there are numerous approaches addressed to one or multiple of these steps (e.g. [Mika et al. 2004], [Hübner et al. 2004], [Lutz 2004]). The key challenge in this process is the identification of *appropriate* services [Timm and Woelk 2003], which is supported by research on semantic web services. However, problems just start to begin when web services have been discovered: *How is the quality of service in highly dynamic environments ensured?*

In this paper, we will propose an approach for third-party certification of quality of service. In the next section, we will outline the fundamental concepts for capability description, service discovery, and quality of service. In the following sections we will present a framework and a resulting architecture for service certification which

T. Eymann et al. (Eds.): MATES 2005, LNAI 3550, pp. 130–140, 2005.

has been implemented prototypically. A first evaluation of this approach is discussed in section 5 and compared to related work in section 6. Finally we will discuss our results and present future research challenges.

2   Rationale

Ensuring quality of service in highly dynamic environments requires the combination of various existing technologies. We propose that the combination of quality of service models, capability representation, and yellow pages services is a promising approach to enable reliable, distributed problem solving. In the following sections, we will outline ongoing research in these three areas.

2.1   Quality of Service (QoS)

Assessing quality of services is crucial to the selection process, i.e., which service is suited *best* for solving a given problem. Quality measures are multi-dimensional and are expressed in a QoS model (e.g. [Liu et al. 2004], [Sheth et al. 2002]). These models distinguish between domain dependent dimensions, specifying specific business criteria, and generic quality criteria, specifying, e.g., execution price, response time, reliability, and reputation of the service and are based on an organisational viewpoint taken in, e.g., the work of [Garvin 1988]. Specific QoS criteria are identified in [Ran 2003], where the author distinguishes four dimensions of quality for web services: run-time related, transaction support related, configuration management and cost related, and security related issues. Here, as part of the configuration management, the completeness criterion is defined as a measure for the discrepancy between a specified and the actual provided set of features of the service. To assess the key quality measure of completeness – whether a service is capable of solving a problem at all, and to what degree – and which is in focus of this paper, an explicit representation of service capabilities and problem descriptions is required.

2.2   Capabilities

Retrieving a service to solve a specific problem implies the existence of a formal description of (a) the offered service capabilities and (b) the given problem. To provide the dynamic selection of distributed services to solve a problem, a standardized protocol to access services is needed. The World Wide Web Consortium (W3C) defines web service architectures and protocols to access those [W3C 2002], e.g., the description language WSDL [Christensen et al. 2001] to define a web service framework. The WSDL defines the web interfaces and the language to access the web service. Describing the capabilities of web services, with respect to using this information for dynamic inference processes, formal description languages, e.g., DAML-S [Ankolekar et al. 2002] and OWL-S [Martin et al. 2004] are needed. The combination of DAML-S and WSDL offers a formal framework to describe semantics of web services. The domain of geospatial information systems is a representative for a sophisticated use of (semantic) web services, i.e. the Open Geospatial Consortium

(OGC) is developing standards for geospatial and location based services[1]. The OGC catalogue service provides service information, metadata and the type of service, encoded in ISO19119. Additionally, the OGC compatible services provide access to mandatory and optional metadata and structure of service data, encoded in XML, using an OGC XML-schema. However, these static descriptions of service capabilities limit the dynamic aspects distributed problem solving essentially. Work on capability management in the multiagent system community focuses on inferences on capabilities in order to enable higher applicability of a provided service (e.g. [Timm and Woelk 2003], [Scholz et al. 2004], [Guttmann and Zukerman 2004]) and thus allowing for enhanced dynamic behaviour of the overall system. Based on a representation of service capabilities, infrastructures like catalogues or yellow pages are used for match-making of service consumers and service providers.

2.3 Yellow Pages Services

In an environment where service providers and consumers are distributed across the internet, infrastructures for catalogue services are required in order to enable the dynamic retrieval of service providers. In the multiagent system community, the FIPA[2] standardizes the directory facilitator (DF) as part of an agent platform [Fipa 2003]. The DF is an implementation of a yellow pages service for agents, managing service descriptions of agents. In the web service community, the Universal Description, Discovery, and Integration of web services (UDDI) is used as a catalogue service [Oasis 2004], which provides a service publishing and an inquiry API. A more sophisticated approach is used within the OGC catalogue services. They support the discovery, access, maintenance and organization of geospatial information and related resources of web services by adding a set of formal metadata descriptions for the services. The identification of the *best*-fitting service is supported by using semantic descriptions of the content of services [Hübner et al. 2004].

Summarizing, yellow pages services integrate basic capability descriptions without inferences in order to perform the match-making process between service consumer and provider. Yet, integration of more sophisticated capability management with a quality of service measure into the catalogue service appears to be a promising approach to enable a framework for reliable distributed computing.

3 Conceptual Framework

Specific requirements for this framework arise from the internet where services are distributed across the net, availability cannot be assured, and there is no authority to guarantee the quality of a provided service. In our approach we propose a conceptual framework with the objective to support integrated identification, evaluation, and selection of services for reliable behaviour of applications using distributed services. On a conceptual level, three main components are mandatory:

- Capability management for the identification of the *best*-fitting service, i.e., services are identified on basis of their capabilities. The problem here is to

---

[1] See http://www.opengeospatial.org/
[2] Foundation for Intelligent Physical Agents, http://www.fipa.org

match a given task to capabilities; in real-life applications this includes not only direct but also fuzzy mappings [Scholz et al. 2004].

- Certification management for the evaluation of the services, i.e., available services need to be evaluated according to the offered capabilities as well as other quality issues resulting in a quality measurement.
- Catalogue management for supporting the service retrieval process, i.e., it integrates capability and certification management for providing a unified service exploration interface for service consumers.

These components are the basis for mapping service consumers to service providers. The process for this mapping includes three steps: service registration, service validation, and service retrieval. The registration at a catalogue is required in order to publish the service for usage by consumers. In order to enable reliable behaviour of the service, the framework requires a service to certify its capabilities prior to registration, which is step two in the mapping process. After certification of abilities, the services are published with their QoS and consumers can query the catalogue for services fulfilling their quality criteria. Additionally, the consumer may provide feedback to the catalogue service about the experienced quality of the used service. When expectations of quality were not met, the catalogue service will re-certify the service.

The key idea of the framework is the agent-based integration of explicit capability representation, certification of capabilities, and publishing of certified services. This approach uses a QoS model with focus on capabilities as a first step, but is easily extended with other QoS measures, e.g., availability, costs or duration to solve the problem.

4 Architecture

To implement the framework, the three main components identified in the prior section have to be agentified and integrated. In Figure 1, the architecture for the agent system realising an integrated catalogue, capability, and certification management is visualised. The agent for catalogue management is implementing the key-role and is responsible for managing service registration inquiries, invocation of the certification process, and providing an exploration interface to query on registered services. It utilises the capability management for the match-making between consumer problems and service problem solving capabilities.

The agent for certification management certifies QoS of service providers with regard to provided capabilities using the capability management agent for inference on capabilities. The certification of problem solving capabilities is performed by putting the service to the test with a set of problems and a standard solution. Problems are domain specific, and are either taken from the problem database (PDB) or created dynamically by a problem generator agent. These agents need to be adapted for each domain in order to generate relevant problems for the certification process. The results from service are evaluated according to a standard solution. On this basis a measure of completeness, which is the QoS for the provided capability, may be derived. The QoS are stored in a database (QoS DB), which is updated in regular intervals with re-certification of the services.

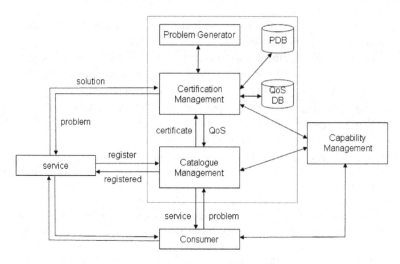

Fig. 1. Architecture for dynamic certification of services

The capability management allows for dynamic inference on capabilities and match-making to problem descriptions. It performs the match-making process between consumer and service by inferences on combination and recombination of singleton to more compositional capabilities to enable classification of problems. This allows for a more sophisticated match-making process, since the capabilities are not only considered at design-time of the system, but also at run-time. For details on the algorithm and representation, please refer to [Scholz et al. 2004].

In the following sections, the processes of registration, validation, and retrieval are discussed in more detail.

4.1 Registration and Validation

Prior to the registration of a service in the catalogue, the provided capabilities of the service have to be certified. This process is explained in **Fig. 2**: The *service* submits a registration requests (*register*) with the catalogue to the *catalogue management*, consisting of the name of the service, its physical address, and the list of capabilities. The catalogue management requests the certification of the service by the *certification management* with the same information as provided in the original request. The certification management uses the capability management implicitly in order to identify the problem domain, and receives standard problems from the problem database or dynamically generated problems from the problem generator. The list of problems is sent to the service requesting the registration. The solved problems are returned to the certification management, which assesses the QoS on basis of standard solutions and notifies the catalogue management of the completion of the certification process. Finally the service is informed, that its registration in the catalogue is completed.

To upkeep the quality of the certificates of available services, they have to be reviewed continuously. The certification management initiates the process and sends out the request to certificate available services and the results are stored in the QoS-database.

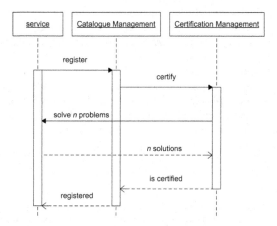

Fig. 2. Process of registration and validation

4.2 Retrieval

A service consumer using the exploration interface of the catalogue management is, in most cases, interested in the services capable of solving its problem with the highest quality. The process of retrieving the service with the highest quality from the catalogue is shown in figure 3: A *consumer* requests a service from the catalogue for problem solving (*query services*). The request consists of the name of the consumer, the physical address, and the problem description based on the capability management. The *catalogue management* matches the problem with help of the capability management to a set of registered services and retrieves their QoS

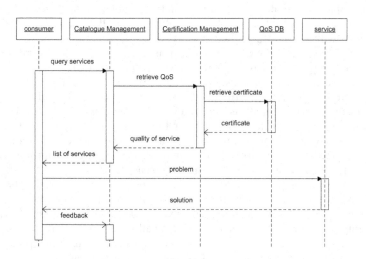

Fig. 3. Process of service retrieval and feedback

information from the *certification management*, which were stored in the QoS Database (*QoS DB*). The list of available services with added QoS information is returned to the service consumer (*list of services*), which selects an appropriate service to solve the problem (*problem, solution*).

Changes in the QoS occurring between the regular re-certification processes are addressed by consumer feedback. Upon reception of the solution, the consumer may evaluate the result and, in case of lacking quality, may inform the catalogue management of the discrepancy between expected and received quality (*feedback*). This would initiate an immediate re-certification of the consulted service by the certification management.

5 Experiments

In order to evaluate the proposed approach, a first set of experiments was launched using a multiagent implementation on basis of Jade 3.2[3]. A user-oriented approach is used, evaluating the benefit of certification and catalogue management.

These experiments include the registration and validation process as well as a first step for the retrieval of services from the catalogue. The feedback from the service consumer to the catalogue management is omitted here, but will be considered in future experiments.

5.1 Design

The experiment is focused on route planning, where the service consumer is looking for the shortest path between two locations. Four sub-optimal search algorithms on graphs were implemented defining four services of this purpose: greedy search, breath-first search, depth-first search, and iterated depth-first search [Russel and Norvig 2003]. The certification management is implemented as defined above, i.e., it uses a problem generator for creating random problem graphs with an increasing number of nodes and edges. In the generated graphs, there may be sub-graphs, not connected with each other. For performance measurement, the optimal search algorithm A* is implemented. The QoS measure is specified as the ratio of optimal solution length (A*) divided by the test service resulting length.

The experimental process is divided into two steps: In the certification step, services are tested by the certification management and QoS results are registered. The catalogue management is realized by the directory facilitator of the agent platform, with the modification that prior to an entry in the DF, a service agent is certified by the certification management agent. After the certification process is completed, the search agents are taken into the DF catalogue with a description of their abilities (search on graphs) and the QoS measure.

In the second step, two virtual service consumers are created. The consumer "certified" uses the service certified as performing best in the catalogue. The second consumer "random" selects a service provider by random. Additionally, they are generating problems, asking for the shortest path in a random graph – with varying amount of nodes (from 5 to 500). Each of the agents is creating 2.500 problem graphs. The results are documented with the QoS measure described above.

---

[3] http://jade.tilab.com

We chose the search problem domain since shortest path algorithms are fully understood, and an optimal algorithm exists creating an objective and valid QoS measure.

5.2 Results

The outcome differences for both consumer types are striking (cf. Fig. 4). Selection on a random base leads to results, varying within the complete interval of [0, 1], i.e., no result found (0) or optimal solution (1). The mean QoS is 0.438 with standard deviation of 0.444. A remarkable proportion of "no results found" caused by use of depth-first search yields a median of 0 for the random agent.

Considering the "certified" consumer, a different picture evolves. The range of results is limited within the upper half of the interval [0, 1]. Especially, the outcome "no results found" never appeared. The mean QoS of certified consumer is 0.880 with standard deviation of 0.133.

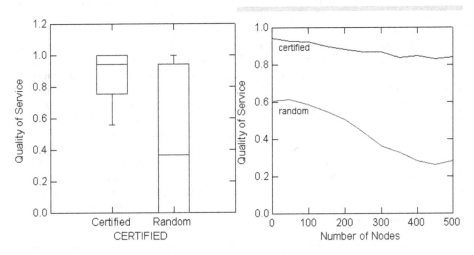

Fig. 4. Box-and-Whisker Plot   Fig. 5. QoS by amount of nodes

There seems to be a benefit using certification for service selection. For validation of this thesis, statistical testing has been performed. The two-sample t-Test for QoS resulted in a highly significant t-value of 47.620 (p-value < 0.001). In order to protect these results from invalid assumptions, a non-parametric test, the Kruskal-Wallis-test, has been computed, too. The resulting p-value is smaller than 0.001 again.

Theoretical considerations of the underlying problem domain, propose decreasing QoS if amount of nodes is increased. A more sophisticated result of the experiment is that this decrease comes out to be different for the consumer types (cf. Figure 5).

Summarizing, there is evidence for the benefit of certification management in this experimental setting. The prototype and experiments may be considered as a feasibility proof of our approach in this specific domain. However, this is a first result and further experiments, especially in different domains, are required for further conclusions.

6 Related Work

The certification and quality of available services is an important issue in current research. In the field of web services, [Sheth et al. 2002] propose a service-oriented middleware which has an integrated QoS model supporting its automatic computation. The QoS measure is proposed to be fine-tuned by simulation of changes in a workflow prior to execute that change. This approach defines a model which lacks an explicit representation of service capabilities and focuses on standard issues like time, cost, and reliability and therefore leaves the question unanswered, whether a service is capable of solving a problem, and to what degree. In [Liu et al. 2004], the authors propose a QoS model, distinguishing between generic and domain dependent quality criteria. The model is used in a QoS registry, where web services are registered with a QoS based on reputation and user feedback. This approach also lacks a formal representation of service capabilities, and focuses on the basic criteria like execution time and pricing. However the approach of multiple QoS measures is considered in our framework; the prototypical implementation uses a domain-specific QoS. [Ran 2003] defines a model for web service discovery with QoS, by introducing a certification component to the common UDDI architecture. The author presents a broad, informal model for QoS, including a completeness measure. Nevertheless, the approach defines a static approach to certification and does not define its process. In the multiagent system community, [Rovatsos et al. 2003] define a communication based performance measure for self diagnosis. The authors define a generic model for measuring the performance of agent communication actions which can be used for self-repairing and self-optimising, which is, to some extend a QoS measure. Nevertheless, this approach focuses on measuring communication efforts and is not suited for measuring quality of service. A different approach to reliable behaviour of distributed services is trust (e.g. [Dash et al. 2004], [Falcone and Castelfranchi 2004]). In these approaches, a trust model, based on, e.g., a service consumer community, is used for assessing the reliability of a service. These approaches are different to the one presented in this paper, since they lack representation of service capabilities and certification mechanisms.

7 Conclusions and Future Work

In this paper, we presented a framework for automated service certification for reliable distributed problem solving. The framework includes a quality of service model integrating capability assessment and problem-based completeness measure for dynamic capability certification. Our proposed agent-based architecture implements the framework and supports agents for registration, certification, and retrieval of services. A first step approach has been implemented and evaluated for the search-problem domain.

The results of the evaluation indicate, that automated certification of service capabilities enhances the overall performance of the system with respect to quality of the distributed problem solving. As a speciality of this domain, relevance increases by problem size. However, this observation is based on a domain which is formally well-understood and moreover on an objective quality measure.

In future work, we are going to adapt this approach to different domains of application: On a technical level, GIS domains will be taken into consideration; on an application level, logistic services will be investigated. These domains allow for a more sophisticated evaluation of the approach with consideration of higher problem complexity and missing objective quality measure. To address the expected problems, multi-dimensional QoS models and explicit trust-models will be integrated. Finally, we are going to apply this approach to agent-based process planning and production control within the IntaPS project.

Acknowledgements

Part of the work was funded by the Deutsche Forschungsgemeinschaft (DFG) in the IntaPS-3 project within the SPP 1083 program as well as the Collaborative Research Center on Autonomous Logistic Processes (SFB 637), and by the European Community in the project GeoShare.

References

[Ankolekar et al. 2002] Ankolekar A., Burstein M., Hobbs J.R., Lassila O., McDermott D., Martin D., McIlraith S.A., Narayanan S., Paolucci M., Payne T. (2002): DAML-S: Web Service Description for the Semantic Web. Proceedings of the 1st International Semantic Web Conference (ISWC 02), 2002. Springer Verlag, Berlin.

[Christensen et al. 2001] Christensen E., Curbera F., Meredith G., and Weerawarana S. (2001): Web Services Description Language (WSDL): http://www.w3.org/TR/2001/NOTE-wsdl-20010315 2001. (last visited 2005/01)

[Dash et al. 2004] Dash R.K., Ramchurn S.D., Jennings N.R. (2004): Trust-Based Mechanism Design. Proceedings of the 3rd International Joint Conference on Autonomous Agents & Multiagent Systems (AAMAS 2004). ACM Press, New York, 2004, pp. 748-755

[Falcone and Castelfranchi 2004] Falcone R., Castelfranchi C. (2004): Trust Dynamics: How Trust is Influenced by Direct Experiences and by Trust itself. Proceedings of the 3rd International Joint Conference on Autonomous Agents & Multiagent Systems (AAMAS 2004). ACM Press, New York, 2004, pp. 740-747

[Fipa 2003] FIPA Agent Discovery Service Specification. Document Nr.: PC00095A, 2003. http://www.fipa.org/specs/fipa00095/ (last visited Jan. 2005).

[Garvin 1988] Garvin D. (1988): Managing Quality: The strategic and Competitive Edge. Free Press, New York, 1988.

[Guttmann and Zukerman 2004] Guttmann C. and Zukerman I. (2004): Towards Models of Incomplete and Uncertain Knowledge of Collaborators' Internal Resources. Proceedings of the 2nd German Conference on Multiagent System Technologies (MATES 2004). Springer Verlag, Heidelberg, 2004, pp. 58-72.

[Hübner et al. 2004] Hübner, S., Spittel, R., Visser, U. & Vögele, T. (2004): Ontology-Based Search for Interactive Digital Maps. IEEE Intelligent Systems 19(3), pp. 80-86, IEEE Computer Society Press.

[Liu et al. 2004] Liu Y., Ngu A.H.H., and Zeng, L. (2004): QoS Computation and Policing in Dynamic Web Service Selection. Proceedings of the WWW2004 Vol. 2, ACM Press, New York, 2004, pp. 66-73

[Lutz 2004] Lutz, M. (2004): Non-taxonomic Relations in Semantic Service Discovery and Composition. 1st "Ontology in Action" Workshop, in conjunction with 16th Conference on Software Engineering and Knowledge Engineering (SEKE 2004), Banff, Canada, pp. 482-485.

[Martin et al. 2004] Martin D., Burstein M., Hobbs J., Lassila O., McDermott D., McIlraith S., Narayanan S., Paolucci M., Parsia B., Payne T., Sirin E., Srinivasan N., Sycara K. (2004): OWL Semantic Markup for Web Services: http://www.w3.org/Submission/2004/SUBM-OWL-S-20041122/ (last visited 2005/01)

[Mika et al. 2004] Mika P., Oberle D., Gangemi A., Sabou M. (2004): Foundations for Service Ontologies: Aligning OWL-S to DOLCE. Proceedings of the WWW2004 Vol. 1, ACM Press, New York, 2004, pp. 563-572

[Oasis 2004] OASIS (2004): UDDIv3 Specification. http://uddi.org/pubs/uddi_v3.htm (last visited 2005/01)

[Ran 2003] Ran, S. (2003): A Model for Web Services Discovery With QoS. SIGecom Exch. Journal 4(1), ACM Press, New York, 2003, pp. 1-10

[Rovatsos et al. 2003] Rovatsos M., Schillo M., Fischer K., Weiß G. (2003): Indicators for Self-Diagnosis: Communication-Based Performance Measures. Proceedings of the 1st German Conference on Multiagent System Technologies (MATES 2003). Springer Verlag, Heidelberg, 2004, pp. 25-37

[Russel and Norvig 2003] Russel S.J. and Norvig P. (2003): Artificial Intelligence – A modern Approach (Second Edition). Pearson Education Inc., New Jersey, 2003

[Scholz et al. 2004] Scholz, T., Timm, I. J., and Woelk, P.-O. (2004): Emerging Capabilities in Intelligent Agents for Flexible Production Control. In: Katalinic et al. (Eds.): Proceedings of the International Workshop on Emergent Synthesis (IWES 2004), Budapest, Hungary.

[Sheth et al. 2002] Sheth A., Cardoso J., Miller J., Kochut K., and Kang M. (2002): QoS for Service-oriented Middleware. Proceedings of the 6th World Multiconference on Systemics, Cybernetics and Informatics (SCI02), July 2002, pp. 528--534

[Solanki et al. 2004] Solanki M., Cau A., Zedan H. (2004): Augmenting Semantic Web Service Description with Compositional Specification. Proceedings of the WWW2004 Vol. 1, ACM Press, New York, 2004, pp. 544-552

[Timm and Woelk 2003] Timm, I. J. and Woelk, P.-O. (2003): Ontology-based Capability Management for Distributed Problem Solving in the Manufacturing Domain, In: Schillo, M. et al. (Eds.): Proceedings of the first German Conference on Multi-Agent System Technologies (MATES 2003), Erfurt. LNAI 2831. Springer: Berlin, pp. 168-179.

[W3C 2002] W3C Web Services Architecture Working Group: Web services Glossary. http://www.w3c.org/TR/2002/WD-ws-gloss-20021114/ (last visited 2005/01)

[Wooldridge 2000] Wooldridge M. J. (2000): Reasoning about Rational Agents. The MIT Press, Cambridge, Massachusetts, 2000.

Engineering a Multi Agent Platform with Dynamic Semantic Service Discovery and Invocation Capability

Oguz Dikenelli[1], Özgür Gümüs[1], Ali Murat Tiryaki[1], and Geylani Kardas[2]

[1] Ege University, Department of Computer Engineering,
35100 Bornova, Izmir, Turkey
{oguzd, gumus, ali_tiryaki}@staff.ege.edu.tr
[2] Ege University, International Computer Institute,
35100 Bornova, Izmir, Turkey
geylani@bornova.ege.edu.tr

Abstract. In this paper, an agent framework, which provides a build in support for dynamic semantic service discovery and invocation within the agent's plan(s), is introduced. To provide such a support, a generic plan structure is defined for semantic service integration. Developer can reuse this generic plan and add it to any agent plan as a task to create semantic service enabled plan(s). The platform executes this kind of plan(s) with its build in support. Also, a case study is developed to show the effectiveness of this approach in terms of integrating agents with web services.

1 Introduction

Web Services can be considered as pluggable software components with language and platform independent interfaces. Hence, other components can use the web services dynamically through the published interfaces. This machine-readable interface description of the web services gives opportunity to autonomous agents to use them when they demand the functionality provided by the service. But, it is not clear how agents will decide to use a web service and how they will discover and invoke the right service in addition to its own duties.

In the literature, Semantic Markup for Web Services (OWL-S, formerly DAML-S) [16] has been extensively used to implement semantic based service discovery and execution of composite services. For example, some semantic service matching engines have been implemented based on the DAML-S profile ontology in [7] and [9]. Also, some works have been conducted to execute composite services using DAML-S process ontology in [11], [12] and [13]. Moreover, some integrated architectures have been proposed based on matchmaking in [10] and [15] and brokering in [14] to handle discovery and invocation together. However, the basic problem still remains: How can a developer build an agent system that uses web services and how he/she integrates and synchronizes these services' execution with other agent related task(s). To solve this problem, first

T. Eymann et al. (Eds.): MATES 2005, LNAI 3550, pp. 141–152, 2005.

of all agent platform must be developed that supports the execution of semantic service integration type of task(s). In this paper, we introduce an implemented agent platform that provides such a support. For this purpose, a generic plan structure is defined using the Hierarchical Task Network (HTN) formalism for semantic service discovery and dynamic invocation. Then, agent's internal architecture is specially designed to execute plan(s) that includes the task(s) derived from this generic plan. Also, a service is implemented within the platform to give the semantic service matching service to the agents in the platform.

The paper is organized in the following manner. In section 2, the general architecture of the platform is given. A design approach for the agent and semantic service integration is discussed in section 3. Section 4 introduces the internal architecture of the agent designed for execution of semantic service enabled plans. The generic plan structure for semantic service integration is explained in section 5 and the last section gives a case study and concludes the work.

2   Software Architecture of the Agent Platform for Semantic Service Integration

To be able to call a multi agent platform as semantic service enabled, agents of the platform must be capable of executing plan(s) that include specific task(s) for semantic service integration. We call this kind of plans as semantic service enabled plans. It is clear that agent(s) requires a specific support from the platform to execute this kind of plans. So, a conceptual architecture, that executes semantic service enabled plans, must be defined first. Fig. 1 illustrates packages of such a conceptual architecture in a layered style. Of course, a general purpose MAS platform requires additional services such as Directory Facilitator, Agent Management Service and such an abstract architecture is defined in FIPA's Abstract Architecture Specification [5]. But, our purpose is only defining and implementing packages which are responsible to execute semantic service enabled plans. So, any platform can be made semantic service enabled by just implementing package responsibilities defined in this paper.

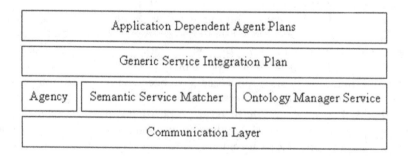

Fig. 1. Packages of platform's software architecture

Bottom layer includes the communication layer that is responsible of abstracting platform's communication infrastructure implementation. It implements FIPA's Agent Communication and Agent Message Transport specifications [5] to handle agent messaging. This layer has been developed and used as part of our FIPA compliant agent development framework [2], [3] and then reused in this implementation.

In our implementation, Agency package includes necessary infrastructure to generate general purpose and goal directed agents similar to JADE [1] and DE-CAF [6] platforms. It provides a build in agent operating system to schedule, execute and monitor agent plan(s) which are defined in HTN formalism [8]. To execute semantic service enabled plans, we have defined a generic HTN structure that is specialized based on the domain requirements. Naturally, this plan can be executed by the agency as the other HTN plans and it can be combined with other plan(s).

Semantic Service Matcher (SSM) can be considered as a bridge between platform and web services hosted outside of the platform. SSM uses service profile concept of the OWL-S ontology for service advertisement and this advertisement knowledge is used by internal semantic service matching engine for discovery of the services upon request. We have used the service capability matching algorithm originally proposed in [9] for semantic service matching engine implementation. Since our discussion on Generic Service Integration Plan in section 5 sometimes uses the concepts of this algorithm, we briefly introduce the concepts used in the algorithm in this section. Capability matching algorithm matches OWL-S profile's input and output concepts of the advertisement and request. Input and output concepts are taken values from specific domain ontology(ies) and the match degree is determined by the minimal distance between the concepts of these ontology(ies). Formally if out_{AD} and out_{REQ} represent the outputs of the advertisement and the request respectively, algorithm defines four types of match on outputs:

- *exact match* when out_{AD} and out_{REQ} are equal or out_{REQ} is subclass of out_{AD}
- *plug-in match* when out_{AD} is more generic than out_{REQ} (out_{AD} subsumes out_{REQ})
- *subsumes match* when out_{AD} is more specific than out_{REQ} (out_{REQ} subsumes out_{AD})
- *fail* when neither of the conditions above satisfies

The scoring function is ordered as exact > plug-in > subsumed > fail. Same can be applied to inputs but matchmaker prefers output matches over input matches and input match scoring is used to sort equivalent output matches. In our implementation, SSM is queried by the platform's agent(s) with FIPA RDF [5] content language using OWL-QL [4] query syntax in argument part of the message. To be able to use the match degree within the QWL-QL, we have extended the QWL-QL for querying the matching of semantic capability. Details of this extension are discussed in section 5.

Ontology Manager Service (OMS) behaves mainly as a central repository for the domain ontologies used within the platform and provides basic ontology management functionality such as ontology deployment, ontology updating, querying etc. But, the most critical support of the OMS for service integration is its translation support between the service or domain ontologies. OMS provides a user interface to define mappings between the selected ontologies and then handles the translation request(s) using the mapping knowledge. Through the usage of the ontology translation support, any agent of the platform may discover and/or invoke the services even if they use different ontologies.

"Generic Service Integration Plan" includes pre-defined tasks for dynamic semantic service discovery and invocation. This generic plan executes standard tasks such as service discovery based on the service capability, selection of matched services and invocation of selected service(s) in a pre-defined order and under the pre-set conditional assumptions. The details of this plan are discussed in section 5. But, it has to be emphasized that behavior of some task(s) may need to be modified depending to the application conditions. In this kind of situations, developers have to modify the specific tasks of this plan to satisfy the application requirements.

Top layer includes the application dependent plans that are defined by agent developers to satisfy the system's goal(s). To make these plans semantic service enabled, "Generic Service Integration Plan" can be added to the plan as service task.

3   A Design Approach for the Agent and Semantic Service Integration

To be able to integrate semantic web services with agents, some well defined activities are needed within the agent development methodology. These activities are conducted to build up the elements of the conceptual architecture defined in section 2. In the following, two activities are defined for this purpose.

Activity 1: *Define the OWL-S based service profiles of each domain specific services that may be used by the agents.*

In the design phase, we must know interface of external services to be able to write the actual agent plans that include service integration. So, an OWL-S service profile is defined for different types of domain specific services that agents may use. These profiles are stored in and build up the knowledge base of the SSM. External services are advertised themselves to the SSM using these predefined service profiles. The problem occurs when input and output parameters of external service interface and profile take values from different ontologies. In this case, service provider must define the mappings between ontologies of these parameters using the transition service of the OMS and agents translate profile values to the actual service interface values before the invocation. In this paper, we do not consider this case since we have not integrated the OMS implementation with the platform yet.

Activity 2: *Specialize the Generic Service Integration Plan for each required service(s).*

Application dependent agent plans may need one ore more external services whose profiles are defined in activity 1. So, developers first identify such services in this activity, then "Generic Service Integration Plan" is specialized for these services using the defined service profiles. Finally, specialized service plans are integrated with the actual application dependent plans.

4   Agent's Internal Architecture

As we stated in section 2, our agent's internal architecture executes plans represented with HTN formalism. HTN structure consists of two types of tasks. Complex task includes a "reduction schema" knowledge that defines the decomposition of the complex task to the sub tasks. The second type of tasks is the primitive tasks (actions) that can be executed by the internal architecture directly. Each task also has "provision/outcome links" that are used to propagate values between the tasks. So, internal architecture dynamically opens the complex task using the "reduction schema" knowledge, identifies input/output values of each task with "provision/outcome links", executes primitive tasks and propagates output values other dependent task(s).

In addition to complex and primitive tasks, we have defined a new task type called as "service" task to execute semantic service enabled plans. "Service" task is different because it always takes values from OWL-S profile concepts. Moreover, input and output concepts of the requested service(s) are mandatory values for "service" task to be able to discover the requested service(s). In HTN formalism, complex and primitive task types propagate data values through its provision link. Similarly, "service" task can take values through provision link if it is dependent to some task(s) which produce the required data. But if input and output of the requested service are not provided by other task(s), it must be provided as constant. So, "service" task is responsible to collect all of the values of input and output concepts from provision link and internal constant values to pass them to subtasks. Hence, this task is handled differently by the internal architecture when it is encountered.

The overall structure of agent's internal architecture is shown in Fig. 2. This architecture is specially designed to execute semantic service enabled plans. But, of course, it can also execute HTN structure(s) that includes only complex and primitive tasks. As it can be seen from Fig. 2, the internal architecture is composed of four functional modules: dispatcher, matcher, scheduler and executer. Each module runs concurrently in a separate Java thread and uses the common data structures. All together, they match the goal extracted from the incoming FIPA-ACL message to an agent plan, schedule and execute the plan following the predefined HTN structure. In the following, we briefly explain responsibilities of each module during plan execution with an emphasis on semantic service integration.

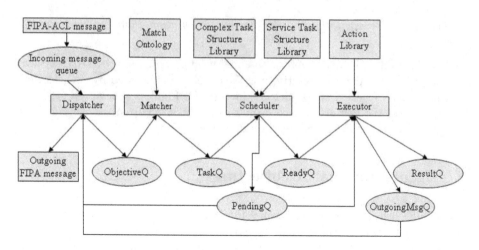

Fig. 2. Agent's internal architecture

When a FIPA-ACL message is put into the incoming message queue by the communication infrastructure layer, the dispatcher is notified. Dispatcher then parses the message and checks whether it is reply of a previous message or not. If it is a reply message, then the dispatcher finds out the task waiting for that reply from the pending queue, sets the provision(s) for that task and puts the task to the ready queue if all the other provisions of task are set. If it is not a reply message, then the dispatcher creates a new objective, puts it to the objective queue and notifies the matcher.

Matcher is responsible for matching the incoming objective to a pre-defined plan by querying the "Match Ontology". There can be two kinds of plans. They are called as service integration plan and ordinary plan. The service integration plan aims only semantic service discovery and invocation. The ordinary plan may include "service" task(s) and becomes semantic service enabled plan or it includes only complex and primitive tasks. The "Match Ontology" is defined in OWL including Match and Template concepts and the method of *QueryManager* interface returns the *MatchedTemplate* object to the matcher. Matcher identifies the type of the plan from *MatchedTemplate* object and creates a *ServiceTemplate* object for service plan or *TaskTemplate* object for ordinary plan by setting its parameters using the returned template. It then puts the created object to the task queue and notifies the scheduler.

Scheduler works differently for complex task and "service" task. If it gets a *TaskTemplate* from the task queue, it understands that it is a complex task. Then, it gets the name of the task from the *TaskTemplate* and creates a *ComplexTask* object by getting its class definition from task structure library. This *ComplexTask* may include "service" task(s). The class definition taken includes the reduction schema which holds the subtasks of the task. Then, the scheduler interprets the reduction schema and puts the ready actions to the ready queue by creating a *ReadyActionTemplate* and notifies Executor. It also places the provision waiting action(s) into the pending queue and the complex task(s) to the task queue by creating a *TaskTemplate* object. If it finds a "service" task in the reduction schema, it creates a *ServiceTemplate* object and puts it into the task queue for execution.

If scheduler gets *ServiceTemplate* object from the task queue, it gets its task structure from service structure library. Service structure library holds only service integration plans that are derived by reusing our generic service integration plan structure. At this point, scheduler creates *ServiceTask* object, it gets OWL-S profiles input and output concepts from *ServiceTask*, and then it passes this knowledge as a parameter to the sub-task found in the reduction schema. Sub-tasks are handled in a same way of complex task scheduling.

Executor first gets the name of the primitive task from the *ReadyActionTemplate* and creates an *Action* object using the class definition that it retrieved from the action library corresponding to the primitive task name. Secondly, it calls the *Do()* method of the *Action* object. The result queue is updated using the outcome of the executed action. One important point is that if there are action(s) waiting for that outcome in the pending queue, the related provisions of these actions are set based on the outcome. These actions are put into the ready queue if their all other provisions are already set, otherwise they continue to wait in the pending queue until all other provisions are set by different outcomes.

5 Generic Plan Structure for Semantic Service Integration

In this section, we introduce the structure of the generic plan that is specially designed for semantic service integration. The workflow of the plan can be described as follows: When an agent requires executing semantic service, it first must discover the desired service using SSM. After that, it must select the most suitable service among the discovered services. Finally, the selected service is invoked directly communicating with its providers. The HTN structure for this workflow is illustrated in Fig. 3. Each node in this HTN structure represents a task of HTN formalism. Provision links are located in the left side of the node and outcome links are in the right side. The sub-task(s) of a complex task is represented with a line drawn between them. The responsibility of each task is written inside of the node.

The top level task is called as "execute semantic web service". This task is a "service" task that may be included to any plan to make it semantic service enabled. Also, "execute semantic web service" tasks can be connected to each other to create composite semantic web services.

"Execute semantic web service" task must include input and output parameters of desired semantic web service and match degree to discover the service. These parameters can be passed through the provision link or defined as constant(s) during the creation of the real plan derived reusing the generic structure. "Execute semantic web service" task propagate the required parameters to its sub-tasks using the provision link structure. After the all tasks are executed,

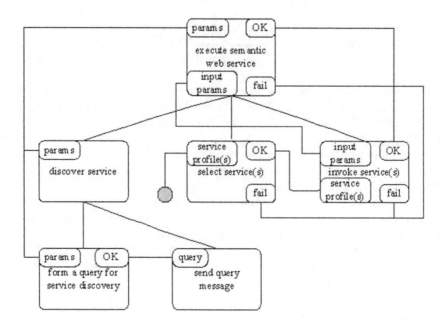

Fig. 3. Generic plan structure for semantic service integration

the result of the "execute semantic web service" task is propagated to other task(s) with OK outcome. If a desired service can not be found or any problem is occurred during the service invocation, it ends with fail outcome.

First sub-task of the "execute semantic web service" is called as "discover service" task which is responsible of discovering the service with the desired capability. It takes input and output parameters of desired semantic web service and match degree from "execute semantic web service" task. "Discover service" task includes two primitive tasks (actions) named as "form a query for service discovery" and "send query message" to inquire the SSM.

"Form a query for service discovery" action inherits the provisions of "discover service" task. This action forms a query using the parameters passed through its provision to discover the desired semantic web service. This query must include input and output parameters of the desired service and a match degree for each parameter since SSM uses this knowledge to semantically match the requested service with the advertised ones. As it is said before, our platform uses OWL-QL to query the SSM for service discovery. Since SSM knows only the OWL-S ontology and match degree is not defined in OWL-S ontology, it's not possible to specify match degree in OWL-QL for querying OWL-S profiles. So, we have extended OWL-QL to be able to prepare queries that include match degree for semantic service discovery. This extension is called as OWL-QL-S. An OWL-QL-S query may include an exact-match parameters list, a plug-in-match parameters list and a subsume-match parameters list. These lists contain URI references that occur in the query, and no URI reference can be an item of more than one of these lists. Thus, an OWL-QL-S query that prepared to discover OWL-S semantic web service(s) is capable of specifying the match degree that will be accepted for every input and output parameter.

"Send query message" action takes the OWL-QL-S query as provision and prepares a FIPA-ACL message to discover the desired service. Then it sends this message to the SSM. FIPA-RDF content language is used to transfer OWL-QL-S query. So, OWL-QL-S query is located in the argument property of the FIPA-RDF action.

"Select service(s)" action is executed when a reply message, which includes matched service profiles, is sent by the SSM. The matched service profiles are passed to this action as external provision. "Select service(s)" action is responsible of selecting the most appropriate service(s) among all the sent ones. In our implementation, SSM returns the matched services by sorting according to match degrees and "select service(s)" selects the first one. But, this task may vary depending to the overall requirements of the plan. For example, an application may require invoking all exactly matched services. In this kind of situation, plan developer has to modify the original action implementation according to the application requirements. At the end of the action, selected service profile(s) is sent with the OK outcome to the "invoke service(s)" action. If no service is selected, "select service(s)" action and consequently "execute semantic web service" task end with fail outcome.

"Invoke service(s)" action takes the selected service profile(s) and values of service's input parameters through the provision links and invokes selected service(s). This version of our implementation is capable to call atomic semantic web services. In other words, invocation of composite semantic web services is not supported yet. To invoke an atomic semantic web service, first of all, the URI of the WSDL document and operation name of service must be obtained from the corresponding OWL-S grounding document. WSDL document contains all the information that is required to invoke a web service dynamically such as network address, operation name, types of input and output parameters etc [17].

6   Case Study

To give ideas in a more concrete way, we designed an agent based information system prototype for tourism domain. We considered only a single scenario in which traveler tries to find and reserve a suitable hotel room for his/her holiday. The system includes a traveler agent that interacts with outside semantic web services to satisfy the requirements of this scenario.

Following our design approach, we first identified possible external domain service profiles that traveler agent can use to satisfy its goal. First of all, this system requires a service to find the hotels which satisfy travel preferences of the user. So, the first service profile is defined for this service and it takes "activity" and "location" as service input parameters and returns "hotel" individuals as output. We have implemented three actual services of this type and registered them to SSM by selecting different "activity", "location" and "hotel" concepts from related domain ontologies. Second service is defined for querying room availability and it takes "date" as input parameter and returns "room availability" as output. We have also created three actual services of this type and registered them to SSM. It must be pointed out that knowledge about the "hotel" individual is stored in the "contactInformation" concept of OWL-S profile during registration of this service and then used in "find a room" service task as service selection criteria. Final service is designed to make reservation. It takes "date" as input parameter and returns "reservation result" individual as output.

After we have defined the service profiles, we try to model traveler agent's plan that uses the defined services to satisfy the scenario at hand. This plan's HTN structure is shown in Fig. 4. As shown in the figure; the plan includes "three" service tasks that are defined considering the service profiles identified as the first activity. At this point, all of these service tasks are created from the generic service integration plan by specializing its actions based on the requirements of the plan.

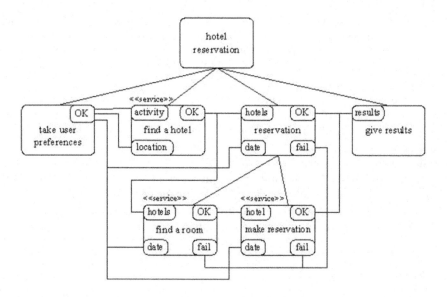

Fig. 4. Hotel reservation plan structure

First action of the plan finds the user's activity and location preferences using the predefined preferences ontology and passes them to the "find a hotel" "service" task for the execution of the "service" task. Since this task reuses the structure of the generic service integration plan, it first executes the "discover service" complex task of the generic plan. Subtasks of "discover service" complex task are reused as is since they require only the input and output parameters of the searched service. "Select service(s)" action is used as is also since SMM sends the matched profiles as sorted. It takes the matched service profiles send by SMM and pass them to the "invoke service(s)" action. "Invoke service(s)" action specialized to invoke the services starting from the top of the list using the values of input parameters. If an invoked service returns a list of hotels successfully, it stops and passes the list of hotels to the next task.

The found hotels are passed to the "reservation" task which includes two "service" sub-tasks, one for finding an available room and one for making reservation. These sub-tasks also reuse the structure of the generic service integration plan. They use sub-tasks of "discover service" complex task as is. However, "find a room" "service" task specializes the "select service(s)" action to select the services that provided by one of the given hotels and "make reservation" "service" task specializes the same action to select the service provided by the given hotel that has an available room. "Find a room" "service" task specializes the invoke service(s) action that continues to invoke selected room availability services until it gets an output indicating an available room. Upon the completion of service invocation, "find a room" "service" task passes the found hotel that has an available room to the "make reservation" "service" task for realizing the reservation. This "service" task uses "invoke service(s)" action as is since only one service is passed to this action from "select service(s)" action. At the end, reservation details are given to the client.

7   Conclusion

Developers can create semantic web service enabled plans using the support provided by the architecture introduced in this paper. Two activities should be performed to develop plans with such a capability. First, service profile of each domain specific service should be defined with use of a service ontology. Those services will be used by platform's agents in their plans. Second, for each required service, the plan called "Generic Service Integration Plan" should be specialized. We believe that the above mentioned support simplifies the semantic service based multi agent system development and bridges the gap between the agent and semantic service worlds.

References

1. Bellifemine, F., Poggi, A., and Rimassa, G.: Developing multi-agent systems with a FIPA-compliant agent framework. Software Practice and Experience, 31 (2001) 103-128.
2. Erdur, R.C. and Dikenelli, O.: A standards-based agent framework for instantiating adaptive agents. In Proceedings of The Second International Joint Conference on Autonomous Agents and Multiagent Systems (AAMAS 2003), pages 984-985, ACM Press, 2003.
3. Erdur, R.C. and Dikenelli, O.: A FIPA-Compliant Agent Framework with an Extra Layer for Ontology Dependent Reusable Behaviour. In Proceedings of Advances in Information Systems, Second International Conference (ADVIS 2002), LNCS 2457, Springer, 2002.

4. Fikes, R., Hayes, P, Horrocks, I.: OWL-QL - A Language for Deductive Query Answering on the Semantic Web. Knowledge System Laboratory, Standford University, 2003, avail-able at http://ksl-web.standford.edu/KSL-Abstracts/KSL-03-14.html

5. FIPA: FIPA Specifications, http://www.fipa.org

6. Graham, J.R., Decker, K.S., Mersic, M.: DECAF - A Flexible Multi Agent System Architecture. Journal of Autonomous Agents and Multi-Agent Systems, 7, 7-27, 2003.

7. Li, L. and Horrocks, I.: A Software Framework for Matchmaking Based on Semantic Web Technology. In Proceedings of the Twelfth International Conference on World Wide Web, pages 331-339. ACM Press, 2003.

8. Paolucci, M. et al.: A Planning Component for RETSINA Agents, Intelligent Agents VI, LNAI 1757, N.R. Jennings and Y. Lesperance, eds., Springer Verlag, 2000.

9. Paolucci, M., Kawamura, T., Payne, T., R., Sycara, K.: Semantic Matching of Web Services Capabilities. In Proc. of the International Semantic Web Conference (ISWC'02), Springer Verlag, Sarddegna, Italy, June 2002.

10. Paolucci, M. and Sycara, K.: Autonomous Semantic Web Services. IEEE Internet Computing, September - October 2003, Published by the IEEE Computer Society

11. Sheshagiri, M., desJardins M., Finin T.: A Planner for Composing Services described in DAML-S. Workshop on Planning for Web Services, Trento, 2003.

12. Sirin, E., Hendler, J., Parsia B.: Semi-automatic Composition of Web Services using Semantic Descriptions. Web Services: Modeling, Architecture and Infrastructure workshop in conjunction with ICEIS2003, April 2003.

13. Sirin, E., Parsia, B., Wu, D., Hendler, J., Nau, D.: HTN planning for web service composition using SHOP2. Journal of Web Semantics, 1(4):377-396, 2004

14. Sycara, K., Paolucci, M., Soudry, J., Srinivasan, N.: Dynamic Discovery and Coordination of Agent-Based Semantic Web Services. IEEE Internet Computing 8(3): 66-73 (2004)

15. Sycara, K., Paolucci, M., Ankolekar, A., Srinivasan, N.: Automated discovery, interaction and composition of Semantic Web Services. Journal of Web Semantics, Elsevier, pp. 27-46, 2003

16. The OWL Services Coalition: Semantic Markup for Web Services (OWL-S), 2004, http://www.daml.org/services/owl-s/1.1/

17. W3C: Web Services Description Language (WSDL) 2.0, http://www.w3.org/TR/wsdl20

Towards a Formal Methodology for Designing Multi-agent Applications

Amira Regayeg[1], Ahmed Hadj Kacem[1], and Mohamed Jmaiel[2]

[1] Faculté des Sciences Économiques et de Gestion de Sfax,
B.P. 1088, 3018 Sfax, Tunisia
{Amira.Regayeg, Ahmed}@fsegs.rnu.tn
[2] École Nationale d'Ingénieurs de Sfax,
B.P.W., 3038 Sfax, Tunisia
Mohamed.Jmaiel@enis.rnu.tn

Abstract. This paper has two purposes. First, it defines a formal language for specifying multi-agent systems. This language is expressive enough to cover individual agent aspects (knowledge, goals, roles, ...) as well as collective aspects of in terms of coordination protocols, organization structure and planning activities. Second, it provides a formal design methodology based on stepwise refinements allowing to develop a design specification starting from an abstract requirements one.

1 Introduction

Several researches tried to face the problem of developing software systems using the agent concept. The majority of the suggested approaches are extensions of either object oriented methodologies like, for example, AOAD [20] and MaSE [2], or knowledge based methodologies, such as CoMoMAS [5]. The major problem of these extensions is that they do not provide appropriate tools to model the specific features of agents, such as mental states and social behaviours. Other attempts, like Gaia [19], SODA [13] and Prometheus [14], sought to focus on the social aspect of an agent group or an organization. These approaches, given that they are based on semi-formal notations, they do not enable formal reasoning about specifications. Approaches which make use of formal methods, like for example, the framework suggested by Luck and d'Inverno using the Z language [10], Concurrent-Metatem [4] based on temporal logic, and SLABS (Formal Specification Language for Systems Agent-Based)[23], concentrate their effort only to the specification phase. Recent work, such as ADK [21], although it based on a formal approach and it covers the specification, design and implementation phases, it completely ignores formal reasoning and particularly the verification phases.

In order to overcome these insufficiencies and to master the inherent complexity of multi-agent development, we suggest a formal design approach of multi-agent systems based on stepwise refinements. It is recognized that the formal approach represents an obvious but attractive challenge for Agent Oriented Software Engineering [22]. Here, we try to take advantage of the potential

T. Eymann et al. (Eds.): MATES 2005, LNAI 3550, pp. 153–164, 2005.
© Springer-Verlag Berlin Heidelberg 2005

of the formal methods in building reliable software. Doing so, we define, on the one hand, a formal specification language which integrates the linear temporal logic in the Z language, and on the other hand, a set of methodological principles and hints which help the user to build in a systematic and incremental way intra and inter agent aspects. This integration is motivated by recent tendencies [15] which are directed towards (1) addressing aspects separated using suitable languages and tools, and (2) integrating various approaches in a unified development process[1]. Indeed, the Z language possesses all ingredients needed to handle static and functional aspects of agents (i.e., the mental state and associated treatments), whereas temporal logic is considered as one of the most eminent formalisms for specifying reactive systems [11]. In addition, approaches based on stepwise refinements [17] proved their impact in developing several software applications [8,3].

In order to provide a formal interpretation for our temporal operators we suggest an operational semantics for multi-agent applications in terms of sequences of system states. The definition of this temporal model within the Z notation enables us to make use of tools supporting pure Z notation, such as Z/EVES [12]. These tools allowed us to perform syntax, type, and domain checking of our specifications and to reason about them by proving desired properties. Our design process is composed of a number of refinement steps where each one provides some methodological guidelines which help the developer to take the suitable design decision as well as rules making it possible to ensure that a refined specification satisfies the initial one.

This paper is organized as follows. Section 2 defines the specification language and its semantics. Then, in section 3 we explain our specification and design approach. Finally, we conclude with drawing some perspectives.

2   The Specification Language

We consider a multi-agent application as a collection of components which evolve in a continuously changing environment containing active agents and passive objects. Accordingly, the specification of a multi-agent application includes descriptions of the environment, the behaviour of individual agents (intra-agent), and the communication primitives as well as the interaction protocols (inter-agent). In addition, we may add to the collective part a description of the organizational structures and planning activities.

For the specification of multi-agent applications, we use an integration of temporal logic in Z schemas as described in our previous work [15]. This integration will enable us to cover all the above mentioned aspects in a unified framework. Indeed, the Z notation allows to describe all components (passive and active) in terms of attributes and related properties. The temporal logic will enrich this description with social behaviour and interaction properties.

2.1   The Z Notation

The Z notation, as presented in [18], is a model oriented formal specification language which is based on set theory and first order predicate logic. This language is used to describe an application in terms of states and operations on them. In order to structure specifications and to compose them Z uses a *schema language*. The latter enables to collect objects, to encapsulate them, and naming them for reuse. A schema consists of two parts: a declaration part and a predicate part constraining the values of the declared variables. A Z schema has the following form:

```
┌─ SchemaName ──────────────────────────────────
│  Declarations
│ ──────────────────────────────────────────────
│  Predicates
└───────────────────────────────────────────────
```

2.2   The Temporal Logic

The linear temporal logic, as presented by Manna and Pnueli [11], is suitable for the specification and the verification of concurrent and interactive systems. Actually, there is a variety of temporal operators that can be used to express agents behavioural properties. However, all these operators can be defined in terms of two basic operators. In this paper, we make use only of the necessary operators for development of our multi-agent applications. In the following, we briefly present these operators with an intuitive explanation. Let P be a logical or a temporal formula:

$\triangledown P$ P holds "now"[1] ($\triangledown$ may be omitted);

$\square P$ "*always*" P, i.e. P holds for the present and for all future points in time;

$\lozenge P$ "*eventually*" P, i.e. P holds at some present or future point in time;

$\bigcirc P$ "*nexttime*" P, i.e. P holds at the next point in time.

In order to integrate these temporal operators in the framework of the Z language, we give the following definition of temporal formulas according to the syntax of Z. We distinguish atomic predicate formulas (*formula*), which are closely related to the application to specify, and temporal formulas (*Tempformula*) which connect predicate formulas with temporal operators.

$$Tempformula ::= \langle\!\langle formula \rangle\!\rangle \mid \bigcirc \langle\!\langle Tempformula \rangle\!\rangle \mid \square \langle\!\langle Tempformula \rangle\!\rangle \mid$$
$$\lozenge \langle\!\langle Tempformula \rangle\!\rangle$$

We will show later that these operators are sufficient to express interesting properties of multi-agent applications.

2.3   The Semantics of Temporal Formulas

In this section we provide evaluation functions defining the semantics of our temporal logic. This step is very significant since it enables us to translate temporal formulae into the pure Z notation. Thus, it becomes easy to exploit the

---

[1] We explain the operators while being based on a concept of "time", but really the fundamental notion is the one of causality.

automatic verification tools, such as Z/EVES or Isabelle, which accept merely the standard syntax of Z.

First, we present the underlying time model. The basic unit of this time model is the agent state. Let $[State]$ be the set of possible agent states. A system state ($SysState$) is defined as the union of the states of the agents belonging to this system:

$$
\begin{array}{|l}
\_SysState _____ \\
\quad SysState : \mathbb{F}\, State \\
\hline
\end{array}
$$

A time model ($Model$) is defined as an axiomatic function that associates to each point of time the corresponding system state, where the time is specified as the set of natural numbers ($Time == \{x : \mathbb{N}\}$):

$$Model == Time \to SysState$$

Second, we provide an axiomatic function (E) which evaluates a temporal formula in a given model at a given point of time:

$$
\begin{array}{|l}
E : Temporalformula \times Model \times Time \to bool \\
\hline
\forall f : Formula;\ m : Model;\ t : Time \\
\quad \bullet\ E((\triangledown f), m, t) = T \Leftrightarrow AtomEval(f, m\,t) = T \\
\forall f : Tempformula;\ m : Model;\ t : Time\ \bullet \\
\quad E((\Diamond f), m, t) = T \Leftrightarrow (\exists\, t1 : Time \mid t1 \geq t \bullet E(f, m, t1) = T) \\
\forall f : Tempformula;\ m : Model;\ t : Time\ \bullet \\
\quad E((\Box f), m, t) = T \Leftrightarrow (\forall\, t1 : Time \mid t1 \geq t \bullet E(f, m, t1) = T) \\
\forall f : Tempformula;\ m : Model;\ t : Time\ \bullet \\
\quad E((\bigcirc f), m, t) = T \Leftrightarrow (E(f, m, (t+1)) = T)
\end{array}
$$

Next, we generalize the function E by making abstraction of the time parameter. Hence, the function (Eva)below interprets temporal formulas with respect to a given model:

$$
\begin{array}{|l}
Eva : Tempformula \times Model \to bool \\
\hline
\forall f : Tempformula;\ m : Model \\
\quad \bullet\ Eva(f, m) = T \Leftrightarrow (\forall\, t : Time \bullet (f, m, t) \in \operatorname{dom} E \wedge E(f, m, t) = T)
\end{array}
$$

We can more generalize the function of evaluation by making abstraction of the model. The following function defines a general interpretation of the temporal operators:

$$
\begin{array}{|l}
Eval : Tempformula \to bool \\
\hline
\forall f : Formula \\
\quad \bullet\ Eval(f) = T \Leftrightarrow (\forall\, m : Model \bullet (f, m) \in \operatorname{dom} Eva \wedge Eva(f, m) = T)
\end{array}
$$

Finally, in order to use the temporal operators in their usual notations (i.e. $\Box$ for always) in the Z schemata it is necessary to introduce them as axiomatic functions defined with the interpretation function *Eval*. Thus, we could establish a logical equivalence between a temporal operator and the corresponding predicate specified in the above function *Eval*. This equivalence is described for the $\Box$ operator as follows:

$$\Box f \Leftrightarrow Eval(\Box f) = T$$

The other temporal operators are introduced with similar equivalences.

3   Formal Design Approach

In order to be useful, a formalism or a set of tools have to be supported with a design approach. This approach should provide some principles that help and guide the design process. In this section, some of those principles are clarified. Indeed, our approach is based on two principal phases. The first one is a specification phase in which we describe, in an abstract way, the user requirements. The second one is a design phase based on a succession of refinements in terms of collective behaviours (inter-agents) as well as individual behaviours (intra-agent). The verification that the developed design specification satisfies the requirements one is considered as essential tasks which is progressively performed during the refinement steps.

3.1   Specification Phase

In this first phase, we specify the requirements which correspond, in the context of multi-agent, to a common objective to be achieved by the agents. In our approach, this stage provides also a description of the environment in which the agents evolve and which includes, generally, the working space, the passive objects, and the active entities representing the agents to be deployed.

1. *Specification of the active entities:* The description of an active entity (agent) consists in presenting, in terms of temporal formulae, its static and dynamic properties. This description is given by a Z schema of the following form:

   ┌─ *Entity* ─────────────────────────────────────
   │ $atr_1 : Type_1,\ atr_2 : Type_2\ \ldots atr_m : Type_m$
   ├──
   │ $Spr_1, \ldots, Spr_n,$
   │ $\quad Cpr_1, \ldots, Cpr_{n'}$
   └──

   Where atr_i corresponds to an attribute, Spr_i represents a static property and Cpr_i represents a behavioural property.
2. *Specification of the system*: The system includes active entities (agents) and passive entities belonging to the working space. This specification is given by a set of formulas relating passive entities with active ones. Generally, this leads to a Z schema of the form:

$$
\boxed{
\begin{array}{l}
\textit{System} \\\hline
obj_1 : TypeObject_1, \ldots, obj_k : TypeObject_k \\
Entities : \textbf{set of } Entity \\\hline
Pr_1,\ Pr_2,\ \ldots,\ Pr_l
\end{array}
}
$$

Where obj_i corresponds to a passive entity, *Entities* represents a set of entities, and Pr_i represents a temporal formula.

3. *Requirements Specification*: This specification describes what we require from the system to develop. In the context of multi-agent application, this corresponds to a set of temporal formulas specifying *the Common Objective (CO)* in terms of the desired future state.

   According to the Z approach, such a specification is well expressed with a specialization of the *System* schema:

$$
\boxed{
\begin{array}{l}
\textit{ReqSpec} \\\hline
System \\\hline
CO_1,\ CO_2,\ \ldots,\ CO_n
\end{array}
}
$$

Where CO_i represents a temporal formula.

3.2   Design Phase

The basic idea consists in performing a sequence of refinements made by specializations of Z schemas for data refinement, and derivation of temporal formulas for behavioural refinement. The refinement steps are supported by a set of rules which help the transitions between specifications. The refinements are carried out at two complementary levels. The first, is the collective level which will be augmented by properties referring, primarily, to collective aspects (inter-agent) characterizing, in particular, organization and communication structures. The second level rather stresses the individual aspects (intra-agent) by extending the specifications of the active entities provided in the first phase.

Collective Level. Designing the collective aspects of a multi-agent application is made, in our approach, within three aspects : (1) cooperation strategy, (2) organization structure and (3) interaction protocol.

1. Cooperation Strategy

   Step 1: *Cooperation Strategy definition*

   Starting from CO and using a hierarchical representation, we iterate the composition, based on logical connections, of the requirements specification (*ReqSpec* schema) until we obtain elementary temporal formulas in a way that each one corresponds to a subgoal.

   That is, for each formula CO_i which composed CO, we generate by decomposition and transformation a finite set of temporal formulas connected by the logical connectors ($\wedge, \vee$). The conjunction $\wedge$ indicates a sequence of subgoals whereas the disjonction $\vee$ presents different subgoals for the achievement of the goal.

Finally, we obtain a list of scenarios for CO_i where each one is described by a sequence of elementary temporal formulas. These formulas represent the different local goals: $\{bl_{i1}, \ldots, bl_{in}\}$.

At the end of this step, we generate a graph and/or which summaries the various decomposition levels.

Each scenario leads to the following specification which corresponds to a refinement of the *ReqSpec* specification:

> *Implementation$_0$* ──────────────────────────
> System
> ─────────
> $bl_{i1}, bl_{i2}, \ldots, bl_{in}$

This refinement step requires the proof of the following theorem for each scenario of CO_i present in the requirements specification:

> **theorem** CoopScenario
> $bl_{i1}, bl_{i2}, \ldots, bl_{in} \vdash CO_i$

2. Organization Structure

The organization structure implicitly defines a control strategy to be respected by these entities. It is, generally, defined in terms of temporal formulas referring to several entities at the same time.

Here, we invent a suitable organization structure for the system to be developed. We, first, identify the necessary roles, then we assign a role for each active entity belonging to the system.

(a) *Social Level*

− *Step 2: Identification of roles*

In our approach, an agent role is formally represented by a set of temporal formulas corresponding to local goals.

Hence, starting form the above defined local goals, we can regroup them according to predicates (actions) present in the various formulas describing the different local goals bl_{ij}. Thus, we will have as many roles as actions describing the various local goals.

> $role_i == \{bl_{i1}, \ldots, bl_{ik}\}$

Where $bl_{i1}, \ldots, bl_{ik}$ present the same action.

This step leads to a refined specification:

> *Implementation$_1$* ──────────────────────────
> Implementation$_0$
> $R : \mathbb{P}_1$ Role
> ─────────
> $\forall bl : BL \bullet \exists r : Role \bullet bl \in r$

This regroupment must respect the following completeness theorem which guarantees that every local goal is associated to a role:

theorem completeness
$$\bigcup_{i=1}^{m} role_i = \{bl_{i1}, bl_{i2}, \ldots, bl_{in}\}$$

– *Step 3: Definition of organization relationships*
At this level, we refer to the model [9] where a Generic organization structure *OrgStructure* is defined by a finite set of relations between the various necessary roles [*OrgRelationship*] for the achievement of a common objective.
Our goal, in this step, is to express how starting from the set of roles defined in the previous step, we find the various possible organization relationships.
We propose, for this definition, to search the common arguments present in the predicates describing the local goals of different roles. A common argument for two or several local goals of different roles proves the existence of an organizational relation between these roles. After a succession of iterations, we obtain a set of organization relationships connecting the various roles.
This step leads to a refined specification:

$$
\begin{array}{l}
\underline{Implementation_2 } \\
Implementation_1 \\
Rorg : \mathbb{P}_1\ OrgRelationship \\
\hline
\forall\, r : Role \bullet \exists\, rorg : OrgRelationship \mid rorg \in Rorg \bullet r \in \mathrm{dom}\ rorg
\end{array}
$$

In this context, a constraint to check is that each role must have at least a relationship to one or more other roles. This is guaranteed by the proof of the following theorem:

theorem RoleRelation
$$\forall\, r \in Role \bullet r \in \mathrm{dom}\ Sorg$$

(b) *Agent Level*
This level consists on defining the agents for which each role will be associated. Then, we instantiate the different organization relationships, defined in the previous level, in order to find the eventually organization links between these agents.

– *Step 4: The role assignation*
This step consists on defining, given a set of roles, the agents which will be charged with each one of these roles.
To find the number of the necessary agents for each role, we need to define the precedence order between the various local goals of the retained roles. This order relation is based on the different temporal operators describing the list of local goals. Thus, we can define a precedence graph for the common objective.

The basic idea consists on referring to precedence order of the different local goals in order to avoid assigning simultaneous local goals to the same agent. Also, one agent can have more than one role provided that the local goals of these various roles are not in contradiction. Thus, several scenarios can arise.

At this level, we can define a first refinement of *Entity* schema where we add the concept of *role*:

$$
\begin{array}{|l}
\hline
\textit{Entity}_1 \\
\hline
\textit{Entity} \\
\textit{roles} : \mathbb{P}_1\ \textit{Role} \\
\hline
\end{array}
$$

Then, we can refine the system specification as follows:

$$
\begin{array}{|l}
\hline
\textit{Implementation}_3 \\
\hline
\textit{Implementation}_2 \\
\hline
\forall\, r : \textit{Role} \mid r \in R \bullet \exists\, e : \textit{Entity}_1 \mid e \in \textit{entities} \bullet r \in e.\textit{roles} \\
\hline
\end{array}
$$

- **Step 5**: *The acquaintances definition (organisation links)*

  The distribution of the roles induces an instantiation of the generic organisation structure, called concrete organisation structure *ConcreteOrg* [9].

  An organization link is defined as follows:

$$
\begin{array}{|l}
\hline
\textit{OrganisationLink} \\
\hline
E : \mathbb{P}\ \textit{Entity} \\
\hline
\#E \geq 2 \\
\hline
\end{array}
$$

An organization link *OrganisationLink* makes it possible to associate two or several agents of different roles. Thus, each relation between two roles, described in the previous level (Step 2.1.b), will be expressed in term of organization links referring to a set of agents.

$$
\begin{array}{|l}
\hline
\textit{Implementation}_4 \\
\hline
\textit{Implementation}_3 \\
\textit{organisationlinks} : \mathbb{P}_1\ \textit{OrganisationLink} \\
\hline
\forall\, Or : \textit{organisationlinks} \bullet \forall\, e : \textit{Entity} \bullet \\
\quad e \in \textit{entities} \Leftrightarrow e \in Or.E \\
\hline
\end{array}
$$

At this stage, the following theorem must be proofed indication that every organization link instantiates an organization relationship:

theorem Instantiation
$$\forall\, OR : \textit{OrgRelationship} \bullet r : \mathbb{P}_1\ \textit{Role} \mid r \in \text{dom}\ OR \bullet$$
$$\exists\, OL : \textit{OrganisationLink} \bullet OL.E.R \in r$$

3. Interaction Protocol:

Step 6: Interaction Protocol definitions

Having his role, each entity have some communication acts whose will be achieved ($CommAct_i$).

Thus we can describe the *Implementation_i* schema:

Implementation_i

$Implementation_{i-1}$

$CommAct_{i1}, CommAct_{i2}, \ldots, CommAct_{in}$

Each formula ($CommAct_i$) is a temporal formula that describes a communication act.

These formulas are found by deriving each $role_i$ formula using the *Achiev* function which associate for each *role* the necessary communication acts *commacts*:

theorem RoleAchiev

$\forall\, role : Role \bullet \exists\, commacts : \mathbb{P}_1\, Action \bullet$
$Achiev(role) = commacts$

Individual Level. The specification of the individual futures is generated by the definition of the different entity capabilities allowing the realization of the actions defined in the collective level as well as cooperative, organizational and interactive actions.

Step 7: Individual Capabilities definitions

In order to execute each communication act, an entity must be equipped by some capabilities as well as send and receive capabilities.

Also, due to the execution of each communication act, an entity have some internal actions whose must be executed as well as the knowledge updates.

We denote by $Behav_i$ these different actions describing the behaviour of each entity.

We obtain the specifications describing the individual properties of each agent which will be regarded as an entity to implement separately.

For each entity, we can found a refined schema as:

EntityImpl

$Entity1$

$Behav_1, Behav_2, \ldots, Behav_l$

Each $Behav_i$ can be derived from one or more communication acts using the *Execute* function which associate to a set of communication acts a behavioural action describing the internal updates due to the execution of these acts :

theorem BehavDerivation

$\exists\, Commacts : \mathbb{P}_1\, CommAct \bullet \exists\, BehavAct : Action \bullet$
$Execute(Commacts) = BehavAct$

The design phase leads to a detailed specification of the environment and detailed behaviours of the active entities. The refinement specification corresponds to the schema for the system (*System*) extended with the union of the properties added at both collective and individual levels.

4   Conclusion

In this paper, we proposed a formal approach for specifying and verifying multi-agent applications. Our main contribution consists in defining a methodology that permits to develop, step by step, in an incremental way, a design from an abstract specification. Some case studies are under realization (e.g. the conflicts control in the air-traffic). The introduction of a temporal model for multi-agent applications in the Z framework enabled us to exploit a Z supporting tool (Z/EVES) for syntax and type checking as well as theorem proving.

However, it is necessary to point out that these first results, even original and promising, constitute a modest contribution to the definition of a formal methodology for the design process of multi-agent applications.

Finally, some future works deserve to be undertaken. Indeed, each proposed step should be supported by verification tools. Also, we intend to provide tools which help to generate more concrete specifications, using process algebra, CSP [6] for example, instead of temporal logic. These more concrete specifications can be implemented using the system SPIN [7]. This latter enables us (1) to simulate the system behaviour, and (2) to verify the desired temporal properties.

References

1. D. Bjorner. New results and trends in formal techniques for the development of software for transportation systems. In G. Tarnai and E. Schnieder, editors, *Proceedings of the FORMS2003: Symposium on Formal Methods for Railway Operation and Control Systems*, pages 69–76, Braunschweig, Germany, 1999.
2. S. Deloach and M. Wood. Analysis and design using mase and agenttool. In *Proceedings of the 12th Midwest Artificial Intelligence and Cognitive Science Conference MAICS 2001*, Miami University, Oxford, Ohio, 2001.
3. F. Erasmy and E. Sekerinski. Stepwise refinement of control software-a case study using raise. In M. Naftalin, T. Denvir, and M. Bertran, editors, *FME'94: Industrial Benefit of Formal Methods*, pages 547–566. Springer, Berlin, Heidelberg, 1994.
4. M. Fisher. A survey of concurrent METATEM – the language and its applications. In *Proc. 1st InternationalConf. Temporal Logic*, Lecture Notes in Computer Science, pages 480–505. Springer-Verlag, 1994.
5. N. Glaser. The comomas methodology and enironment for multi-agent system development. In *DAI*, pages 1–16, 1996.
6. C.A. Hoare. *Communicating Sequential Processes*. Prentice Hall International, 1985.
7. G.J. Holzmann. *The Spin Model Checker: Primer and Reference Manual*. Addison-Wesley, 2003.
8. M. Jmaiel and P. Pepper. Development of communication protocols using algebraic and temporal specifications. *Computer Networks Journal*, 42:737–764, 2003.

9. M. Loulou, A. Hadj-Kacem, and M. Jmaiel. Formalization of cooperation in MAS: Towards a generic conceptual model. In *The IX Ibero-American Conference on Artificial Intelligence (IBERAMIA 2004)*, volume 3315 of *Lecture Notes in Artificial Intelligence*, pages 43–52. Springer-Verlag, 2004.

10. M. Luck and M. d'Inverno. A formal framework for agency and autonomy. In *Proceedings of the first international conference on Multi-Agent Systems*, pages 254–260. AAAI Press/MIT Press, 1995.

11. Z. Manna and A. Pnueli. *The Temporal Logic of Reactive and Concurrent Systems*. Springer-Verlag, 1992.

12. I. Meisels and M. Saaltink. The Z/EVES 2.0 reference manual. Technical Report TR-99-5493-03e, ORA Canada, Canada, 1999.

13. A. Omicini. Soda: Societies and infrastructures in the analysis and design of agent-based systems. In *AOSE*, pages 185–193, 2000.

14. L. Padgham and M. Winikoff. Prometheus: A methodology for developing intelligent agents. In *AOSE*, pages 174–185, 2002.

15. A. Regayeg, A. Hadj-Kacem, and M. Jmaiel. Specification and Verification of Multi-Agent Applications using Temporal Z. In *Proceedings of IEEE/WIC/ACM International Conference on Intelligent Agent Technology (IAT'04)*, pages 260–266, Beijing, China, September 2004.

16. A. Regayeg, A. Hadj-Kacem, and M. Jmaiel. Towards a formal methodology for developing multi-agent applications using temporal Z. In *The 3rd ACS/IEEE International Conference on Computer Systems and Applications (AICCSA'05)*, Cairo, Egypt, January 2005.

17. D. Sannella. Algebraic specification and program development by stepwise refinement. In *Proc. 9th Intl. Workshop on Logic-based Program Synthesis and Transformation, LOPSTR'99*, volume 1817 of *Lecture Notes in Computer Science*, pages 1–9. Springer, 2000.

18. M. Spivey. The Z notation (second edition). *Prentice Hall International*, 1992.

19. M. Wooldridge, N. Jenning, and D. Kinny. The Gaia methodology for agent-oriented analysis and design. *Autonomous Agents*, 3, 2000.

20. M. Wooldridge, N. R. Jennings, and D. Kinny. A methodology for agent-oriented analysis and design. In Oren Etzioni, Jörg P. Müller, and Jeffrey M. Bradshaw, editors, *Proceedings of the Third International Conference on Autonomous Agents (Agents'99)*, pages 69–76, Seattle, WA, USA, 1999. ACM Press.

21. H. Xu and S. M. Shatz. A framework for model-based design of agent-oriented software. *IEEE Transactions on Software Engineering*, 29(1):15–30, January 2003.

22. F. Zambonelli and A. Omicini. Challenges and research directions in agent-oriented software engineering. *Autonomous Agents and Multi-Agent Systems*, 9(3):253–283, 2004.

23. H. Zhu. A formal specification language for agent-oriented software engineering. In *Proceedings of AAMAS'2003*, pages 1174–1175, Melbourne, Australia, 2003.

LEADSTO: A Language and Environment for Analysis of Dynamics by SimulaTiOn

Tibor Bosse[1], Catholijn M. Jonker[2], Lourens van der Meij[1], and Jan Treur[1]

[1] Vrije Universiteit Amsterdam, Department of Artificial Intelligence,
De Boelelaan 1081a, 1081 HV Amsterdam, The Netherlands
{tbosse, lourens, treur}@cs.vu.nl
http://www.cs.vu.nl/~{tbosse, lourens, treur}
[2] Nijmegen Institute for Cognition and Information, Division Cognitive Engineering,
Montessorilaan 3, 6525 HR Nijmegen, The Netherlands
C.Jonker@nici.kun.nl

Abstract. This paper presents the language and software environment LEADSTO that has been developed to model and simulate the dynamics of Multi-Agent Systems (MAS) in terms of both qualitative and quantitative concepts. The LEADSTO language is a declarative order-sorted temporal language, extended with quantitative means. Dynamics of MAS can be modelled by specifying the direct temporal dependencies between state properties in successive states. Based on the LEADSTO language, a software environment was developed that performs simulations of LEADSTO specifications, generates simulation traces for further analysis, and constructs visual representations of traces. The approach proved its value in a number of projects within different domains of MAS research.

1 Introduction

Two important phases in the development of Multi-Agent Systems are the Design phase and the Implementation phase. In principle, the result of the Design phase is a high-level description (a model) of the system to be developed which, when encoded in some programming language, solves a particular problem. To this end, the problem is decomposed into modules, of which the functions and interfaces are specified in detail [10]. Then, the result of the Design phase, the (technical) specification, can serve as a starting point for the Implementation phase. However, an important problem is the validation of this specification: can it be proven that the specification shows the expected behaviour (e.g. as described by requirements) before it is actually implemented? Especially when the specification is given in terms of abstract high-level concepts this is a non-trivial task.

To contribute to the validation of Multi-Agent System specifications, this paper introduces the language and software environment LEADSTO. LEADSTO can be used to model the *dynamics* of systems to be designed, on the basis of highly abstract process descriptions. If those dynamics are modelled correctly, the LEADSTO software environment can use them for *simulation* of the desired behaviour of the system. Although such simulations are no formal proof, they can contribute to an informal vali-

T. Eymann et al. (Eds.): MATES 2005, LNAI 3550, pp. 165–178, 2005.

dation of the specification: by performing a number of simulations, it can be tested whether the behaviour of the specification is satisfactory. Therefore, LEADSTO may be an important tool to bridge the gap between the Design and the Implementation phase.

Generally, in simulations various formats are used to specify basic mechanisms or causal relations within a process, see e.g., [1], [5], [9]. Depending on the domain of application such basic mechanisms need to be formulated quantitatively or qualitatively. Usually, within a given application explicit boundaries can be given in which the mechanisms take effect. For example, "from the time of planting an avocado pit, it takes 4 to 6 weeks for a shoot to appear".

As mentioned above, in order to simulate a system to be designed, it is important to model its *dynamics*. When considering current approaches to modelling dynamics, the following two classes can be identified: *logic-oriented* modelling approaches, and *mathematical* modelling approaches, usually based on difference or differential equations. Logic-oriented approaches are good for expressing qualitative relations, but less suitable for working with quantitative relationships. Mathematical modelling approaches (e.g., Dynamical Systems Theory [9]), are good for the quantitative relations, but expressing conceptual, qualitative relationships is very difficult. In this article, the LEADSTO language (and software environment) is proposed as a language combining the specification of qualitative and quantitative relations.

In Section 2, the LEADSTO language is introduced. Section 3 provides examples from existing case studies in which LEADSTO has been applied. Section 4 describes the tools that support the LEADSTO modelling environment in detail. In particular, the LEADSTO Property Editor and the LEADSTO Simulation Tool are discussed. Section 5 compares the approach to related modelling approaches, and Section 6 is a conclusion.

2   Modelling Dynamics in LEADSTO

Dynamics can be modelled in different forms. Based on the area within Mathematics called calculus, the Dynamical Systems Theory (DST) [9] advocates to model dynamics by continuous state variables and changes of their values over time, which is also assumed continuous. In particular, systems of differential or difference equations are used. This may work well in applications where the world states can be modelled in a quantitative manner by real-valued state variables and the world's dynamics shows continuous changes in these state variables that can be modelled by mathematical relationships between real-valued variables.

Not for all applications dynamics can be modelled in a quantitative manner as required for DST. Sometimes qualitative changes form an essential aspect of the dynamics of a process. For example, to model the dynamics of reasoning processes in Intelligent Agents usually a quantitative approach will not work. In such processes states are characterised by qualitative state properties, and changes by transitions between such states. For such applications often qualitative, discrete modelling approaches are advocated, such as variants of modal temporal logic; e.g., [6]. However, using such non-quantitative methods, the more precise timing relations are lost too.

For the approach used in this paper, it was decided to consider time as continuous, described by real values, but to allow both quantitative and qualitative state properties. The approach subsumes approaches based on simulation of differential or difference equations, and discrete qualitative modelling approaches, but also combines them. For example, it is possible to model the exact (real-valued) time interval for which some qualitative property holds. Moreover, the relationships between states over time are described by either logical or mathematical means, or a combination thereof. This is explained below in more detail.

Dynamics is considered as evolution of states over time. The notion of state as used here is characterised on the basis of an ontology defining a set of properties that do or do not hold at a certain point in time. For a given (order-sorted predicate logic) ontology Ont, the propositional language signature consisting of all *state ground atoms* (or *atomic state properties*) based on Ont is denoted by APROP(Ont). The *state properties* based on a certain ontology Ont are formalised by the propositions that can be made (using conjunction, negation, disjunction, implication) from the ground atoms. A *state* s is an indication of which atomic state properties are true and which are false, i.e., a mapping S: APROP(Ont) → {true, false}.

To specify simulation models a temporal language has been developed. This language (the LEADSTO language) enables one to model direct temporal dependencies between two state properties in successive states, also called *dynamic properties*. A specification of dynamic properties in LEADSTO format has as advantages that it is executable and that it can often easily be depicted graphically. The format is defined as follows. Let α and β be state properties of the form 'conjunction of atoms or negations of atoms', and e, f, g, h non-negative real numbers. In the LEADSTO language the notation $\alpha \twoheadrightarrow_{e, f, g, h} \beta$ (also see Figure 1), means:

If state property α holds for a certain time interval with duration g, then after some delay (between e and f) state property β will hold for a certain time interval of length h.

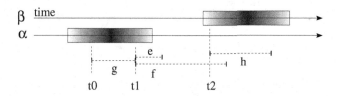

Fig. 1. The timing relationships

An example dynamic property that uses the LEADSTO format defined above is the following: "observes(agent_A, food_present) $\twoheadrightarrow_{2, 3, 1, 1.5}$ belief(agent_A, food_present)". Informally, this example expresses the fact that, if agent A observes that food is present during 1 time unit, then after a delay between 2 and 3 time units, agent A will believe that food is present during 1.5 time units. In addition, within the LEADSTO language it is possible to use sorts, variables over sorts, real numbers, and mathematical operations, such as in "has_value(x, v) $\twoheadrightarrow_{e, f, g, h}$ has_value(x, v*0.25)".

Next, a *trace* or *trajectory* γ over a state ontology Ont is a time-indexed sequence of states over Ont (where the time frame is formalised by the real numbers). A LEADSTO expression α →→$_{e, f, g, h}$ β, holds for a trace γ if:

∀t1: [∀t [t1−g ≤ t < t1 ⇒ α holds in γ at time t] ⇒ ∃d [e ≤ d ≤ f & ∀t' [t1+d ≤ t' < t1+d+h ⇒ β holds in γ at time t']

An important use of the LEADSTO language is as a specification language for simulation models. As indicated above, on the one hand LEADSTO expressions can be considered as logical expressions with a declarative, temporal semantics, showing what it means that they hold in a given trace. On the other hand they can be used to specify basic mechanisms of a process and to generate traces, similar to Executable Temporal Logic (cf. [1]).

Finally, the LEADSTO format can be graphically depicted in a causal graph-like format, such as in Figure 2. Here, state properties are indicated by circles and LEADSTO relationships by arrows. An arc denotes a conjunction between state properties. Agents are indicated by dotted boxes. Circles that are depicted within an agent denote its internal (mental) state properties. Circles that are depicted on the left or right border of an agent denote, respectively, its input and output state properties, and circles that are depicted outside an agent denote state properties of the external world. Notice that this simple form leaves out the timing parameters e, f, g, h. A more detailed form can be obtained by placing the timing parameters in the picture as labels for the arrows. For more details about the LEADSTO language, see Section 4.

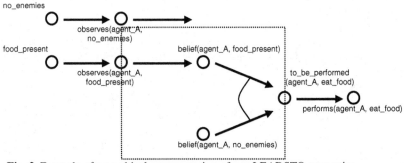

Fig. 2. Example of a graphical representation of two LEADSTO properties

3 Applications

The LEADSTO environment has been applied in a number of research projects in different domains. In this section, an example LEADSTO specification is given for a specific domain: a Multi-Agent System for ant behaviour, adopted from [3]. The world in which the ants live is described by a labeled graph as depicted in Figure 3. Locations are indicated by A, B,..., and edges by E1, E2,... The ants move from location to location via edges; while passing an edge, pheromones are dropped. The objective of the ants is to find food and bring this back to their nest. In this example there is only one nest (at location A) and one food source (at location F).

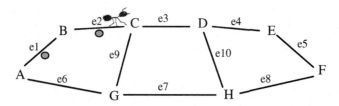

Fig. 3. An ants world

In [3], the dynamics of this system are formalised in LEADSTO, and some simulations are shown for different situations. A number of LEADSTO expressions that have been used for the simulation are shown in Box 1. For the complete specification, see [3].

In Figure 4 an example of a resulting simulation trace is shown. The upper part of the figure shows qualitative information; the lower part shows quantitative information. Time is on the horizontal axis. In the upper part, the state properties are on the vertical axis. Here, a dark box on top of the line indicates that the property is true during that time period, and a lighter box below the line indicates that the property is false. For example, the state property to_be_performed(ant2, pick_up_food) is true from time point 20 to 21. Because of space limitations, only a selection of important state properties was depicted. In the lower part, different instantiations of state property pheromones_at_E1(X) are shown, with different (real) values for X. For example, from time point 1 to 7 the amount of pheromones on E1 is 0.0.

LP5 (Selection of Edge)

This property models (part of) the edge selection mechanism of the ants. It expresses that, when an ant a observes that it is at location l coming from edge e0, and there are two other edges connected to that location, then the ant goes to the edge with the highest amount of pheromones. Formalisation:

observes(a, is_at_location_from(l, e0)) and neighbours(l, 3) and connected_to_via(l, l1, e1) and observes(a, pheromones_at(e1, i1)) and connected_to_via(l, l2, e2) and observes(a, pheromones_at(e2, i2)) and e0 ≠ e1 and e0 ≠ e2 and e1 ≠ e2 and i1 > i2 →→$_{0,0,1,1}$ to_be_performed(a, go_to_edge_from_to(e1, l1))

LP9 (Dropping of Pheromones)

This property expresses that, if an ant observes that it is at an edge e from a location l to a location l1, then it will drop pheromones at this edge e. Formalisation:

observes(a, is_at_edge_from_to(e, l, l1)) →→$_{0,0,1,1}$ to_be_performed(a, drop_pheromones_at_edge_from(e, l))

LP13 (Increment of Pheromones)

This property models (part of) the increment of the number of pheromones at an edge as a result of ants dropping pheromones. It expresses that, if an ant drops pheromones at edge e, and no other ants drop pheromones at this edge, then the new number of pheromones at e becomes i*decay+incr. Here, i is the old number of pheromones, decay is the decay factor, and incr is the amount of pheromones dropped. Formalisation:

to_be_performed(a1, drop_pheromones_at_edge_from(e, l1)) and ∀l2 not to_be_performed(a2, drop_pheromones_at_edge_from(e, l2)) and ∀l3 not to_be_performed(a3, drop_pheromones_at_edge_from(e, l3)) and a1 ≠ a2 and a1 ≠ a3 and a2 ≠ a3 and pheromones_at(e, i) →→$_{0,0,1,1}$ pheromones_at(e, i*decay+incr)

Box 1. Example LEADSTO specification

Although this picture provides a very simple example (involving only three ants), it demonstrates the power of LEADSTO to combine (real-valued) quantitative concepts with (conceptual) qualitative concepts.

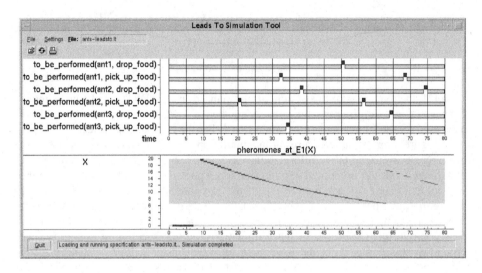

Fig. 4. Example simulation trace

Thus, Figure 4 shows an easy to read (important for the communication with the domain expert), compact, and executable representation of an informal model for ant behaviour. Moreover, the example demonstrates the power of conceptual modelling based on highly abstract process descriptions. In less than 3 pages of code, the global dynamics of ant behaviour are so well defined that the specification actually runs. The specification took only a couple of days to construct, making the LEADSTO approach valuable for proof-of-concept simulations, thus important for Agent-Oriented Software Engineering.

Finally, note that the ant example does not fully exploit the power of to use real-valued time parameters (in fact, most of the rules use the values 0,0,1,1 for the parameters e, f, g, h, see Box 1). Nevertheless, in a number of other domains the use of real-valued time parameters turned out to be beneficial, since it allows for more realistic simulations of dynamic processes. An example domain where this was the case, is the domain of adaptive agents based on classical conditioning, see [2].

4 Tools

In this section, the LEADSTO software environment is presented. Basically, this environment consists of two programs: the *Property Editor* (a graphical editor for constructing and editing LEADSTO specifications) and the *Simulation Tool* (for performing simulations of LEADSTO specifications, generating data-files containing traces for further analysis, and showing traces). Apart from the LEADSTO language constructs introduced in Section 2 the LEADSTO software has a number of other language constructs. Section 4.1 discusses some details. Next, Section 4.2 introduces the Property Editor and Section 4.3 deals with the Simulation Tool. Section 4.4 describes the algorithm used to generate simulations. Finally, Section 4.5 provides some implementation details and discusses possible improvements for the future.

4.1 Details of the LEADSTO Language

There are various representations of LEADSTO specifications. A graphical representation is shown in Section 4.2 when discussing the Editor. In this section all language constructs are discussed using a formal representation, based on the way specifications are stored.

Variables. The language uses typed variables in various constructs. A variable is represented as <Var-Name>:<Sort>.

Sorts. Sorts may be defined as a set of instances that may be specified: sortdef(<Sort-Name>, [<Term>,...]). There are also built-in sorts such as integer, real, and ranges of integers represented as for example between(2,10).

Atoms. Atoms may be terms built up from names with argument lists where each argument must be a term or a variable, for example: belief(x:AGENT, food_present).

LEADSTO rules. LEADSTO rules are introduced in Section 2. They are represented as:

leadsto([<Vars>,] <Antecedent-Formula>, <Consequent-Formula>, <Delay>, where
<Delay> := efgh(<E-Range>,<F-Range>, <G-Range>,<H-Range>))[1]
<Vars> := "[" <Variable>,... "]"

For example, $\alpha \rightarrow\!\!\!\!\rightarrow_{0,\,0,\,1,\,1} \beta$ is represented as leadsto(alfa, beta, efgh(0,0,1,1)). Variables occurring in LEADSTO rules must be explicitly declared as <Variable> entries.

Formulae. LEADSTO rules contain formulae. The current implementation allows conjunctions and universal quantification over typed variables. Some variables are global, encompassing the whole rule. Other - local - variables are part of universal quantification of some conjunction. The first kind of variables may be of infinite types. Currently, local variables must be of finite types. Some of these restrictions – such as on not allowing disjunction – will be removed in a next version. This will have no effect on the performance of the algorithm discussed in Section 4.4, but will make the details of the algorithm more complex. Other restrictions with respect to variables of infinite type will remain.

Time/Range. Time and Range values occurring in LEADSTO rules and interval constructs may be any number or expression evaluating to a number.

Constants. Constants may be defined using the following construct: constant(<Name>, <Value>). A constant(C1, a(1)) entry in a specification will lead to C1 being substituted by a(1) everywhere in the specification.

Intervals. During simulation, some atom values will be derived from LEADSTO rules. Others are not defined by rules but represent constant values of atoms over a certain time range. They are expressed as: interval([<Vars>,]<Range>,<LiteralConjunction>).

---

[1] The reason for grouping the delay is to make it easier to use delay constants.

Periodically   reoccurring   constant   values   are   represented   as: peri-
odic([<Vars>,]<Range>,<Period>,<LiteralConjunction>), where
    <Range> := range(<Start-Time>,<End-Time>)
    <Vars> := "[" <Variable>,... "]"
    <Period> : an expression or constant or variable representing a number.
    <LiteralConjunction> := <Literal> { and <Literal> }*
    <Literal> := <Atom> I not <Atom>

For example, an entry interval([X:between(1,2)], range(10,20), a(X)) makes a(1) and a(2)
true in the time range (10,20). Likewise, an entry periodic(P, range(0,1), 10) makes P
true in time ranges (0,1), (10,11), (20,21), and so on.

Simulation Range. The time range over which the simulation must be run is expressed by means of the constructs start_time(<Time>) and end_time(<Time>).

Visualisation of Traces. The construct display(<Tag-Name>, <Property>) is used to specify details of how to display the traces. The <Tag-Name> argument makes it possible to
define multiple views of a trace. The active view may be specified from within the
User Interface of the Simulation Tool. A number of properties may be specified, for
showing or hiding certain atoms, for sorting atoms, for grouping atoms into a graph,
and so on.

4.2 Property Editor

The Property Editor provides a user-friendly way of building and editing LEADSTO
specifications. It was designed in particular for laymen and students. The tool has
been used successfully by students with no computer science background and by
users with little computer experience. By means of graphical manipulation and filling

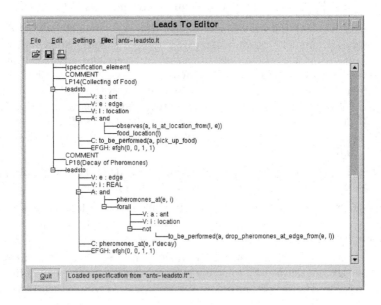

Fig. 5. The LEADSTO Property Editor

in of forms a LEADSTO specification may be constructed. The end result is a saved LEADSTO specification file, containing entries discussed in section 4.1. Figure 5 gives an example of how LEADSTO specifications are presented and may be edited with the Property Editor. This screenshot corresponds to (part of) the specification given in Box 1.

4.3 Simulation Tool

Figure 6 gives an overview of the Simulation Tool and its interaction with the LEADSTO Property Editor.

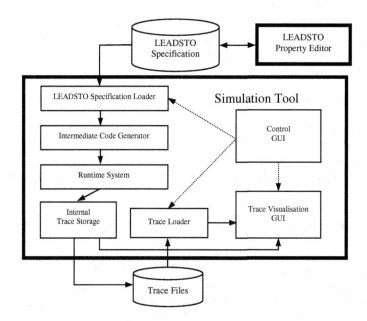

Fig. 6. Simulation Tool Architecture

The bold rectangular borders define the separate tools. The lines with arrows represent data transport; the dashed arrows represent control. The Property Editor is used to generate and store LEADSTO specification files. The Simulation Tool loads these specification files. The overall control of the Simulation Tool is handled by the *Control-GUI* component. The Simulation Tool can perform the following activities:

- Loading LEADSTO specifications, performing a simulation and displaying the result.
- Loading and displaying existing traces (without performing simulation).
- Adjusting the visualisation of traces.

Loading and simulating a LEADSTO specification is handled in four steps:

1. The *Specification Loader* loads the specification.
2. The *Intermediate Code Generator* initialises the trace situation with values defined by interval and periodic entries in the specification. The LEADSTO rules

are preprocessed: constants are substituted, universal quantifications are expanded and the rules are partially compiled into Prolog calls.

3. The actual simulation is performed by the *Runtime System*. This is the part that contains the algorithm, discussed in the next section.

4. At the end of a simulation the result is stored internally by the *Internal Trace Storage* component. The result can be saved as a trace file containing the evolution over time of truth values of all atoms occurring in the simulation, and will be visualised by the *Trace Visualisation GUI*. In principle, traces are three-valued, using the truth values true, false, and unknown. Saved trace files can be inspected later by the simulation tool and can be used by other tools, e.g., for automated analysis.

Note that visualisation of traces is integrated into the Simulation Tool through the *Trace Visualisation GUI* component. It is possible to select what atoms must be shown and in what order (sorting) etc. Figure 4 is an example of the visualisation of the result of a simulation.

4.4 Simulation Engine Algorithm

In this section a sketch of the simulation algorithm is given. The core of the semantics is determined by the LEADSTO rules, for example leadsto(alpha,beta, efgh(e, f, g, h)) or (in the notation of Section 2) $\alpha \rightarrow\!\!\!\twoheadrightarrow_{e, f, g, h} \beta$. The state properties α, β are internally normalised. Currently, only state properties that can be simplified to conjunctions of literals are allowed.

Restrictions on delays
The parameters g and h are time intervals, they must be >= 0. The algorithm allows only causal rules, e,f >= 0. Allowing e,f < 0 would lead to non-causal behaviour (any trace situation could have an effect arbitrarily in the past) and an awkward simulation algorithm. The causal nature of the semantics of LEADSTO rules results in a straightforward algorithm: at each time point, a bound part of the past of the trace (the maximum of all g values of all rules) determines the values of a bound range of the future trace (the maximum of f + h over all LEADSTO rules).

Outline of the algorithm
First all interval and periodic entries are handled by setting the ranges of atoms according to their definition. Next, for the algorithm a time variable HandledTime is introduced: all LEADSTO rules with antecedent range up to HandledTime have fired. The idea is to propagate HandledTime until HandledTime >= EndTime[2] via the following steps:

1. At a certain HandledTime, a value for NextTime is calculated. This will be the first time in the future after HandledTime that firing of a LEADSTO rule with its g-interval (see Figure 1) extending past HandledTime may have effect in the form of some consequent atom set. The time increment will be at least as big as the minimum of e + h over all LEADSTO rules.

2. An (optional) Closed World Assumption is performed for all selected atoms in the range (HandledTime, NextTime), i.e., all unknown atoms in this range are made false.

---

[2] EndTime is the time up to which the simulation should be run.

3. All LEADSTO rules are applied for which the range of the antecedent ends before or overlaps with NextTime.
4. Set HandledTime := NextTime
5. Continue with step 1 until HandledTime >= EndTime

4.5 Implementation Details

The complexity of the current algorithm is proportional to the number of LEADSTO rules in the specification, to the number of incremental time steps of the algorithm (which is at most equal to the length of the simulation divided by the minimum of e + h over all LEADSTO rules) and (at most) to the number of matching antecedent atoms per LEADSTO rule (limited by the number of atoms set during the simulation). A number of optimizations already improve the performance, such as only considering antecedent atoms that have matching values in the (HandledTime, NextTime) time range and not considering LEADSTO rules that have been tested to not fire until some time in the future.

The software was written in SWI-Prolog/XPCE, and consists of approximately 20000 lines of code. The approach for the design and implementation has been to first focus on a complete implementation that is easily adaptable, with acceptable performance for the current users. For an impression of the performance: the simulation of Section 3 took two seconds on a regular Personal Computer. More complex LEADSTO simulations have been created that take about half an hour to run. For example: one simulation with 170 LEADSTO rules, 2000 time steps, with 15000 atoms set, took 45 minutes.

There is room for further performance improvement of the algorithm. One possible improvement is to increase the time increment NextTime − HandledTime introduced in the algorithm above. Global analysis of dependency of LEADSTO rules should improve the performance, for instance by trying to eliminate simple rules with small values of their e + h parameters. Furthermore, the LEADSTO language is being extended with constructs for probabilistic rules, and with constructs for systematically generating traces of LEADSTO specifications for a range of parameters.

5 Related Work

In the literature, a number of modelling approaches exist that have similarities to the approach discussed in this paper. Firstly, there is the family of approaches based on differential or difference equations (see, e.g., [9]). In these approaches, to simulate processes by mathematical means, difference equations are used, for example, of the form: $\Delta x = f(x) \Delta t$ or $x(t + \Delta t) = x(t) + f(x(t)) \Delta t$. This can be modelled in the LEADSTO language as follows (where d is Δt): has_value(x, v) $\rightarrow\!\!\!\rightarrow_{d, d, d, d}$ has_value(x, v+f(v)*d). This shows how the LEADSTO modelling language subsumes modelling approaches based on difference equations. In addition to those approaches the LEADSTO language allows to express qualitative and logical aspects.

Another modelling approach, Executable Temporal Logic [1], is based on temporal logic formulae of the form φ & $\chi \Rightarrow \psi$, where φ is a past formula, χ a present formula and ψ a future formula. In comparison to this format, the LEADSTO format is more expressive in the sense that it allows order-sorted logic for state properties, and allows one to express quantitative aspects. Moreover, the explicitly expressed timing parameters go beyond Executable Temporal Logic. On the other hand, within Executable Temporal Logic it is allowed to refer to different past states at different points in time, and thus to model more complex relationships over time. For the LEADSTO language the choice has been made to model only the basic mechanisms of a process (e.g., the direct causal relations), like in modelling approaches based on difference equations, and not to model the more complex mechanisms.

The Duration Calculus [11] is a modal logic for describing and reasoning about the real-time behaviour of dynamic systems, where states change over time and are represented by functions from time (reals) to the Boolean values (0 and 1). It is an extension of Interval Temporal Logic [7], but with continuous time, and uses integrated durations of states as interval temporal variables. Assuming finite variability of state functions (i.e., between any two time points only a finite number of state changes occurs), the axioms and rules of Duration Calculus constitute a complete logic (relative to Interval Temporal Logic). A number of interesting tools have been created around (subsets of) Duration Calculus, see, e.g., [8] for information on model checking duration calculus formulae. Duration Calculus itself is not directly used for creating executable models, but environments for executable code exist (e.g., PLC automata, see [4]) for which a semantics is given in Duration Calculus.

Another family of modelling approaches based on causal relations is the class of *qualitative reasoning* techniques (see, e.g., [5]). The main idea of these approaches is to represent quantitative knowledge in terms of abstract, qualitative concepts. Like the LEADSTO language, qualitative reasoning can be used to perform simulation. A difference with LEADSTO is that it is a purely qualitative approach, and that it is less expressive with respect to temporal and quantitative aspects.

6   Conclusion

This article presents the language and software environment LEADSTO that has been developed to model and simulate the dynamics of Multi-Agent Systems on the basis of highly abstract process descriptions. If those dynamics are modelled correctly, the LEADSTO software environment can use them for simulation of the desired behaviour of the system. Although such simulations are no formal proof, they can contribute to an informal validation of the specification: by performing a number of simulations, it can be tested whether the behaviour of the specification is satisfactory. Therefore, LEADSTO may be an important tool to bridge the gap between the Design and the Implementation phase.

Within LEADSTO, dynamics can be modelled in terms of both qualitative and quantitative concepts. It is, for example, possible to model differential and difference equations, and to combine those with discrete qualitative modelling approaches. Existing languages are either not accompanied by a software environment that allows simulation of the model, or do not allow the combination of both qualitative and quantitative concepts.

The language LEADSTO is a declarative order-sorted temporal language extended with quantitative notions (like integer, and real). Time is considered linear, continuous, described by real values. Dynamics can be modelled in LEADSTO as evolution of states over time, i.e., by modelling the direct temporal dependencies between state properties in successive states. The use of durations in these temporal properties facilitates the modelling of such temporal dependencies. In principle, accurately modelling the dynamics of processes may require the use of a dense notion of time, instead of the more practiced variants of discrete time. The problem in a dense time frame of having an infinite number of time points between any two time points is tackled in LEADSTO by the assumption of "Finite Variability" (see Section 5 and, e.g., [11]). Furthermore, main advantages of the LEADSTO language are that it is executable and allows for graphical representation.

The software environment LEADSTO was developed especially for the language. It features a dedicated Property Editor that proved its value for laymen, students and expert users. The core component is the Simulation Tool that performs simulations of LEADSTO specifications, generates simulation traces for further analysis, and visualises the traces.

The approach proved its value in a number of research projects in different domains. It has been used to analyse and simulate behavioural dynamics of agents in cognitive science (e.g., human reasoning, creation of consciousness, diagnosis of eating disorders), biology (e.g., cell decision processes, the dynamics of the heart), social science (e.g., organisation dynamics, incident management), and artificial intelligence (e.g., design processes, ant colony behaviour). LEADSTO is so rich that it can be used to model phenomena from diverse perspectives. It has, for example, been used to model cognitive processes from a psychological/BDI perspective and from a physical/neurological perspective. For more publications about these applications, the reader is referred to the authors' homepages.

References

1. Barringer, H., M. Fisher, D. Gabbay, R. Owens, & M. Reynolds (1996). *The Imperative Future: Principles of Executable Temporal Logic*, Research Studies Press Ltd. and John Wiley & Sons.
2. Bosse, T., Jonker, C.M., Los, S.A., Torre, L. van der, and Treur, J., Formalisation and Analysis of the Temporal Dynamics of Conditioning. In: J.P. Mueller and F. Zambonelli (eds.), *Proc. of the Sixth Int. Workshop on Agent-Oriented Software Engineering, AOSE'05*. To appear, 2005.
3. Bosse, T., Jonker, C.M., Schut, M.C., and Treur, J, Simulation and Analysis of Shared Extended Mind. In: Davidsson, P., Gasser, L., Logan, B., and Takadama, K. (eds.), *Proc. of the First Joint Workshop on Multi-Agent and Multi-Agent-Based Simulation, MAMABS'04*, 2004, pp. 191-200.
4. Dierks, H. PLC-automata: A new class of implementable real-time automata. In M. Bertran and T. Rus, editors, *Transformation-Based Reactive Systems Development (ARTS'97)*, volume 1231 of Lecture Notes in Computer Science, pages 111-125. Springer-Verlag, 1997.
5. Forbus, K.D. *Qualitative process theory*. Artificial Intelligence, vol. 24, no. 1-3, 1984, pp. 85-168.

6. Meyer, J.J.Ch., and Treur, J. (volume eds.), *Agent-based Defeasible Control in Dynamic Environments*. Series in Defeasible Reasoning and Uncertainty Management Systems (D. Gabbay and Ph. Smets, series eds.), vol. 7. Kluwer Academic Publishers, 2002.
7. Moszkowski, B., and Manna, Z. Reasoning in Interval Temporal Logic. In Clarke, E., and Kozen, D., editors, *Proceedings of the Workshop on Logics of Programs*, volume 164 of LNCS, pages 371–382, Pittsburgh, PA, June 1983. Springer Verlag.
8. Pandya, P.K., Model checking CTL[DC].   In: *Proceedings of TACAS 2001*, Genova, LNCS 2031, Springer-Verlag, April 2001.
9. Port, R.F., Gelder, T. van (eds.) (1995). *Mind as Motion: Explorations in the Dynamics of Cognition*. MIT Press, Cambridge, Mass.
10. Vliet, H., van. *Software Engineering: Principles and Practice*. John Wiley & Sons, Ltd, 2000.
11. Zhou, C., Hoare, C.A.R., and Ravn, A.P. *A Calculus of Durations*, Information Processing Letter, 40, 5, pp. 269-276, 1991.

Towards a Distributed Tool Platform Based on Mobile Agents

Kolja Lehmann, Lawrence Cabac, Daniel Moldt, and Heiko Rölke

University of Hamburg, Department of Computer Science,
Vogt-Kölln-Str. 30, D-22527 Hamburg
{8lehmann, cabac, moldt, roelke}@informatik.uni-hamburg.de

Abstract. Nowadays many software development (SD) projects are placed in a distributed setting, concerning both the software itself and the resources, processes and actors needed to create or maintain the software. Therefore, tools and methods to support software engineering should be distributed as well.

In a SD project many different actors play different roles, all interacting with one another. The software engineering paradigm most suited for this kind of organization in which autonomous actors act and interact is the paradigm of agent-oriented software development (AOSE).

This article presents a MAS-based tool platform (cooperative infrastructure) which integrates different tools that are distributed over several agent platforms.

The eventual goal of this platform is to create a distributed software development environment. This should easily allow interaction, coordination and cooperation between different participating parties in a software development process, by allowing them to communicate, negotiate, synchronize resources, etc. in a transparent, distributed and dynamic setting.

Keywords: Multi-agent system, agent, AOSE, distributed IDE, distributed software development, software development tools, MULAN, nets-within-nets, Petri nets, Plug-in Agent, RENEW.

1 Introduction

Software development processes today are getting increasingly more distributed and shared among multiple organizations. Parts of software can be manufactured offshore to reduce costs, while central components are left for more trusted companies with a better reputation. Design, specification and quality assurance (QA) might be performed in yet another place. Therefore, new tools are needed to support the collaboration between different people in different organizations working together towards a common goal, namely the production or maintenance of a software product. These software tools need to integrate the different views of the stakeholders on the software and to allow them to work together.

Current integrated development environments are well suited to support a single user in the development process. However, in increasingly dynamic settings

T. Eymann et al. (Eds.): MATES 2005, LNAI 3550, pp. 179–190, 2005.

of distributed development teams, flexibility and support for collaborative work is still not adequately integrated.

In our view the agent-oriented software development paradigm is best suited for this kind of challenge for a couple of reasons. By applying the AOSE paradigm it is possible to provide a similar structure of the application domain model and the technical domain model. This is of advantage for the construction of complex highly dynamical software systems [22]. The AOSE paradigm is designed to integrate different autonomous software entities: agents, that all have their own goals and are interacting to achieve these goals.

For example a customer has the goal to obtain a software that meets his or his companies needs. A developer wants to have all information and resources at hand to perform his work. The QA department needs access to the test-ready releases and communication channels to communicate the problems found. All these different users can be further integrated by applying a flexible work-flow management system that delegates tasks between the involved parties. This workflow system can be distributed within the multi-agent system as well.

Our approach for the development of this kind of distributed development environment is described in this article. It is based on different kinds of interacting agents on a fine-grained level. Every user is represented by an agent, but also all functionality is provided by different kinds of *Tool Agents*, that plug into the users *User Agent* and interact with each other to provide the desired functionality. Other agents within the multi-agent system provide additional functionality like persistence of agents between sessions, user authentication and tool creation.

Our approach also incorporates the notions and concepts from plug-in system architectures [2,3,4]. These concepts allow to construct large, flexible and adaptable systems from smaller composable elements, in which functionality can be extended or altered by adding, changing or removing plug-ins. The combination of both leads to the concept of pluggable agents or Plug-in Agents.

This article describes first steps that have been made towards the development of such a system, the architecture implemented so far and envisioned for the future. Therefore, Section 2 will introduce the basics on which this work is based, especially our MAS framework MULAN, Section 3 describes the architecture of the system. It focusses on the aspects that have already been implemented and hints at the direction of further development. Since mobile agents are used for the deployment of services, Section 4 describes the way mobility is implemented using our architecture based on the framework MULAN.

2   Basic Concepts

In this section we will introduce the agent system architecture MULAN together with the CAPA extension. MULAN is implemented using the reference net formalism (and Java) so we start with an overview on reference nets.

2.1   Reference Nets

Reference Nets [11] are expressive high-level Petri nets that allow nets to be nested within nets in dynamical structures (nets-within-nets [20]). In contrast to ordinary Petri nets, where tokens are passive elements, tokens in nets-within-nets are active elements, i.e. Petri nets. In general we distinguish between two different kinds of token semantics: value semantics and reference semantics. In value semantics tokens can be seen as direct representations of nets. This allows for nested nets that are structured in a hierarchical order because nets can only be located at one location. In reference semantics arbitrary structures of net-nesting can be achieved because tokens represent references to nets. These structures can be hierarchical, acyclic or even cyclic.

Reference Nets are object-oriented nets, which may be modelled and executed using the Petri net-IDE RENEW [12]. Similar to objects in object-oriented programming languages, where objects are instantiations of classes, net instances are instantiations of net templates. Net templates define the structure and behavior of nets just like classes define the structure and methods of objects. While the net instance has a marking that determines its status, the net template determines only the behavior and initial marking that is common to all net instances of one type.

Communication between different nets (net instances) is possible via synchronous channels. Synchronous channels resemble method calls in object-oriented programming languages, but they are more powerful. They temporarily fuse two (or more) transitions and allow the passing of arguments in either directions. Furthermore, the enabledness of the channel is determined by all participating transitions, not only by one caller.

2.2   The Multi-agent System Mulan

Today, agents and multi-agent systems (MAS) are one of the most important structuring concepts for complex software systems. By including attributes like autonomy, cooperation, adaptability and mobility, agents go well beyond the concept of objects and object-oriented software development.

The multi-agent system architecture MULAN [14] is based on the nets-within-nets paradigm, which is used to describe the natural hierarchies in an agent system. MULAN is implemented in Reference Nets using RENEW [12]. MULAN has the general structure as depicted in Figure 1: Each box describes one level of abstraction in terms of the net hierarchy. Each upper level net contains net

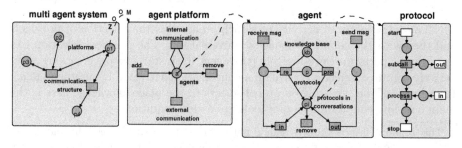

Fig. 1. Agent system as nets-within-nets

tokens, whose structures are made visible by the ZOOM lines.[1] The figure shows a simplified version of MULAN, since for example several inscriptions and all synchronous channels are omitted. Nevertheless, MULAN is an executable model.

The Multi-agent System View. The net in the upper left of Figure 1 describes an agent system, whose places contain agent platforms as tokens. The transitions describe communication or mobility channels that build up the infrastructure. The multi-agent system net shown in the figure is just an illustrating example, the number of places and transitions or the interconnections have no further meaning.

The Platform View. By zooming into the platform token on place p1, the structure of a platform becomes visible, shown in the upper right box. The central place agents hosts all agents that currently reside on this platform. Each platform offers services to the agents, some of which are indicated in the figure.[2] Agents can be created (transition add) or destroyed (transition remove). Agents can communicate by message exchange. Two agents of the same platform can communicate by the transition internal communication, which binds two agents, the sender and the receiver, to pass one message over a synchronous channel. Transition (external communication) only binds one agent, since the other agent is bound on a second platform somewhere else in the agent system. Also mobility facilities are provided on a platform: agents can leave the platform (via the transition new) or enter the platform (via the transition destroy).

In the diagram some details of the platform are hidden for the reason of simplicity. An important feature that cannot be seen is that a platform may itself act as an agent. By this means, arbitrary hierarchies of agents and platforms are possible, in particular a platform is able to encapsulate its agents from the outside world.

The Agent View. An agent is a message processing entity. It must be able to receive messages, possibly process them and generate messages of its own. Each agent consists of exactly one *agent net* that is its interface to the outside world (in the lower right corner of the figure) and an arbitrary number of *protocols* (lower left corner) defining its behavior. The agent may exchange messages with other agents via the platform. This is done using the transitions receive message and send message. These two transitions are the only interconnection of the agent to the rest of the (multi-) agent system, so the agent is a strongly encapsulated entity.

The central point of activity of a such an agent is the selection of protocols and therewith the commencement of conversations. The protocol selection can basically be performed pro-actively (the agent itself starts a conversation) or reactively (protocol selection based on a conversation activated by another agent). In the case of the pro-active protocol selection, the place knowledge base is the main enabling condition, the protocols are a side condition.

---

[1] This zooming into net tokens should not to be confused with place refinement.

[2] Note that only mandatory services are mentioned here. A typical platform will offer more and specialized services, for example implemented by special service agents.

The Interaction View. The activities of an agent are modeled as protocol Petri nets (or short: protocols) – an example is given in the lower left corner of the figure. The variety of protocols ranges from simple linear step-by-step plans to complex dynamic workflows. Petri nets are well suited for the modeling of procedures or process flows, which can be seen by their wide-spread use in the area of (business) process modeling [21].

2.3 Capa

CAPA (Concurrent Agent Platform Architecture) [6] is a partial re-implementation of the MULAN framework. CAPA ensures the compatibility of the MULAN framework to the FIPA specifications [7]. The internal structure of the agents and the possibilities sketched above are not touched by CAPA.

A part of the compliance to the FIPA specifications concerns the management of an agent platform. In particular, an AMS (agent management system) and a DF (directory facilitator) have to be provided. This is done by placing special agents on each platform that offer the mandatory services. Additional services may be offered by agents residing on the platform. Agents migrating to a platform may offer new services previously lacking on this platform.

3   Tool Platform Architecture

This section describes the static and dynamic architecture of the tool platform. It is comprised of different interacting agents, that fulfill different tasks. Figure 2 shows the interaction of these agents. The first architecture of the platform has been proposed in [15].

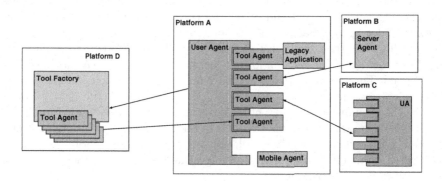

Fig. 2. Architecture of the tool platform

The goal here is to achieve a flexible, adaptable system architecture that is capable of supporting the collaborative work of flexibly and dynamically structured groups. For this the system needs to be extensible and should also be similarly structured as the application domain.

First we will introduce our notion of extensibility, then we will go into detail how this extensibility can be included into the MULAN / CAPA framework. Finally, we discuss how mobility of MULAN agents can provide more flexibility for the system to achieve that reflects a highly dynamical setting in a distributed work environment.

3.1 Extensibility

In software engineering, components have been introduced as units of extensibility [19, p. 68]. Likewise, extensibility in the agent-oriented view is a first-order concept. In our notion we integrate the two notions into a concept of a migrating agent and a pluggable component to form a Plug-in Agent. A Plug-in Agent is capable of extending the functionality of another agent or component [2,3,4]. To achieve the possibility to extend the functionality offered by an agent or a group of agents – sometimes on remote, distributed platforms – the agent uses mobility, which is another first order concept in the agent-oriented paradigm. In this case mobility is a very useful concept that bridges the gap between flexible / adaptable and distributed systems.

3.2 Tool Agent Registration

The system consists of a number of interconnected agent platforms. For example, a user who wishes to use the system will start a new platform on his local system. This platform can contain any number of agents, but to start with, the user creates only an instance of the User Agent (UA). This agent acts as a local representative of the user in the distributed system. It is equipped with protocols to discover and register with Tool Agents (TAs), that perform some kind of task on behalf of the user.

In order to register a new Tool Agent, the User Agent first needs to find out where to get it. To that end, it queries the platform's Directory Facilitator agent (DF) for agents that offer a "Tool Factory" service. On request, the Tool Factory (TF) will then send a list of tools it is able to provide. At the moment, the list of tool agents is static, a format for the description of TAs still needs to be designed. This description also needs to include a description of dependencies between these agents.

The UA then displays the list of tools to the user who chooses the functionality for his session. The UA sends a request to the Tool Factory, which instantiates the new TA, sends it to the UA's platform if necessary and performs the mutual registration. The actual process of migrating the TA to another platform is described in detail in Section 4.

In order to acquire a new Tool Agent, the User Agent sends a request message to a Tool Factory Agent (TF), which knows the different kinds of TAs and is capable of generating new instances on behalf of the user. At this point the TF can also perform checks on the access rights of the user to determine whether or not the requested tool is accessible to the user or perform some kind of customization of the tool agent. For example, if the TA needs to communicate with some kind of server agent, the Tool Factory could instantiate the TA with the address of the server. These are common instantiation features in a dynamical / pluggable system.

3.3 Tool Agents

Tool Agents provide the functionality that the system has to offer. This functionality can be provided in different ways (see Figure 2): As a wrapper around a legacy application, by contacting some kind of server agent (as in the Whiteboard example in Section 5.2), by directly communicating with another TA connected to a different UA (as in the chat example in Section 5.2) or all by itself.

Additionally a TA can provide extension points for other TAs registered with the same UA. By using this mechanism, more complex functionality can be flexibly built as a combination of simpler agents,[3] leading to a dynamically adaptable system through (self-)composing plug-ins.

3.4 User Interface

The basic user interface is provided by the User Agent and consists of not much more than a frame that can be filled with content and in the simplest case a list of TAs to register.

Once a Tool Agent is registered with a User Agent it sends a reference of its user interface part to the UA. There are in principle several different ways to approach the UI-integration. One is to have the TA send only a description of UI-elements, like input fields, buttons, etc. and leave it up to the User Agent to render those elements. The UA listens for events on the UI and sends those events as ACL-Messages to the Tool Agent, that can be located on an arbitrary platform. The Tool Agent then decides how to handle these events [15].

However, this mechanism is too slow for a real time user interaction. It also prevents a flexible UI. Another more tightly coupled mechanism was chosen for the implementation. Here the TA[4] is required to reside on the same agent platform, more exactly within the same Java Virtual Machine as the User Agent, so that its user interface can directly be referenced.

The exact ways in which different Tool Agents can work together and share parts of the User Interface still needs to be defined. At the moment every Tool Agent's specific UI is realized as a tab of its own within a tab folder in the User Agent's UI.

4 Mobility

One characteristic that is often mentioned in the definition of agents is the notion of agent mobility. However, mobile agents are not very often implemented

---

[3] Examples for different kinds of plug-in-mechanisms are the IDE Eclipse [1] and the RENEW engine [13]. The difference here is that the plugins are realized on a higher level by dynamic composition of agents.

[4] Or at least its UI part.

because this comes with a number of difficult problems, security being among the most important ones. On the other hand the practical use of mobile agents is often not very clear. Therefore, other aspects of agency, like autonomy and interaction are more widely implemented in agent systems.

Our tool platform uses mobile agents as a means to distribute functionality within the system. Mobility is provided by MULAN / CAPA, using protocols to control the migration processes. Tool Agents are created at central locations within the system and then migrated to the spot where they are needed. However, those centrally located services can be redundant and distributed.

4.1 Uses of Mobility

The individual working environment of a user of the platform can be seen as his configuration of connected Tool Agents and their internal states. Mobility comes into play at two points: First, when a user first requests a new Tool Agent, it is created by a Tool Factory agent, which is a central service provider and will often reside on a different platform than the user requesting the TA, comparable to a web-service.[5] Before the TA can provide functionality to the user, it needs to migrate to that user's platform.

Secondly, when a user quits his work, he can decide to store his workspace in a central repository, so he can recall it later and continue working in his configuration on another desktop if needed. Therefore, the configuration of Tool Agents needs to be migrated to some kind of agent base (repository), from where it can later be recalled.[6] That way the problems of mobility and persistence are solved in one go, as persistence is merely declared as a special case of mobility. At the moment, this repository agent is not yet implemented, though.

Other applications of mobility in this context are automated version control or software distribution.

4.2 Protocols for Migration

The basic migration process (see Figure 3) only transmits the knowledge base of an agent and not the protocols (i.e. the code) that are referenced from within the knowledge base. This has different implications, mainly empowering the receiving platform. The agent platform can decide which protocols to offer to an agent on this platform and which versions of these protocols. This is an important decision with regard to security (see Section 4.3).

On the other hand, it is possible that an agent will not work as expected on another platform if protocols are present in another version or are completely missing. This problem could be solved by using dynamic protocol composition. As almost all MULAN-protocols are made up of Netcomponents[5], a possible way to go would be the specification of protocols as a combination of Netcomponents that are authorized by the platform.

---

[5] Generally it would be sufficient to have one Tool Factory for an organization, but with several cooperating organizations there could be multiple instances, maybe offering different kinds of TAs.

[6] For example by providing a username and password.

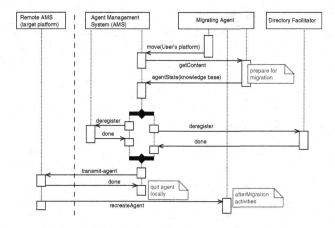

Fig. 3. Agent Interaction Protocol for the Migration Process

Another possibility is sending the protocol code along with the agents. This would however weaken the position of the platform. As we are using Petri nets for protocols, mechanisms to check compliance of protocols to certain rules could be grounded on Petri net properties, like invariants and liveness properties [16].

4.3 Security

Probably the most difficult aspect of mobile software agents are the different security issues. All of them cannot be extensively discussed here, but merely mentioned together with some points on how to handle them. These issues can be grouped into message level security, protection against malicious agents and protection against malicious hosts. These issues have partially been treated for our agent Petri net-based approach in earlier publications (see [9,10]).

5   Implementation and Example Applications

This section describes the current status of implementation of the tool platform, together with some example Tool Agents that have been implemented so far. There is a basic User Agent, a Tool Factory Agent and two different Tool Agents, along with the necessary ontologies and protocols to have them work together.

For communication there is an ontology defined for all issues concerning the management of Tool Agents, which must be understood by all agents. Additionally every class of Tool Agents can define their own ontologies for their special purposes.

5.1   Protocols

The behavior of agents in MULAN is specified by protocols that are executed by these agents. Like the ontologies, there are general protocols of the platform as well as individual protocols for different types of Tool Agents. The protocols of the platform concern the finding, creating and registering of Tool Agents.

The User Agent will find the Tool Factory by means of the directory facilitator agent, which is part of every FIPA-compliant platform. To distribute this work over multiple platforms, the CentralDF was developed, a mechanism of hierarchically integrating DFs on different agent platforms [8].

5.2   Example Tool Agents

Two example Tool Agents have been implemented with this platform to explore the possibilities for its use. The first one is a simple chat application, the second one is a white-board that allows several users to simultanously work on a document. The functionality of these applications is not very elaborate, because the main focus was a proof of concept study.

The chat tool only needs one type of tool agent, the Chat Agent. It offers the user a window where he can select other users to communicate with. To find those, first the platforms's directory facilitator is queried for agents that implement the `ChatAgent` service. Those are then asked for the names of the User Agents they are connected to.

After selecting a chat partner, another window is opened for the communication between the two agents, which is then simply accomplished by sending ACL inform messages between the agents, containing the statements in a format defined in the ontology.

While the chat application is an example for functionality provided by a TA communicating with another TA on a different UA, the White-board application uses a dedicated White-board Server Agent that controls a shared resource. The system can contain any number of server agents that can hold different documents. The TAs can check out a copy of this document and provide the user with an interface to edit it. Changes can then be checked in with the server agent and published to the other TAs.

This shows how different communication patterns can be applied within the basic architecture to achieve different results. Other patterns are of course possible, for example the communication of TAs that are connected to the same UA to provide a functionality together or communication with resources outside the multi-agent system, like a web-service.

6   Results and Conclusion

This article has presented the basics of a distributed tool platform based on mobile MULAN agents. For a more intuitively structured design we provide generic User Agents and Tool Agents that can be adapted for specific application needs. The goal of the system is to present a software development environment that is distributed and facilitates distributed work. The current status of the project and the tools implemented so far have been shown. This study has shown that an integrated application to support cooperative work in a flexible and application-reflective manner can be implemented by the means of a multi-agent system, respectively agent technologies. This allows for the adaptation of the software to the needs of users.

Our solution provides the basic features that are needed in such an environment: flexibility, extensibility, adaptability and the possibility for individual configuration. This can be extended to form an integrated environment for collaborative, distributed work, which can eventually lead to an agent technology-based IDE for the development of agent application. Technological aspects have been covered by providing an architecture with the focus on distributed agent-based workflows [18]. This architecture allows for inter-organizational coordination of activities. Furthermore, we have provided a smooth integration of agent concepts with Web Services in [17]. This will allow us to use appropriate technological means to support the conceptual work presented here.

References

1. Bolour Computing Azad Bolour. Notes on the eclipse plug-in architecture. `http://www.eclipse.org/articles/Article-Plug-in-architecture/plugin_architecture.html`, July 2003.
2. Lawrence Cabac, Michael Duvigneau, Daniel Moldt, and Heiko Rölke. Agent technologies for plug-in system architecture design. In *Proc. of AOSE*, LNCS, Utrecht, Netherlands, 2005. Springer-Verlag. accepted poster presentation / to be published.
3. Lawrence Cabac, Michael Duvigneau, Daniel Moldt, and Heiko Rölke. Modeling dynamic architectures using nets-within-nets. In *Proc. of ICATPN*, LNCS, Miami, 2005. Springer-Verlag. accepted paper / to be published.
4. Lawrence Cabac, Michael Duvigneau, Daniel Moldt, and Heiko Rölke. Multi-agent concepts as basis for dynamic plug-in software architectures. In *Proc. of AAMAS*, Utrecht, Netherlands, 2005. ACM. to be published.
5. Lawrence Cabac, Daniel Modt, and Heiko Rölke. A Proposal for Structuring Petri Net-Based Agent Interaction Protocols. In Wil van der Aalst and E. Best, editors, *Proc. of ATPN*, volume 2679 of *LNCS*, pages 102–120, Eindhoven, Netherlands, June 2003. Springer-Verlag.
6. M. Duvigneau, D. Moldt, and H. Rölke. Concurrent architecture for a multi-agent platform. In Fausto Giunchiglia, James Odell, and Gerhard Weiß, editors, *Proc. of AOSE 2002*, volume 2585 of *LNCS*, Berlin, 2003. Springer Verlag.
7. FIPA. Foundation for Intelligent Physical Agents. `http://www.fipa.org`, June 2004.
8. Foundation for Intelligent Physical Agents. Distributed directory facilitator - a proposal for the fipa adhoc first cft. `http://www.fipa.org/docs/input/f-in-00063/`, May 2002.
9. Thomas Jacob, Olaf Kummer, Daniel Moldt, and Ulrich Ultes-Nitsche. Implementation of Workflow Systems using Reference Nets – Security and Operability Aspects. In Kurt Jensen, editor, *Proc. of CPN*, 2002. DAIMI PB: Aarhus, Denmark, August 28–30, number 560.
10. Michael Köhler and Heiko Rölke. Modelling Sandboxes for Mobile Agents using Nets within Nets. In N. Busi and F. Martinelli, editors, *Workshop on Issues in Security and Petri Nets (WISP'03) at ATPN*. University of Eindhoven, 2003.
11. Olaf Kummer. *Referenznetze*. Logos-Verlag, Berlin, 2002.
12. Olaf Kummer, Frank Wienberg, and Michael Duvigneau. Renew – The Reference Net Workshop. `http://www.renew.de`, June 2004. Release 2.0.

13. O. Kummer et. al. An extensible editor and simulation engine for Petri nets: Renew. In Jordi Cortadella and Wolfgang Reisig, editors, *Proc. of ICATPN 2004*, number 3099 in LNCS, pages 484–493, Berlin, 2004. Springer Verlag.

14. Michael Köhler, Daniel Moldt, and Heiko Rölke. Modelling the structure and behaviour of Petri net agents. In *Proc. of ICATPN 2001*, volume 2075 of *LNCS*, pages 224–242, Berlin, 2001. Springer Verlag.

15. Kolja Lehmann and Vanessa Markwardt. Proposal of an Agent-based System for Distributed Software Development. In Daniel Moldt, editor, *Proc of MOCA 2004*, pages 65–70, Aarhus, Denmark, October 2004.

16. Kolja Lehmann and Daniel Moldt. Modelling and Analysis of Agent Protocols with Petri Nets. In Gabriela Lindemann, Jörg Denzinger, and Ingo J. et al. Timm, editors, *Proc. of MATES 2004*, volume 3187 of *LNCS*, page 85, Erfurt, Germany, 2004. Springer-Verlag.

17. Daniel Moldt, Sven Offermann, and Jan Ortmann. A petri net-based architecture for web services. In *Proceedings of the Workshop on Service-Oriented Computing and Agent-Based Engineering, AAMAS*, Utrecht, Netherlands, 2005. accepted paper / to be published.

18. C. Reese, J. Ortmann, S. Offermann, D. Moldt, K. Lehmann, and T. Carl. Architecture for distributed agent-based workflows. In *Proceedings of the Workshop on Agent-Oriented Information Systems, AAMAS*, Utrecht, Netherlands, 2005. accepted paper / to be published.

19. J. Sametinger. *Software Engineering with Reusable Components*. Springer Verlag, Berlin, 1997.

20. Rüdiger Valk. Petri Nets as Token Objects - An Introduction to Elementary Object Nets. In J. Desel and M. Silva, editors, *19th International Conference on Application and Theory of Petri nets, Lisbon, Portugal*, number 1420 in LNCS, pages 1–25, Berlin, 1998. Springer-Verlag.

21. Wil van der Aalst, Jörg Desel, and Andreas Oberweis, editors. *Business Process Management: Models, Techniques, and Empirical Studies*. Number 1806 in LNCS. Springer-Verlag Berlin, 2000.

22. Heinz Züllighoven. *Object-Oriented Construction Handbook*. Morgan Kaufmann Publishers and dpunkt.verlag, Heidelberg, Germany, 2005.

The Distributed Weighing Problem:
A Lesson in Cooperation Without Communication

Tibor Bosse[1], Mark Hoogendoorn[1], and Catholijn M. Jonker[2]

[1] Vrije Universiteit Amsterdam, Department of Artificial Intelligence,
De Boelelaan 1081a, 1081 HV Amsterdam, The Netherlands
{tbosse, mhoogen}@cs.vu.nl
[2] Radboud Universiteit Nijmegen, Nijmegen Institute for Cognition and Information,
Montessorilaan 3, 6525 HR Nijmegen, The Netherlands
C.Jonker@nici.ru.nl

Abstract. Cooperative problem solving without communication is an often-studied field within multi-agent research. Realistic problems investigated in this particular field are complex and difficult to model, and therefore not suitable for education. This paper presents the distributed weighing problem as a novel problem to be used for educational purposes within the domain of cooperation without communication. An example agent-based architecture is developed of which parts can be provided to students as a starting-point for practical exercises in cooperative problem solving without communication. Two example strategies are discussed and implemented using this example architecture. Moreover, it is shown how such strategies can be tested and formally validated against a number of desired properties. The educational benefits of the distributed weighing problem are presented as observed in a course for 6 groups of each 3 students.

1 Introduction

Coordination and cooperation between agents has been a topic of research for many years (see for example [5] and [9]), and is a part of everyday life. For instance, within the port of Rotterdam coordination is essential [14]. The port has approximately 24 terminals and about 120 sea vessels and barges are continuously loading and unloading containers. Coordination is needed to determine routes for the vessels and barges in such a way that they do not have to wait too long for other ships when they arrive at a certain terminal.

In the above example, the port authorities communicate with the ships to determine a schedule that is satisfactory for all parties. However, in a number of cases of cooperation between agents, no communication takes place (see also [7]). For instance, without communication people often coordinate their actions so that they do not bump in to each other on the street. Management games such as the broken squares problem [1] have been developed to train people in cooperation without communication. The broken squares problem requires the players to each construct a square out of a set of given parts. The parts, however, are distributed randomly across the individuals, therefore they need to forward those broken parts to other players for

T. Eymann et al. (Eds.): MATES 2005, LNAI 3550, pp. 191–203, 2005.
© Springer-Verlag Berlin Heidelberg 2005

which those parts are useful. The problem is solved when all individuals have formed their individual goal square. Also in the domain of software agents cooperation with limited or no communication plays a role. Agents might not have all the information or abilities they need to reach a certain goal. They may need to cooperate with other agents to be able to reach that goal. The problem solving capacity of the overall system increases with the cooperation capacity of the agents in the system. However, the communication load increases with the number of agents, which makes it attractive to solve the cooperation problem using limited communication.

As the examples show, in a number of cooperation problems communication is not possible or unnecessary. Students in the fields of artificial intelligence, computer science, information science, and management need to be familiar with solving such problems. Especially, the IT-related students need to be trained in the development of cooperative software agents. Suitable problems for educational purposes are problems that can easily be modelled. Scalability of the problem allows for testing the generality of the solution. Problems identified in the literature for cooperation without communication are often very hard to model. The broken squares problem for example entails modelling the different shapes of the pieces of the puzzle, the shapes that can be created when combining pieces of puzzles, and so on. Therefore it is hard to get students to study this type of problem in depth.

To improve the quality of education in cooperation without communication, this paper introduces a problem that is purely cooperative and can be solved without communication. The problem is derived from the *twelve balls problem* (see [11]), also known as the twelve coins problem. It involves twelve balls, each with the same appearance, of which one has a deviating weight which can either be lighter or heavier compared to the other balls. The balls can be put on a balance and weighed against each other. The goal of the problem is to find the deviating ball, and determine how it deviates from the rest (whether it is heavier or lighter). An additional restriction applies: The maximum number of weighings allowed is three.

The twelve balls problem, which is initially a centralized problem, can easily be modelled as a distributed problem without communication. To this end, each ball is represented by one agent that can decide to jump on the balance or not. The common goal is to derive the solution for the problem. The agents representing the balls are not allowed to communicate with each other. As the emphasis is on cooperation and not on efficiency of the solution, the requirement of solving the problem within three weighings is dropped. To ensure the eventual solution of the problem, no repetition of weighings is allowed, so the combined strategy of the agents should always result in performing a different weighing than before. In the rest of the paper this distributed problem is addressed as the *distributed weighing problem*. The number of balls can easily be scaled to any preferred number.

The distributed weighing problem is explained in more detail in section 2. Section 3 describes an example design of a component-based multi-agent system that models the problem. This design can serve as a starting-point in practical assignments in cooperation without communication. Example strategies that can be used by the agents are shown in more detail in section 4. Section 5 shows how such strategies can be tested and formally validated against a number of desired properties. Experiences in using the problem in education are discussed in Section 6. Section 7 compares the work with related literature and presents conclusions.

2   The Distributed Weighing Problem

This section describes the distributed weighing problem at a more detailed level, including the assumptions that agents are allowed to make on the behaviour of other players in the puzzle. Two possible protocols for the problem are introduced, and their differences discussed. Thereafter, a theoretical overview is presented of the possible types of agents one can encounter when solving the problem.

2.1   Puzzle Design

The distributed weighing problem is a derivative of the twelve balls problem, explained in the introduction, in which an arbitrary number of balls is used. Each ball is represented by an agent. All balls but one have exactly the same weight. The deviating ball is either heavier or lighter than the others. The goal of the game is to determine which ball is the deviating ball and to determine the deviation (heavier of lighter). The puzzle is solved when at least one ball knows the answer. Actions of a ball are observable to others. A ball has the following options:

1. **join_left.** If not already on the balance, the ball agent can select this option when it wants to join the left scale.
2. **join_right.** If not already on the balance, the ball agent can perform this action in case it wants to join the right scale.
3. **do_nothing.** This option can be used in case the ball agent is satisfied with the current balance configuration. If the agent is already on the balance, this is its only course of action. This design choice simplifies the problem of detecting that an agent decides not to join any scale.

A balance is available to perform the weighings determined by the balls. The game begins with an empty balance. After a weighing is performed, all agents are automatically removed from the balance.

The weighing process is performed according to a *sequential* protocol. In this protocol all balls get turns in a predetermined order. At the beginning an empty balance is observed by the first ball in line. After a ball has performed the chosen response action (possibly the observable "do_nothing"), the next ball observes the new situation. For example, ball B observes a situation with ball A on the left scale and an empty right scale. After all agents have performed the "do_nothing" action after each other, the balance performs the weighing and the agents observe the result of the weighing (i.e., one scale heavier than the other, or both scales equal). When playing this protocol, each ball knows after which other agent it has the turn. The first ball knows it has the turn at the beginning of the game.

In fact, the sequential protocol reflects a specific type of cooperation without communication. In such cooperation problems, where the parties involved contribute to the problem sequentially, their main concern is *what* action they have to perform. In cooperation problems where the parties involved contribute to the problem in parallel, an additional concern is *when* to perform the action. In future work, the distributed weighing problem will be used to study parallel cooperation as well.

2.2 Types of Agents

In order to ensure success, the agents are allowed to assume that the other agents will also behave with some intelligence and with the same goal in mind. In this section (and only this section) this assumption is dropped for the purpose of identifying all possible kinds of agents. In principle, three different types of agents can be identified:

A. Nasty. This agent tries to cause loops. A loop means that the same weighing is done over and over again. Nasty agents do not meet the benevolent requirement presented in [13] which roughly states that agents want to help each other whenever possible.

B. Dummy. A dummy agent performs arbitrary moves without any notion of previous weighings, or the possible consequences of his moves. Therefore the strategy can non-intentionally cause loops. Such an agent might also confuse agents that try to solve the problem in a more intelligent fashion.

C. Progressive. Progressive agents are those who always move towards the solution. Three basic strategies can be distinguished in the behaviour of the agent:

C-a. Non-repetitive. An agent that follows a non-repetitive strategy tries to prevent a weighing that has already been done. If the other agents are also non-repetitive, no loops will emerge during the problem solving process. Success is ensured if the agents keep performing weighings until they know the answer.

C-b. Information-eager. Agents following an information-eager strategy only aim for weighings from which new information can be derived. For example, a first weighing of ball A and B on the left scale against ball C and D on the right scale results in a balance. Therefore, it is known that all the balls are non-deviant, and a weighing of ball A against ball B would not add any information and is not accepted in the information-eager strategy.

C-c. Efficient. For each number of balls there is a minimal number of weighings that is always enough to find a solution. For the general problem (from [10]) with a maximum of n weighings the maximum number of balls for which the solution can be determined, m, is defined as: $m \leq (3^n - 3) / 2$. In case of the twelve balls problem that is always three weighings. An agent that follows an efficient strategy aims at finding the solution in that amount of weighings.

For educational purposes the focus is on agents of type C. Agents of type A and B are considered less interesting, because they do not cooperate. When strictly following the strategies of type C, the robustness relationships depicted in Table 1 hold. Robust means that the agents find a solution. As the table shows, strict C-a agents are robust against all other C agents, since these also try to prevent repetition. Strict C-b agents are robust against other strict C-b agents and strict C-c agents, but not against strict C-a agents. This is because a strict C-b agent assumes that the others are also information-eager. If this is not the case, a situation might occur which the agent cannot handle. For example, consider the situation sketched above when it is known that ball A and B are non-deviant. Then, a strict C-a agent might still propose a weighing of ball A against B, whilst a strict C-b agent will not allow this. As a result, the C-b agent will not be able to derive any appropriate action for the situation. For similar reasons, strict C-c agents are only robust against other strict C-c agents.

Section 4 presents the strategies of a type C-a and of a type C-b agent. A type C-c agent is not considered, since the focus is on finding a solution using a simple strategy, not on finding it in an efficient manner. It is however easy to incorporate such a strategy in the design presented in the next section.

Table 1. Robustness of C-strategies

	C-a	C-b	C-c
C-a	+	+	+
C-b	-	+	+
C-c	-	-	+

3 Example Design of a Multi-agent System for the Distributed Weighing Problem

This Section presents an example design of a multi-agent system for the distributed twelve balls problem. Students can, based on their experience in modelling and designing multi-agent systems, be provided with parts of this model as a starting-point for the exercise.

3.1 Top Level

The multi-agent system is designed using the component-based agent modelling approach DESIRE; cf. [3]. The highest level of abstraction consists of the agents representing the balls (called *ball_A*, *ball_B*, and so on) and the *External World*. The agents can perform actions in the external world, and observe the external world.

The execution of actions generated by the agents is modelled as follows. After an agent generates a certain action to be performed (e.g., jump on the left scale of the balance), this action is transferred to the external world, where the result of the action will occur (e.g., ball A is currently on the left scale of the balance). Thus, the execution of physical actions by the agents is modelled as part of the component external world. The action *do_nothing* represents the fact that an agent does not move for a certain period of time. Introducing this as an action makes the problem of knowing when an agent finished his turn easy.

Besides performing actions, the agents can observe the world. In the simplest model, these observations are not modelled explicitly (i.e., the agents do not have to determine pro-actively when to observe what). Instead, every relevant aspect of the world is transferred automatically from the external world to the agents in the form of *observation results*. These observation results include the current position of the balls on the balance, the results of weighings, and the actions performed by others.

3.2 Agent Level

The composition of the agents is based on the generic agent model as described in [3]. In the current model, four of the generic agent components are used, namely *Own Process Control*, *World Interaction Management*, *Maintenance of Agent Information*, and *Agent Specific Task*.

According to the generic agent model, the task of the component *Own Process Control* is to control the agent's own activities (e.g., determining, monitoring and evaluating its own goals, plans and characteristics). In the current domain, this is done by maintaining the following information: the agent's own name, the name of the current protocol, and other information associated with the protocols. For example, for the sequential protocol, the agent needs to know either the order in which the agents are allowed to perform actions (e.g., A-B-C-D-E-F-G-H-I-J-K-L-A), or the name of the agent ahead of it.

The component *World Interaction Management* takes care of the processes involved in interaction with the external world, i.e., observation interpretation, directed observation initiation, and action performance. The component passes actions and observation results (e.g., concerning the current position of the balls on the balance) from the relevant other components to the world and vice versa.

The task of the component *Maintenance of Agent Information* is to maintain (partial) agent models, containing relevant information about the state of the surrounding agents. In most applications, this information is obtained in two different ways: by observing the other agents and by communicating with them. Obviously, in the distributed weighing domain only the first approach occurs. For this domain, the agent models are restricted to the assumed weights of the agents (including itself). At any time, to each agent exactly one of the following values is assigned: {unknown, neutral, heavier_or_neutral, lighter_or_neutral, heavier, lighter}. Initially, each agent gets the value unknown. In later stages of the process, these values are updated in accordance with the observed weighing results. A number of knowledge rules are used to perform this modification:

- each ball occurring in a *balanced* weighing gets the value neutral
- each ball *not* occurring in an *unbalanced* weighing gets the value neutral
- each ball occurring on the *lower* scale in one weighing, and occurring on the *higher* scale in another weighing, gets the value neutral
- each unknown ball occurring on the *lower* scale in a weighing gets the value heavier_or_neutral
- each unknown ball occurring on the *higher* scale in a weighing gets the value lighter_or_neutral
- if one ball is lighter_or_neutral and all other balls are neutral, then this ball gets the value lighter
- if one ball is heavier_or_neutral and all other balls are neutral, then this ball gets the value heavier

Moreover, it is assumed that all agents have perfect recall.

Within the generic agent model specific tasks (e.g., design, diagnosis, information retrieval) can be modelled in the component *Agent Specific Task*. For the current domain, the specific task can be described as the determination of actions to be performed, based on the current situation of the balance. Thus, the output of this component is a proposal of the form join_left, join_right, or do_nothing. The exact knowledge used within Agent Specific Task depends on the strategy used by the agent, as described in the next section.

4   Example Strategies

This section describes a concrete example of a strict non-repetitive and a strict information-eager strategy. These examples show that the problem is relatively easy to solve. Moreover, they illustrate what comes into play when designing such strategies. The current strategies were used to construct strict C-a and strict C-b type agents that were tested in different combinations (see Section 5).

4.1 Non-repetitive Strategy

Non-repetitive strategies require looking ahead at the possible options that can still be performed without resulting in repetition. Without these calculations it is impossible to determine whether jumping on a scale can or cannot result in a new weighing of m to m balls, for some m. Two solutions are considered here: (1) Generate all possible weighings; (2) Use a mathematical formula to calculate the amount of options left.

A first option is to generate all possible weighings that might result after jumping on one of the scales, until you find one that has not been done in the past. If such a weighing cannot be found, try the same for jumping on the other scale. If that does not work either, then don't jump on any scale. However, its exponential character makes this option unsuitable for scaling to larger numbers.

A second option is to mathematically calculate how many possible weighings can be constructed in total, considering the current balance after an action of the agent (i.e. join_left, join_right, do_nothing), and the amount of balls still not on the balance. Thereafter, sum up the amount of past weighings of which the current proposal combined with the action of the agent is a subset. If there are more possible weighings than past weighings, the action for which the calculation was done is allowed to be performed. The number of possible weighings can be calculated as follows: Choose a type of weighing: m:m, where m varies from 1 to half the number of balls in the game. Let l denote the amount of available places on the left side of the balance with respect to your choice m, and r the amount of available places on the right side again with respect to m. For example, if you aim for a 3:3 weighing, and there is already one ball on the right scale, then r is 2. The amount of balls not on the balance is n. A formula to calculate the number of possible weighings w given these parameters is:

$$ w = \frac{\left(\prod_{i=0}^{l-1} (n-i) \right)}{l!} \times \frac{\left(\prod_{j=l}^{l+(r-1)} (n-j) \right)}{r!} $$

This number can be calculated for every possible value of m. The specific strategy determines which value is attempted first. The agent has the following arbitrary preference: (1) join_left; (2) join_right; (3) do_nothing.

4.2 Information-Eager Strategy

An agent that follows an Information-Eager strategy aims at weighings that provide some new information. Thus, if all agents are of this type, such weighings will indeed be performed until one of the agents solves the problem. In other words, after an Information-Eager agent has performed an action, the possibility to obtain a weighing that provides new information is still open (unless this was already impossible before the agent's action). A strategy of this type does not need to consider all remaining possibilities, because it can make use of its knowledge about the weights of the existing balls. For example, if a certain agent has the value lighter_or_neutral, and there is a ball with value heavier_or_neutral on the left scale, then it may be wise to join this ball on the left scale, because the resulting weighing is guaranteed to change the value of one of these balls (as long as other balls "complete" the weighing to ensure that both scales contain an equal amount). A number of different strategies of this type can be implemented. The strategy that is described in this section uses a two-step algorithm. In the first step the current situation is classified. In the second step an appropriate action is selected, based on the current situation.

In the first step, a number of different situations can be distinguished. The main distinction is between *advantageous* weighings and *non-advantageous* weighings. A weighing is advantageous if it is guaranteed to provide new information, no matter what the other balls do (as long as they "complete" the weighing, which is assumed). Advantageous weighings are weighings that (1) contain an unknown ball, (2) contain a heavier_or_neutral and a lighter_or_neutral ball on one scale, (3) contain a heavier_or_neutral ball on both scales, or (4) contain a lighter_or_neutral ball on both scales. Examples of the non-advantageous weighings are the case that all balls are neutral, the case that one ball is heavier_or_neutral and the rest is neutral, and so on.

When the current situation is classified, an appropriate action can be determined. In order to do this, the current strategy uses the algorithm depicted in Figure 1. As can be seen in the figure, first an agent has to verify whether it is already on the balance, because then the only possible action is do_nothing. When the agent is not on the balance, it checks whether one of the scales contains the *maximally allowed* number of balls, which is exactly half of the total number of balls (e.g. for the twelve balls problem, it is 6). If this is the case, the agent has to jump on the other scale in order to complete the weighing. The next step is to check whether an action exists that immediately results in an advantageous weighing. For example, if a certain agent has the value lighter_or_neutral, and there is already a ball with value lighter_or_neutral on the left scale, then join_right is such an action.

However, if such an action cannot be found, then the action to be performed depends on the specific situation. For reasons of space, the knowledge used in this last step is not represented completely in Figure 1. However, an example sketch of such a knowledge rule is the following: "if I am neutral, and the left scale contains more balls than the right scale, and there are still two lighter_or_neutral balls **not** on the balance, then I will join_left". The idea of this rule (and of many similar rules) is that the agent leaves empty spaces for the balls of which it is known that they will contribute to an advantageous weighing. Note that in general, this strategy has a preference for jumping on the balance when possible. An advantage of this approach is that the action do_nothing is often avoided, which minimizes the risk of accidentally accepting a non-advantageous weighing.

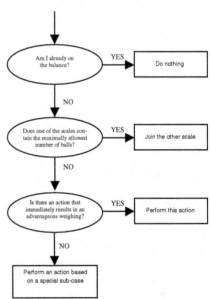

Fig. 1. Action selection algorithm

5 Testing Strategy Performance

The system described in the previous sections has been used to run a complete set of simulation experiments for six balls. The different parameters used in the experiments were the strategy used by each agent (i.e., either non-repetitive or information-eager), the name of the deviating ball, and the type of the deviating ball (i.e., either lighter or heavier). Hence, 768 (= 2^6 * 6 * 2) experiments have been performed in total. In all experiments, the sequential protocol was used for performance of actions. Similar experiments can be performed with student implementations to determine how well their strategies perform.

After performing the experiments, the resulting traces were automatically translated to a format that is suitable for the LEADSTO environment [2]. This environment has an automated checker, which offers the possibility to formally verify dynamic properties against traces. This checker takes a formally specified property and a set of traces as input, and verifies whether the property holds for the traces. For formal specification of the properties, the Temporal Trace Language TTL was used, cf. [12]. This language is based on sorted first-order predicate logic, and allows making explicit references to time points and traces. Using the automated checker, relevant properties can be checked against traces generated by a particular implementation of the distributed weighing problem. Hence, using such tools enables automatic performance measurement of the strategies that have been implemented (e.g. by students). Some examples of such properties are the following (both in informal and in formal TTL notation):

reasoning_successfulness(γ:trace)
In trace γ, eventually there will be a time point t on which some ball knows the solution. Formalisation:
$\exists$t:time $\exists$b1,b2:ball $\exists$ v:value
  [state(γ, t) |= belief(b1, has_value(b2, v), pos) $\wedge$ state(γ, t) |= deviating_ball(b2, v)]

no_repetition(γ:trace)
In trace γ, no weighing w will be performed twice. Formalisation:
$\forall$t1:time $\forall$w:weighing
  [state(γ, t1) |= to_be_performed(w) $\Rightarrow$ $\neg\exists$t2:time [t2>t1 $\wedge$ state(γ, t2) |= to_be_performed(w)]]

reasoning_continuation(γ:trace)
In trace γ, as long as there is no ball that knows the solution, a new weighing w will be performed. Formalisation:
$\forall$t1:time $\forall$b1,b2:ball
  [[state(γ, t1) |=/= belief(b1, has_value(b2, heavier), pos) $\wedge$
   state(γ, t1) |=/= belief(b1, has_value(b2, lighter), pos)] $\Rightarrow$
     $\exists$t2:time $\exists$w:weighing [t2>t1 $\wedge$ state(γ, t2) |= to_be_performed(w)]]

strong_new_information(γ:trace)
In trace γ, after each observation result, each ball will update the agent model of at least one of the balls before the next observation result is available. Formalisation:
$\forall$t1:time $\forall$o1:obs_result $\forall$b1:ball
  [state(γ, t1) |= observation_result(o1, pos) $\Rightarrow$
     $\exists$t2,t3:time $\exists$b2:ball $\exists$v1,v2:value
       [t2<t1<t3 $\wedge$ v1$\neq$v2 $\wedge$ state(γ, t2) |= belief(b1, has_value(b2, v1), pos)
       $\wedge$ state(γ, t3) |= belief(b1, has_value(b2, v2), pos)
       $\wedge$ $\neg$[$\exists$t4:time $\exists$o2:obs_result
           t1<t4<t3 $\wedge$ o2$\neq$o1 $\wedge$ state(γ, t4) |= observation_result(o2, pos)]]]

efficiency(γ:trace)

In trace γ a solution is found within 3 weighings. Formalisation:
reasoning_successfulness(γ)∧
∃ t1,t2,t3:time ∃ w1,w2,w3:weighing
    [state(γ, t1) |= to_be_performed(w1) ∧ state(γ, t2) |= to_be_performed(w2) ∧
    state(γ, t3) |= to_be_performed(w3) ∧ t1<t2<t3 ∧
    ([[t4:time (w4:weighing
        state((, t4) |= to_be_performed(w4) (t4 (t1 (t4 (t2 (t4 (t3]]

A summary of the results of the evaluation of the example strategies introduced in Section 4 can be found in Table 2. The properties are on the vertical axis, whereas three different categories of traces are on the horizontal axis. The cells indicate the percentages of generated traces for which a particular property holds. As can be seen in this table, the experiments in which all agents use the non-repetitive calculation strategy (C-a) of Section 4 were always successful (100%). Moreover, in these traces no repetition of weighings occurs, and the reasoning continues until the solution is known. As could be expected, not all of these traces (66.7%) satisfy the property strong_new_information. The reason for this is that these agents do not care whether they always derive new information, as long as there is no repetition of weighings. As a result, these traces do not always satisfy the property efficiency either. However, remember that the efficiency of the process is not considered as a measure of successful cooperation. On the other hand, the traces where all agents use the information-eager strategy (C-b) as given in Section 4 always derive new information. Of course, these traces are still not always efficient. Furthermore, these traces always satisfy the properties reasoning_successfulness, no_repetition, and reasoning_continuation.

Table 2. Results of the automated checks - percentage of traces for which the property holds

	all agents C-a	all agents C-b	some C-a, some C-b
reasoning successfulness	100	100	74.6
no repetition	100	100	78.8
reasoning continuation	100	100	95.8
strong new information	66.7	100	70.4
efficiency	50.0	33.3	41.7

The most interesting category is the set of "mixed" traces (where some agents used strategy C-a, and some agents used C-b). Table 2 shows that none of the properties succeeded for all of these traces. To be specific, 25.4% of the mixed traces was not successful. In fact, there were two reasons for failure: in 21.2% of the cases the same weighing was repeated forever (i.e., the property no_repetition failed), in 4.2% of the cases the reasoning stopped because an agent could not derive an action at all (i.e., the property reasoning_continuation failed). Closer examination of the unsuccessful traces led to the conclusion that the agent causing the failure was always of type C-b. In addition, the reason of failure had always to do with the agent's assumption that the other agents were also of type C-b. Based on this assumption, a strict information-eager agent can only deal with those situations where it is still possible to derive new information. In case a strict information-eager agent encounters another situation, it can show unpredictable behaviour (e.g., leading to repetition of weighings, or to termination of the reasoning).

Based on the above, it may be concluded that an agent using the non-repetitive strategy of Section 4.1 can successfully cooperate with other agents that use this strategy (although they do not always derive new information) and with agents that use the information-eager strategy of Section 4.2. On the contrary, agents using the information-eager strategy can cooperate with other agents of this strategy, but not always with agents of the non-repetitive strategy. This confirms the predictions about robustness made in Section 2.2. This is an important finding, because it has consequences for the requirements that may be defined when using the problem for educational purposes. For example, when students implement an agent of type C-b, it will not always have to be successful when cooperating with an agent of type C-a.

6   Educational Results

Six groups of each three 3rd year Bachelor students in Artificial Intelligence were given the assignment to implement the distributed weighing problem within 4 weeks time. They were each provided with an implemented external world and had to design and implement the agents representing the balls, including their strategies. The assignment required that their agent should be of type C (i.e., either C-a, C-b or C-c).

The solutions of the groups were tested in different settings, and evaluated using the properties described in Section 5. First the solutions were tested when all agents in the system used the same solution strategy (i.e., implemented by the same group). In this test the systems of three of the six groups only solved the problem in some settings (i.e., not for all possibilities of deviation). This indicates that they must have made some mistake, since it follows from Table 1 that agents should always be robust against agents using the same strategy. The other three groups succeeded in all settings. The second test consisted of using agents designed by different groups in one multi-agent system. Here, again in some cases no solution was found. In a subset of these cases this was to be expected. For example, when a C-b agent tried to cooperate with a C-a agent (see again Table 1). However, there were also some failures in cases where agents of the same type tried to cooperate. The most common types of failure in these cases were: (1) Derivation of multiple actions (e.g., an agent trying to jump on both scales at the same time); (2) No derivation of an action at all. The experiments were shown to all groups in a joint session. The students found it difficult to believe that the others would not follow the same line of reasoning as they did. After letting them explain to one another what kind of strategy they incorporated into their agent, the students understood that the assumptions they had made regarding the strategy of other agents were too strong. This gave them an important insight into the difficulties accompanying cooperation without communications.

Besides evaluating the performance of the strategies, students were also graded for the documentation they had written regarding their agent design and strategy. A standard evaluation form has been developed for this purpose, which comprises elements such as analysis, conceptual design, detailed design and rationale.

7   Discussion and Conclusion

The distributed weighing problem introduced in this paper has been designed with the goal of creating a cooperation problem without communication that is scalable, that is relatively easy with respect to meta-reasoning required of the agents, and for which it is easy to create a simulated environment.

Other (educational) problems from the field of logic (e.g., the muddy children problem [8]) and from the field of distributed problem solving (e.g., the mutual exclusion problem [6]) do not have all these advantages. The muddy children problem is scalable, and simulating the environment is easy, but the problem is heavy in terms of reasoning. The mutual exclusion problem, on the contrary, is a too easy in terms of reasoning. In the mutual exclusion problem, the parties involved do not have to reason at all about the consequences of their actions. The distributed weighing problem offers a nice alternative, since it requires a bit of reasoning about consequences of actions. However, explicit meta-reasoning (see for example [4]) is unnecessary, because of the assumption that all agents will aim for non-repetitive weighings, and the allowance of suboptimal solutions. Under these circumstances the problem can be solved by agents that operate according to the following: "my move aims for non-repetitive weighings, and I assume other agents do the same".

An example solution to the problem was implemented in an agent-based framework, and rigorously tested for two example strategies of levels believed suitable for educational purposes. The two strategies were discussed and compared. Moreover, a methodology was presented to evaluate the performance of strategies, based on formal validation of properties. Using this methodology, the example strategies put forward were formally validated with respect to a number of desired properties.

The educational use of the problem was promising. The students found the problem interesting and challenging, and were confronted with their own faulty assumptions on other students' reasoning. To be able to design correct strategies for the problem, it turned out to be essential to make adequate assumptions about other agents, and to maintain some model of future possibilities. Therefore, the distributed weighing problem showed to be an appropriate problem for the education of cooperation without communication.

References

1. Bavelas, A. The five squares problem - An instructional aid in group cooperation. *Studies in Personnel Psychology*, 5, 29-38.
2. Bosse, T., Jonker, C.M., Meij, L., van der, and Treur, J. LEADSTO: a Language and Environment for Analysis of Dynamics by SimulaTiOn. *Proc. of the Third German Conference on Multi-Agent System Technologies, MATES 2005*. Lecture Notes in AI, Springer Verlag, 2005 (this volume).
3. Brazier, F.M.T., Jonker, C.M., and Treur, J., Principles of Component-Based Design of Intelligent Agents. *Data and Knowledge Engineering*, vol. 41, 2002, pp. 1-28.
4. Corkill, D., Lesser, V., The use of meta-level control for coordination in a distributed problem solving network. In *Proceedings of the Eighth International Joint Conference on Artificial Intelligence*, Karlsruhe, Germany, August 1983, pp. 748 – 756.
5. Dignum, F., Agent Communication and Cooperative Information Agents. In M. Klusch and L. Kerschberg (eds.) *Cooperative Information Agents IV - The Future of Information Agents in Cyberspace (LNCS-1860)*, Springer-Verlag, 2000, pages 191-207.

6. Dijkstra, E.W. Co-operating Sequential Processes. In: Programming Languages, Genuys, F. (Ed), London, Academic Press, 1965.
7. Doran, J.E., Franklin, S., Jennings, N.R., Norman, T.J., On Cooperation in Multi-Agent Systems, *The Knowledge Engineering Review*, 1997 (3), pp. 309-314.
8. Fagin, R., Halpern, J.Y., Moses, Y., and Vardi, M.Y. *Reasoning About Knowledge*. The MIT Press: Cambridge, MA, 1995.
9. Genesereth, M.R., Ginsberg, M.L., and Rosenschein, J.S., Cooperation Without Communication, *The National Conf. on AI*, Philadelphia, PA., August 1986, pp. 51-57.
10. Goodstein, R.L., Find the penny, *Mathematical Gazette*, December 1945, pp. 227-229.
11. Grossman, H.D., The Twelve-Coin Problem, *Scripta Mathematica*, vol. 11, December 1945, pp. 360-363.
12. Jonker, C.M., Treur, J., and Wijngaards, W.C.A., A Temporal Modelling Environment for Internally Grounded Beliefs, Desires and Intentions. *Cognitive Systems Research Journal*, vol. 4(3), 2003, pp. 191-210.
13. Rosenschein, J., Genesereth, M. Deals among rational agents. In *Proc. of the Ninth Int. Joint Conference on Artificial Intelligence*, LA, California, August 1985, pp. 91-99.
14. Schut M.C., Kentrop M., Leenaarts M., Melis M., and Miller I., APPROACH: Decentralised Rotation Planning for Container Barges. In: Lopez de Mataras R. and Saitta L., editors, *Proceedings of the Sixteenth European Conference on Artificial Intelligence (ECAI 2004)*, IOS Press, 2004, pp. 755-759.

An Adaptive Reputation Model for VOs

Arturo Avila-Rosas

Instituto Mexicano del Petróleo,
Eje Central 152, México DF, CP 07730, México
aavilar@imp.mx

Abstract. Because Virtual Organisations (VOs) essentially involve co-operating two or more organisations or agents to pursue a common objective, satisfactory cooperation is vital to their success. However, before an agent made the decision to go ahead with the VO, it needs to be *confident* that the rest of the potential partners will be act cooperatively. We show that reputation is a basic ingredient in the formation of VOs. Reputation is computed using an adaptive algorithm, so agents can learn and adapt their reputation models of their partners according to their recent behaviour. Our approach is especially powerful if the agent participates in a VO in which the members can change their behaviour to exploit their partners. The reputation model presented in this paper deals with the questions of deception and fraud that have been ignored in current models of VO formation.

1 Introduction

Recently, a large number of new collaborative, networked organisations have emerged, having as motivation the explosive progress in computer networks and communication systems, but also as a reaction to market pressures that demand customised, high quality products and services at lower costs and, at the same time, shorter production and marketing times. Promising greater flexibility, resource optimisation and responsiveness in *competitive open environments*, VOs are an example of this trend that has pervaded not only business domains but other areas such as e-science. The concept of a VO has been used to describe the aggregation of autonomous and independent organisations connected through a network and brought together to deliver a product or service in response to a customer need [3]. What distinguishes VOs from other forms of organisation is the full mutual dependence of their members to achieve their goal and therefore the need for cooperation. However, open environments in which VOs are embedded involve organisations and individuals that do not necessarily share the same objectives and interests that they might not know in advance, and where they might not trust each other, but should work together and help each other to achieve a common goal. One of the key omissions in the computational representation of VOs relates to the need to take into account more subjective facets like the *reputation* of the individuals, which helps to cope with heterogeneity, autonomy and diversity of interests among members. We observe that current

T. Eymann et al. (Eds.): MATES 2005, LNAI 3550, pp. 204–209, 2005.

solutions underestimate the possibility of swindle in VOs. A common flaw is assuming that the partners selected are fully competent and honest. Since partners represent organisations or individuals who want to maximise their utilities by joining a VO, they have a strong incentive to misrepresent the value of their contributions and enjoy more benefits of cooperative associations [1]. Further, partners are selected in relation to the abilities they claim to have, but it is possible that they do not have such abilities. However, due to lack of information about past interactions, it is difficult to detect and control these situations. This paper considers the introduction of reputation into VOs, by providing a reputation model based on the adaptive evaluation of direct experiences to identify trustworthy individuals to join VO.

The remainder of this paper is organised as follows. The requirement for reputation systems for VOs are discussed in Section 2. In Section 3 we present our reputation model for VOs which is based on reinforcement learning techniques. Section 4 reviews related work, and Section 5 present our conclusions.

2 Requirements

The objective of this section is to delineate the requirements for building a reputation system in order to serve as a decision-making variable in the selection of partners, promote cooperation, produce trust and induce *good* behaviour in the members of a VO.

1. *Distributed reputation management.* Because VOs do not depend on the presence of any centrally trusted authority, there is a need for distributed mechanisms that enable the partners in a VO to collect, store, manage and disseminate reputation in a personalised fashion.
2. *Dynamism.* Due to limitations in time and intense task pressures, partners in a VO should be able to quickly use a reduced number of interactions to estimate the reputation of a partner and; at the same time, take partner selection decisions without having a significant impact, in terms of time consumption, on the formation of a VO.
3. *Adaptability.* Reputation must be updated dynamically to adapt the values of reputation towards true quality of service. This suggests that the updating process should be a *learning* process about another's true abilities, that captures the observed performance through the reputation of the partner. This leads to discarding updating methods that diminish the impact of strategic changes in partner behaviour that intend to milk *high* values of reputation by intentionally deteriorating the provision of the service.
4. *Predictability.* Reputation must provide information to predict the future performance of a partner and eventually the risk involved of interacting with it. That is, based on a partner's previous performance, reputation must provide an indication of its future performance and willingness to accomplish a task.

3   Direct Reputation Model

In this section we introduce our model of reputation, which is based upon SPO-RAS. SPORAS was chosen because some of its design guidelines are consistent with our specific requirements. Particularly, since SPORAS is an adaptive reputation model that updates the reputation values after each interaction, removing the effects of *obsolete* data in some manner, it is ideal for environments where the behaviour of VO members is changing through the time because the relationships among them are themselves changing as a function of their interests and goals. We start by defining mathematically the concepts of reputation and impressions. Next we describe the methods used in our model for updating reputation.

3.1   Reputation

We define the reputation of an agent as *a perception regarding its intention and competences, which is held by other agents through the formation and dissemination of subjective evaluations based on experiences and observations of past actions.* Here, these evaluations are called *impressions*. From the definition, the observed behaviour of others is collected through: (i) direct experiences, with interaction histories serving as a strong evidence for estimating someone reputation or (ii) via the testimony of others, known as *recommenders*. On the basis of the source of reputation, two concepts of reputation may be derived, namely *direct reputation* and *social reputation*. The concept of social reputation is beyond the scope of this paper.

3.2   Direct Reputation

Direct reputation (DR) is defined as the weighted average evaluation that an agent makes of another's competence, and gives the extent to which the target is *good* or *bad* with respect to a given behaviour or action. Direct reputation is context-dependent so that an agent is reputed according to the service provided. In our algorithm we adopt the ideas of Shapiro [5], then direct reputation is computed as the average of *impressions* received within the most recent time window,

$$W = [t - \epsilon, t],\qquad(1)$$

where ϵ defines a time interval that limits the set of interactions and in which impressions are used to compute a direct reputation value. Impressions are weighted from 0 to 1 to indicate the notion of importance of an impression in relation to others for calculating reputation. The direct reputation values vary in the range of $[0,1]$ and are used only to represent comparative values in this continuous space from bad reputation (values near 0) to good reputation (values near 1). The direct reputation of i in the perspective of j in context k is represented as:

$$DR_{ij}^k \in [0,1].$$

3.3   Impression

We define an impression as an evaluative opinion that is formed by any entity (individual, organisation, etc.) based on a discrete experience with another partner, coupled with the partner's performance. An impression is related with a dimension that describes just one of the qualities of the service as required by agent j. Mathematically, the impression appear as follows,

$$imp_{ij}^d \in [0,1],$$

$$Q_{ij} = \{d \in k \,|\, k \ is \ a \ context\}, \tag{2}$$

where i is the service provider whose interaction with the service consumer j left in it the strong impression imp in relation to dimension d, and Q_{ij} is the set of dimensions for evaluating a service provider in context k. The numbers used for impressions are merely reference values for making comparisons, each consumer establishes a personal threshold of *acceptable* values for the dimension d evaluated.

3.4   Updating Direct Reputation

Each agent updates its reputation value of a service provider every time it receives impressions from either direct (immediate or observed interactions) or indirect experiences. In order to update the reputation values (after receiving t rated experiences or impressions) we use the following reinforcement learning based action update rules:

$$DR_t = DR_{t-1} + \alpha \cdot [imp_t - DR_{t-1}]. \tag{3}$$

Reputation, in Eq.(3), can be interpreted as the aggregation of the previous value of reputation plus a factor that strengthens or weakens that value. This factor indicates the proximity of the recent impression to the past reputation, and shows of how well the previous reputation predicts the latest given impression. The update rule in Eq.(3) is a linear function which is required in an open environment where the number of prior interactions may be reduced, and reputation cannot be updated in the long term through a non-linear function because an agent could cheat on many occasions before the reputation is updated. Now, if α is near 1 then all the previous history will be forgotten, otherwise, if α is near 0 then the previous history will be preserved.

The factor α is also known as a learning rate, and is an indicator of how long past experiences will last in the memory of the system. For our purposes, we consider α as a function $\alpha(DR_{t-1}, imp_t)$ with the following properties that are based on the ideas of Carbo et al. [2]:

- The function $\alpha(DR_{t-1}, imp_t)$ determines how fast the reputation value changes after an experience and how this affects the memory of the system. This depends on the accuracy of the predictions suggested by the *impressions* received; that is, how much similarity exists between the expectation formed by the previous reputation values and the last rating.

- Similarity will be estimated through a similarity function $\beta(DR_{t-1}, imp_t) \in (0,1)$:

$$\beta(DR_{t-1}, imp_t) = 1 - e^{-10 \cdot ABS(E-imp)}, \tag{4}$$

where E is the estimated rating based on the past reputation and rating:

$$E = \frac{DR_{t-1} + imp_{t-1}}{2}. \tag{5}$$

- Finally, the function $\alpha(DR_{t-1}, imp)$ is updated as follows:

$$\alpha(DR_t, imp) = \frac{\alpha(DR_{t-1}, imp) + \beta(DR_{t-1}, imp)}{2}. \tag{6}$$

4   Related Work

Zacharia and Maes in [6] present SPORAS, which is a *centralised* reputation system that establishes reputation for users in an on-line community (for example chat rooms, auctions or newsletters groups), based on the aggregation of *rates* given by users after each transaction. Reputation in SPORAS aims to predict future performance of the users. In order to make accurate predictions using a small computational space, a recursive and adaptive algorithm for updating reputation is used. This aggregation method then allows newer rates to count more than older ones. Because SPORAS is a centralised reputation system, it is not viable for VOs where partners need personalised reputation values calculated from assembled rates of those they trust already rather than those they do not know. Moreover, mediators are designed and operated by parties whose interests may sometimes diverge from those of the electronic community. Although the assumption made in SPORAS to make reputation values dependent on the reputation of the entity who is providing a feedback is correct, it mixes two different dimensions of reputation. While a user can be reputed as completely unable to cheat on deals, nonetheless that same user may be a bad evaluator of other users. That is, being an excellent service provider does not mean being an honest evaluator.

REGRET is a reputation system developed by Sabater and Sierra [4] that adopts a sociological approach for computing reputation in societies of agents trading well defined products inside an e-commerce environment. Although RE-GRET provides a very simple method for aggregating rates (or *impressions* that are the result of evaluating direct interactions) based on the weighted sum of the impressions (more relevance is given to the recent ones), its major contribution is the vision of reputation through of three dimensions. These dimensions are called the *individual dimension*, *social dimension* and *ontological dimension*. As discussed earlier, VOs require to a certain extent that the reputation of a partner is assessed in a *reactive* form to detect possible opportunistic behaviour. However, REGRET's main idea consists of emphasising the freshness of information. Computations in REGRET give a *fixed* high relevance to recent rates over older ones according to a time dependent function, and, moreover the rates are aggregated in a way that can be sensitive to noise since they are simply summed.

5 Conclusions and Future Work

We have provided a critical overview of the state of the art in the field of VOs and reputation. We argue that subjective aspects of partners such as their *competences* and *trustworthiness* should be taken into account in partner selection decisions, since these aspects ultimately influence cooperation between partners. Moreover, we assert that reputation plays an important role in VOs when members decide who to interact with and when to interact, by providing information about the past behaviour of potential partners, their abilities and reliability. In particular, we assert the importance of reputation not only in the formation process of VO but in the operation process.

Additionally, we discussed the requirements for building reputation systems that pursue three basic objectives in the formation and operation of VOs: (1) they provide useful information about potential partners for selecting the most *appropriate*, and eventually enable the formation of VOs; (2) they foster trust among the partners of the VO by revealing each partner's capabilities and predicting its future behaviour; and (3) they offer a means for enhancing cooperation by detecting and deterring deceptive behaviour through imposing *collective sanctions* on defectors.

Although this paper has answered how reputation is relevant to recognise cooperative partners through direct interactions, it opens up more research opportunities and questions that are unanswered. Moreover, there are other issues that were not faced in this paper, due to the bounds imposed on the research, and still need to be addressed.

References

1. S. Braynov and T. Sandholm. Trust revelation in multiagent interaction. In *Proceedings of CHI'02 Workshop on Philosophy and design of Socially Adept Technologies*, pages 57–60, Minneapolis, USA, 2002.
2. J. Carbo, J. Molina, and J. Davila. Trust management through fuzzy reputation. *International Journal of Cooperative Information Systems*, 12(1):135–155, 2003.
3. E. Oliveira and A. Rocha. Agents advanced features for negotiation in electronic commerce and virtual organisations formation processes. In *Agent Mediated Electronic Commerce, the European AgentLink Perspective*, volume 1991 of *Lectures Notes in Artificial Intelligence*, pages 77–96, 2000.
4. J. Sabater and C. Sierra. Reputation and social network analysis in multi-agent systems. In *Proceedings of the First International Joint Conference on AAMAS*, pages 475–482, Bologna, Italy, 2002.
5. Carl Shapiro. Consumer information, product quality, and seller reputation. *The Bell Journal of Economics*, 13:20–35, 1982.
6. G. Zacharia and P. Maes. Trust management through reputation mechanisms. *Applied Artificial Intelligence*, 14(8):881–907, 2000.

Realising Reusable Agent Behaviours with ALPHA

Rem Collier[1], Robert Ross[2], and Gregory M.P. O'Hare[1]

[1] Practice & Research in Intelligent Systems & Media (PRISM) Laboratory,
Department of Computer Science, University College Dublin (UCD),
Belfield, Dublin 4, Ireland
{rem.collier, gregory.ohare}@ucd.ie
[2] Department of Computer Science,
University of Bremen, Germany
robertr@tzi.de

Abstract. This paper describes how roles have been used to engender reuse within the ALPHA agent programming language.

1 Introduction

In many programming paradigms, how to support the reuse of program code has long been considered a central issue. This is not the case for Agent-Oriented Programming (AOP) languages, where researchers are still focusing on answering the question: *what are the most appropriate features for an agent programming language?* However, with the emergence of more mature languages, such as 3APL [4] and Nuin [6], there is a growing need to investigate how reuse might be supported. This issue was highlighted with respect to the Zeus [9] agent platform, where the lack of support for reuse was a significant problem for the commercial developers who used earlier versions of the tool [7].

One approach to reuse is through the concept of a *role*. Roles are widely recognized as a key concept in the analysis and design of multi-agent systems [1, 14] and are often viewed as a valuable level of abstraction, which can be used to define common behaviours that may be reused in the design of many different types of agent. This has led some researchers to argue that there is a need for a new class of *Role-Oriented Programming Environment* [10]. However, a recent survey of role-based approaches for agent development [2], found that the notion of a role is less well established with respect to the implementation of agents. Two exceptions to this are [7] which describes a role-based approach to the fabrication of Zeus agents, and *Role EP* [13], which uses roles to support the programming of travelling/collaboration tasks for mobile agents.

In terms of AOP, [5] presents a role-based extension to the pre-existing 3APL programming language [4]. Underpinning this extension is a formal model of a role that combines information received, objectives, and rules that define conditional norms and obligations. This model is used first to motivate the design of a role-playing agent, whose structure is formally specified, and then to drive the design of a revised agent interpreter. However their work does not consider how this model might be used to engender reuse within the language.

T. Eymann et al. (Eds.): MATES 2005, LNAI 3550, pp. 210–215, 2005.
© Springer-Verlag Berlin Heidelberg 2005

This paper builds on the work presented in [5] by discussing the role-based approach to reuse that has been engendered in the ALPHA programming language [12], which sits at the heart of the Agent Factory framework [3]. Specifically, we explore how OOP reuse mechanisms such as inheritance, composition, and aggregation can be applied to AOP. To achieve this, we model an agent as a set of role templates that can be instantiated as appropriate. This approach is based on practical experience gained from the use of the ALPHA programming language in the development of a number of real world application domains [11] [8].

2   ALPHA - A Language for Programming Hybrid Agents

ALPHA [12] is an agent programming language that supports the development of agents that use a mental state architecture to reason about how best to act. Due to space constraints, only a brief summary of ALPHA is presented here. For a detailed overview of the formal model that underpins the language, see [3].

ALPHA supports the fabrication of agents whose mental state is comprised of *beliefs*, *goals*, and *commitments*. Beliefs describe - possibly incorrectly - the state of the environment in which the agent is situated, goals describe future states of the environment that the agent would like to bring about, and commitments describe the activity that the agent is committed to realising. The behaviour of the agent is realised primarily through a purpose-built execution algorithm that is centred about the notion of *commitment management* [3].

Within ALPHA, commitments are viewed as the mental equivalent of a contract. As such, they define a course of action/activity that the agent has agreed to, when it must realise that activity, to whom the commitment was made, and finally, what conditions, if any, would lead to it not having to fulfil the commitment. Commitment management is then a meta-level process that ALPHA agents employ to manipulate their commitments based upon some underlying strategy known as a *commitment management strategy*. This strategy specifies a set of sub-strategies that define how an agent adopts, refines, and realises its commitments.

The principal sub-strategy that underpins the behaviour of ALPHA agents is commitment adoption. Commitments are adopted either as a result of a decision to realise some activity, or through the refinement of an existing commitment. The former type of commitment is known as a *primary commitment* and the latter as a *secondary commitment*. The adoption of a primary commitment occurs as a result of one of two processes: (1) in response to a decision to attempt to achieve a goal using a plan of action, or (2) as a result of the triggering of a *commitment rule*. Commitment rules define situations (a conjunction of positive and negative belief atoms) in which the agent should adopt a primary commitment.

A key feature of ALPHA, which differentiates it from other agent programming languages, is the inclusion within the language of a set of programming constructs that allow the developer to explicitly specify how each agent can interact with its environment. Specifically, ALPHA includes a PERCEPTOR and an ACTUATOR construct, which specify how the agent senses and effects its environment respectively. These constructs associate Java classes that implement the sensors and effectors of an agent with the behaviour of that agent which is specified in ALPHA.

The set of actuators and perceptors that are specified for a given agent is known as the *embodiment configuration* of that agent.

3 Supporting Roles in ALPHA

As is described in the previous section, an ALPHA agent program traditionally takes the form of a set of commitment rules together with an initial mental state and an embodiment configuration. The ability to compose new ALPHA agent programs from pre-existing programs that are stored in different physical files, known as *role files*, was previously supported via the USE_ROLE construct. The initial motivation for the inclusion of this construct was to support the decomposition of ALPHA agent programs into their constituent roles, facilitating the reuse of those roles at compile time. However, this approach, whilst flexible, has proven to be inadequate for a number of reasons: (1) the concept of a role only exists up to compile time; hence the agent is not aware, at run-time, of the role(s) that it is playing; (2) the relationship that exists between the different roles is not clear - it can be viewed as either a weak form of inheritance or as composition depending on the nature of the underlying code; and (3) lack of support for the templatisation of the roles makes the specification generic role implementations more difficult.

Perhaps the main cause underlying the inadequacy of this approach is that the USE_ROLE construct is, in essence, the equivalent of the #include construct of C. Such a construct is insufficient to provide support for the composition, extension, and templatisation of roles. As a result, the construct has since been re-cast as an IMPORT construct, and ALPHA has been re-engineered to provide explicit support for roles through the inclusion of a *ROLE construct*.

3.1 Role Templates

The primary construct for defining behaviours in ALPHA is the commitment rule. Traditionally, these rules were located in the body of an agent program. However, in our new framework, behaviours are defined via roles. To facilitate this, we have defined a *ROLE construct*. This construct combines a unique *role identifier*, a set of commitment rules that define the behaviour that underpins the role and a set *trigger conditions* that cause the activation of the role. The identifier provides a unique way of referring to a role, and takes the form of a first-order structure whose arguments are variables; commitments rules take the same form as before, with the exception that their scope is now restricted to the role in which they are defined; and finally, the trigger conditions outline situations in which the role should be activated. Allowing the identifier to take variable arguments is the mechanism by which the role is templatised.

The instantiation of a role template is achieved through the generation of a set of variable bindings that map the arguments of the identifier to constants. This may occur in one of two ways: (1) via the satisfaction of a trigger condition, or (2) via the `activate(?role)` action. In the former case, the variable bindings are generated from the trigger condition (that is, each argument of the identifier must occur within each trigger condition). Conversely, in the latter case, the relevant variables must occur within the action definition. We illustrate the ROLE construct through an example that defines a Subscriber facilitator role:

```
ROLE Subscriber(?agent, ?item) {
  TRIGGER BELIEF(fipaMessage(request, sender(?name, ?addr), subscribe(?item)));

  BELIEF(fipaMessage(inform, ?sender, ?item)) =>
  COMMIT(Self, Now, BELIEF(true), inform(?agent, ?item));

  BELIEF(fipaMessage(inform, sender(?agt, ?addr), cancelSubscription(?item))) =>
  COMMIT(Self, Now, BELIEF(true), deactivate(Subscriber(?agt, ?item)));
}
```

The activation of this role can occur either as the result of a message from another agent or via the `activate(…)` action. For example, an agent that had enacted the Subscriber role was to perform the action `activate(Subscriber(Rem, fuelLevel(?level))`, then the Subscriber role would be instantiated and activated using the following variable binding `{?agent/Rem, ?item/fuelLevel(?level) }`. This would result in all occurrences of the variable `?agent` in the commitment rules associated with the role being replaced by `Rem` and all the occurrences of `?item` being replaced by `fuelLevel(?level)`. Also, the instance will be assigned the identifier `Subscriber(Rem, fuelLevel(?level))`. This differentiates role templates from roles and enforces the condition that each role instance must have a unique identifier.

3.2 Inheritance of Roles

In OOP, inheritance refers to the extension of an existing class to include additional, or polymorph existing, behaviour/properties. In the context of AOP, the provision of such a technique would allow the developer to identify common behaviours and to reuse those behaviours by extracting them into an abstract role and then reusing that abstract role in the definition of concrete roles. In ALPHA, we consider only the inclusion of additional behaviours/properties. When an existing role is extended, the developer may specify additional commitment rules and trigger conditions in the sub-role. Additionally, the developer may include additional variables in the identifier of the sub-role. Whenever an instance of the sub-role is activated, the variable binding is applied to both the sub-role and all parent roles.

Use of the extension mechanism is realised through the optional EXTENDS keyword as is shown in the example below which illustrates how a Senior Lecturer role can be defined in terms of a Lecturer role:

```
ROLE SeniorLecturer(?subjects, ?admin) EXTENDS Lecturer(?subjects) {
  ... role body defined here ...
}
ROLE Lecturer(?subjects) {
  .. role body defined here ...
}
```

3.3 Composition of Roles

From an OOP perspective, composition and aggregation are similar techniques for building a composite object out of a number of other objects. The primary difference between these techniques arises from the lifetime of the component objects. With composition, the component objects cannot exist without the composite object. That is, if object A is composed from object B and C, then object A must be created before objects B and C, while objects B and C must be destroyed before A can be destroyed. Conversely, with aggregation, the component objects can exist before the aggregated object is created. In ALPHA, we consider only composition of roles, and support this through the inclusion of a *USES* construct. This construct is used within the body of a role to specify any component roles that are used by that role. For example, consider the estate agent role discussed above. The segment of code below illustrates how this role can be represented in ALPHA:

```
ROLE EstateAgent(?area) {
  USES Valuer, Auctioneer, Salesman;
  ... role body defined here ...
}
```

This code specifies that that an Estate Agent role uses three component roles: a Valuer role, an Auctioneer role, and a Salesman role. The main purpose of the construct is to ensure, at run-time, that the agent has the necessary component roles required to realise the composite role.

4   Discussion

This paper presents a framework for reuse in AOP languages that is founded on the notion of a role. Specifically, this framework presents a model of agents whose behaviour is specified as a set of roles that can be dynamically activated and deactivated at run-time. In addition, we argue that the most appropriate approach to representing the roles that an agent can play is through the use of role templates. These templates are, in essence, parameterised definitions of the expected behaviours that an agent playing that role should realise. Further, we have motivated the inclusion of two reuse mechanisms, namely composition and inheritance. These mechanisms enable developers to easily construct new roles that are based upon pre-existing roles.

A key difference between the approach presented here, and that presented in [5] arises from their specification, which seems to limit an agent to only one active role at a time. Once activated, this role exclusively drives the agents subsequent behaviour, and will continue to do so until it is deactivated and another role is activated. This is in contrast with the more widely accepted view that an agent will potentially have (1) many activated roles at any given instant in time [14], and (2) some of those activated roles may be different instantiations of the same role.

This work introduces the first AOP language that implements support for reuse through a combination of role templates and OOP inspired reuse mechanisms such as inheritance and composition. It is out view that the inclusion of such support is vital if AOP languages are to become a viable option for the development of agent-oriented applications.

References

[1]   B. Bauer, J. P. Muller, and J Odell. *Agent uml: A formalism for specifying multiagent interaction.* In Paolo Ciancarini and Michael Wooldridge, editors, *Agent-Oriented Software Engineering.* Springer Verlag, 2001.

[2] G. Cabri, L. Ferrari, L. Leonardi, F. Zambonelli, *Role-based Approaches for Agent Development*, in Proceedings of the 3rd International Joint Conference on Autonomous Agents and Multi-Agent Systems (AAMAS-04) , NY, 2004

[3] R. W. Collier. *Agent Factory: A Framework for the Engineering of Agent-Oriented Applications*. PhD Thesis, Dept. of Computer Science, Univ. College Dublin, 2001.

[4] M. Dastani, B. van Riensdijk, F. Dignum, and J-J Meyer. *A programming language for cognitive agents: Goal directed 3apl*. In Proc. of AAMAS2003, Melbourne, 2003.

[5] M. Dastani, M. Birna van Riems-dijk, J. Hulstijn, F. Dignum, and J. Ch. Meyer. *Enacting and deacting roles in agent programming*, In Proceedings of the 2nd International Workshop on Programming Multi-Agent Systems *PROMAS2004*), 2004.

[6] I. Dickinson and M. Wooldridge. *Towards practical reasoning agents for the semantic web,* In 2nd Int. Joint Conf. on Autonomous Agents and Multi-Agent Systems (AAMAS-03), Melbourne, Australia, 2003.

[7] A. Karageorgos, S. Thompson and N. Mehandjiev, *Specifying Reuse Concerns in Agent System Design Using a Role Algebra.* In: Agent Technologies, Infrastructures, Tools, and Applications for e-Services. ecture Notes in Artificial Intelligence LNAI, 2592. Springer-Verlag.

[8] C. Muldoon, G.M.P. O'Hare, D. Phelan, R. Strahan, R. Collier, *ACCESS: An Agent Architecture for Ubiquitous Service Delivery*, Proc 7th Int'l Workshop on Cooperative Information Agents (CIA2003), Helsinki, 2003.

[9] H. Nwana, D. Ndumu, L. Lee, and J. Collis. *Zeus: A toolkit for building distributed multi-agent systems*. Applied Artificial Intelligence Journal, 13(1):129–186, 1999.

[10] J. Odell, H. Van Dyke Parunack, S. Brueckner, and J. Sauter. *Temporal aspects of dynamic role assignment*, in Proceedings of the 4th International Workshop on Agent-Oriented Software Engineering (AOSE2003), 2003.

[11] G. M. P. O'Hare and M. J. O'Grady, *Gulliver's Genie: A Multi-Agent System for Ubiquitous and Intelligent Content Delivery*, In Press, Computer Communications, Elsevier Press, 2003.

[12] R. Ross, R. Collier, and G. O'Hare. *Af-apl: Bridging principles & practices in agent oriented languages*, in Proc. 2nd International Workshop on Programming Multiagent Systems Languages and tools (PROMAS2004), New York, USA, 2004.

[13] N. Ubayashi and T. Tamai, *RoleEP: role based evolutionary programming for cooperative mobile agent applications,* in the International Symposium on Principles of Software Evolution, Kanazawa, Japan, November 2000.

[14] M. Wooldridge, N. R. Jennings, and D. Kinny, *The gaia methodology for agent-oriented analysis and design*, Autonomous Agents and Multi-Agent Systems, 3(3):285–312, 2000.

Multi-agent System Specification Using TCOZ

Tim Miller and Peter McBurney*

Department of Computer Science,
The University of Liverpool, Liverpool, L69 7ZF, UK
{tim, peter}@csc.liv.ac.uk

Abstract. TCOZ is a specification language that combines the strengths of Object-Z and Timed CSP with the goal of specifying distributed systems containing objects that act independently and concurrently. Such goals are similar to the goals of the autonomous agent paradigm, in which agents are entities in an environment that act independently of one another, concurrently, and work proactively to achieve certain goals. This paper discusses the suitability of several TCOZ constructs in specifying multi-agent systems.

1 Introduction

Autonomous agents are software entities that have control, to a greater or lesser extent, over their own execution. With the recent rise of the Internet and of distributed computing systems, the autonomous agent paradigm has become important in designing, understanding and managing complex computer systems.

While much research into formal agent logics and languages is focused on modelling beliefs, desires, intentions, and knowledge of both individual agents and groups of agents, [13] languages for specifying and designing agent systems have received far less attention. In addition, much of the research in this area has focused on logic programming languages for agents, such as AgentSpeak(L) [9], or extending existing graphical languages to include the agent paradigm, such as the Agent UML [1]. Our focus is on the formal specification and verification of entire multi-agent systems and the environment in which they operate, with the aim that these specifications can be used as a starting point for system design. A formal specification of a system provides a precise and unambiguous description of the system's behaviour, and can serve many purposes, for example: providing a starting point for the design and implementation of the system; allowing developers to prove that certain properties hold or certain properties are achieved; and providing a starting point for test case and test sequence generation.

---

* The authors are supported by the *Personalized Information Platform for Health and Life Sciences (PIPS)* Project (EC-FP6-IST-507019) and from the UK EPSRC *Market Based Control of Complex Computational Systems* Project (GR/T10657/01), respectively.

T. Eymann et al. (Eds.): MATES 2005, LNAI 3550, pp. 216–221, 2005.
© Springer-Verlag Berlin Heidelberg 2005

There are examples of agent specification languages that provide good support for specifying agent systems, including the interactions between agents. AgentZ [2] is an agent-oriented extension to Object-Z, which includes concepts such as roles, agents, and environments. The OZS notation [5] is a hybrid of Object-Z and statecharts. Object-Z is used to specify the states and operations of an agent, and statecharts are used to specify the reactive properties of the agents. SLABS [14] is an agent-specific formal specification language that has constructs resembling classes and objects. While all of these languages are useful for modelling the states of agents, little support is provided for asynchronous, concurrent, autonomous behaviour. Concurrent METATEM [4] allows specification of agents using executable temporal logic, but state and composition are not as straightforward to model as the state-based approaches above.

In this paper, we present an existing language called *Timed, Communicating Object-Z* (TCOZ) [7], which is used for modelling real-time, concurrent systems by combining the strength of Object-Z [11], a state-based, object-oriented specification language, with Timed CSP [10], a real-time, concurrent language for modelling processes and their interactions. The goals of TCOZ (providing distributed, timed, concurrent, active objects) are similar to that of the agent paradigm. We discuss some of the constructs available in TCOZ that we believe are useful in specifying multi-agent systems. In an extended version of this paper [8], we evaluate TCOZ as a specification language for multi-agent systems by specifying a small, yet non-trivial example of a multi-agent system for handling resource allocation.

2   TCOZ for Agents

In this section, we present some aspects of the TCOZ language, and discuss why we believe this is suitable for modelling software agents in a multi-agent environment.

2.1   Object-Z and State

Object-Z is an extension of the well-known Z specification language [12]. Among other things, Object-Z extends Z by the addition of a *class paragraph*, which resembles the class construct found in the object-oriented programming paradigm. A class consists of a state, which declares the state variables and their set of possible values, an initial predicate, which constrains the initial state value, and zero or more operations, which define transitions over the state.

Figure 1 shows the specification of a clock class, whose scope is defined by the box named *Clock*. The unnamed box in the class represents the state of class, and contains a variable $time : \mathbb{N}$, representing the current time. The *INIT* schema contains a predicate restricting the initial value of the clock's time to 0. The operation *Tick* increments the time by one, and the operation *SetTime* allows the environment to set the time via the input variable *time?*. Object-Z follows the style of Z by decorating input, output, and post-state variables with ?, !, and ′ respectively.

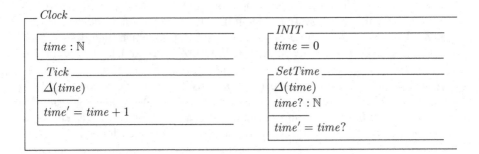

Fig. 1. *Clock* Class in Object-Z

We can create an instance of *Clock* by using a variable declaration $c : Clock$. The commonly used "dot" notation is used to reference the state variables, for example, $c.time$, and to invoke operations, for example, $c.SetTime$. Operation variables can be renamed using the same notation as Z's variable renaming. For example, if we have a variable $newTime$ in scope, we can set the time to the value of $newTime$ like so: $c.SetTime[newTime/time?]$, which will substitute $newTime$ for all occurrences of the name $time?$ in the operation.

These features of Object-Z are suitable for modelling the internal state of agents, such as the perceptions that an agent has of its environment. While it may be non-trivial to model beliefs about the environment, particularly nested beliefs (that is, beliefs about other agents' beliefs), many multi-agent systems, especially containing only software agents, need not model beliefs, and when they do, their beliefs are simple enough that they can be modelled using Object-Z.

2.2 Processes

Timed CSP [10] is an extension of CSP [6]. A specification of a process in CSP contains the set of events in which the process can take part, called the *alphabet* of the process, and the set of possible event traces that the process can perform, including communication between other processes (discussed further in Section 2.4). A specification of a system in CSP is the combination of those processes, which can be either synchronous or asynchronous. Throughout the section, we assume that P and Q are processes, a and b are events, and A is a set of events.

$a \rightarrow P$ is a process that is enabled when a occurs, and then behaves like process P. The environment can choose between two processes using the *external choice operator*: $\square$. Using this, $a \rightarrow P \square b \rightarrow Q$ specifies an event in which either a or b is chosen to occur by the environment, and then behaves as either P or Q respectively. The distributed choice operator allows the choice between an arbitrary number of events: $\square\, a : A \bullet P(a)$ specifies the process in which an environment chooses an event in A to occur, and then behaves as the process $P(a)$.

Internal choice, which allows the process itself to make the choice, can be specified in the same way as external choice, except using the $\sqcap$ and $\prod$ operators respectively.

Two processes can be combined to behave in parallel asynchronously using the $|||$ operator, which specifies that $P ||| Q$ execute concurrently without any synchronisation. A distributed version of the operator is available, used like so: $||| \, a : A \bullet P(a)$.

Processes provide an excellent way to model agents in a multi-agent environment, because they allow agents to have their own thread of control; something that is not possible using a state-based approach such as Object-Z.

2.3   Timing

Timed CSP extends CSP by adding the set $\mathbb{T}$, denoting the set of all moments of time, and timing primitives. The set $\mathbb{T}$ is a subset of the reals, so we can use the Z toolkit's arithmetic operators on time. For example, in the *Clock* class in Figure 1, we can replace all references to $\mathbb{N}$ with $\mathbb{T}$, while still using the arithmetic operator $+$.

TCOZ supports several of the Timed CSP timing primitives, but the only one relevant to this paper is $P \bullet \textsc{WaitUntil}\, t$, which enforces that if P takes less than t units of time to execute, then delay the process until t seconds has passed from the start of P. Other timing primitives include deadlines and events occurring at a particularly time.

This allows us to model timing properties in agents. While this is not so important in most multi-agent systems, it is not difficult to find examples in which timing is important. The case study in the extended technical report version of this paper [8] is such an example.

2.4   Communication Channels

Communication between CSP process is achieved using *channels*. TCOZ allows channels to be declared in the state of an object. If a channel c is declared like so: $c : \textbf{chan}$, then the event $c.v$ is defined as v being sent on channel c. Channels are untyped, and can therefore carry any expression. As with CSP, TCOZ uses the notation $c?v$ to specify that a process receives v on channel c, and $c!v$ to specify that a process sends v on channel c.

Using communication channels in TCOZ enables modelling of communication between agents. The object-oriented paradigm commonly discusses operation invocation as message passing, that is, invoking an operation on an object is defined as passing a message to that object. However, explicit communication channels provides agents with a way to pass messages to agents that are not visible to them, and a way of modelling the way the communication in the system will actually occur.

2.5   Active Objects

TCOZ allows the specification of two types of object: *passive* and *active*. Passive objects are objects that are controlled either by the environment or other objects in the system. Active objects have their own thread of control, and their operations are hidden from all other objects. Dong and Mahony [3] discuss active objects in detail.

Specifying active objects is achieved by declared a operation called MAIN. MAIN operations are non-terminating processes that define the behaviour of objects. For example, our clock example in Figure 1 can be improved such that it updates its own time by the addition of the following MAIN operation:

$$\text{MAIN} == \mu\ C \bullet (\textit{Tick} \bullet \text{WAITUNTIL } 1s) \,\mathring{,}\, C$$

In this definition, we use CSP's μ operator to specify a unique solution within the set of possible traces. The $\mathring{,}$ operator in this definition is sequential composition of operations. So, the behaviour of the clock is to *Tick* once, and then wait until 1 unit of time has passed (*Tick* is constrained to take less than 1 unit of time), and recurse this behaviour. Any objects using this clock need not (cannot!) invoke *Tick* to update the time; any instances of *Clock* will keep time themselves.

Active objects are central to the reason that we have evaluated TCOZ for agents. One of the primary differences between objects and agents is that agents are autonomous. That is, they maintain their own thread of control, and do not necessarily act when asked to perform a task. Active behaviour is a way to operationalise autonomy. It also provides a way for an agent to be *proactive*. That is, it's behaviour is directed by the goals that it wants to achieve. By relying on other agents to send it messages, an agent can never be proactive.

3   Conclusion

In this paper, we discuss the use of TCOZ for modelling multi-agent systems. We believe that TCOZ, which combines the strengths of Object-Z and Timed CSP, provides many of the necessary constructs for specify multi-agent software systems, both at a level of individual agent specifications, and at a higher level of specifying interactions and cooperation between agents. These constructs include: state, which allows agents to record their aims and their perceptions of their environment; process primitives, which allow us to specify agents as having independent threads of control; communication channels, which allow us to specify the interactions between agents at a message passing level; and active objects, which allow us to specify agents as entities that are active and autonomous, and unable to be controlled by the environment in which they reside.

In the extended technical report version of this paper [8], we evaluate TCOZ by specifying a non-trivial example of a multi-agent system being used to allocate resources. While TCOZ may not provide all of the necessary constructs to specify agents systems, it is clear that the goals of TCOZ (providing distributed, timed, concurrent, active objects) are similar to those of the agent paradigm.

3.1   Future Work

This preliminary paper leaves us with several important areas of future work:

- Investigate ways for TCOZ to support additional agent-specific constructs, such as roles and protocols.

- Investigate ways to model more complex agent states such as knowledge, beliefs, desires, and intentions, to increase the scope of possible agent systems that can be specified using TCOZ.
- Examine ways that libraries of complex interactions can be specified in TCOZ for use in specifications.
- Evaluate TCOZ's applicability to agent development frameworks.

References

1. B. Bauer, J. P. Müller, and J. Odell. Agent UML: A formalism for specifying multiagent interaction. In *Agent-Oriented Software Engineering*, pages 91–103. Springer: Berlin, Germany, 2001.
2. A.A.F. Brandao, P. Alencar, and C.J.P. de Lucena. Extending (Object-)Z for multi-agent systems specification. In *International Bi-Conference Workshop on Agent-Oriented Information Systems*, LNAI. Springer-Verlag, 2004.
3. J.S. Dong and B. Mahony. Active objects in TCOZ. In *Proc. of the 1998 IEEE International Conference on Formal Engineering Methods*, pages 16–25. IEEE Computer Society Press, 1998.
4. M. Fisher. A survey of concurrent METATEM — the language and its applications. In *Temporal Logic — Proc. of the First International Conference (LNAI Volume 827)*, pages 480–505. Springer-Verlag, 1994.
5. V. Hilaire, O. Simonin, A. Koukam, and J. Ferber. A formal approach to design and reuse agent and multiagent models. In *Agent Oriented Software Engineering*, volume 3382 of *LNCS*, pages 142–157. Springer, 2004.
6. C. A. R. Hoare. *Communicating Sequential Processes*. Prentice-Hall International, 1985.
7. B. Mahony and J.S. Dong. Timed Communicating Object-Z. *IEEE Transactions on Software Engineering*, 26(2):150–177, Feb 2000.
8. T. Miller and P. McBurney. Multi-agent system specification using TCOZ. Technical Report UCLS-05-007, Department of Computer Science, University of Liverpool, 2005.
9. A. S. Rao. AgentSpeak(L): BDI agents speak out in a logical computable language. In *Proc. of the Seventh Workshop on Modelling Autonomous Agents in a Multi-Agent World*, pages 42–55. Springer-Verlag, 1996.
10. S. Schneider and J. Davies. A brief history of Timed CSP. *Theoretical Computer Science*, 138:243–271, 1995.
11. G. Smith. *The Object-Z Specification Language*. Advances in Formal Methods. Kluwer Academic Publishers, 2000.
12. J. M. Spivey. *The Z Notation: A Reference Manual*. International Series in Computer Science. Prentice-Hall International (UK) Ltd, second edition, 1992.
13. M. J. Wooldridge. *Reasoning about Rational Agents*. Intelligent Robotics and Autonomous Agents. MIT Press, Cambridge, MA, USA, 2000.
14. H. Zhu. SLABS: a formal specification language for agent-based systems. *International Journal of Software Engineering and Knowledge Engineering*, 11:529–558, Nov 2001.

ABACO, Coordination of Autonomous Entities

René Schumann[1] and Jürgen Sauer[2]

[1] OFFIS, Escherweg 2 26121 Oldenburg Germany
`rene.schumann@offis.de`
[2] University Oldenburg, Computer Center, 26121 Oldenburg, Germany
`juergen.sauer@uni-oldenburg.de`

Abstract. This paper presents an approach for the coordination of scheduling systems in production networks, where the schedulers are seen as autonomous entities using different scheduling systems for their own but shall also achieve the common goals of the network. We assume that the order of actions in which to achieve a certain goal is fixed and known. The task is to distribute the actions among the agents, so that the common goal is achieved in an efficient way. ABACO carries out this distributed scheduling, additionally it offers the possibility of reactive scheduling and improving the global schedule. The challenging thereby is to maintain the autonomy of the entities. ABACO was designed to do so. That is why the ABACO method may be useful in other contexts for coordinating the scheduling systems of autonomous agents itself, too.

1 Introduction

We present a method for coordinating the scheduling systems of autonomous entities. To point out the advantages of the method we chose the coordination of scheduling systems of autonomous entities in a production network as scenario. A production network is formed by a set of possibly independent enterprises, e.g. production companies, whose production process is distributed among the entities. A supply chain is an example of such a network (see e.g. [1]). The coordination task is to schedule the activities that have to be completed for achieving a common goal, for example to fulfil a single order.

An important point in the coordination of such autonomous entities is to preserve the autonomy of each entity. The coordination of autonomous entities is addressed in fields of research like multi-robot coordination and application of multi-agent systems (MAS) in the supply chain management (SCM).

Among coordination methods for multi-robot scenarios the level of preserved autonomy among robots can widely differ [2]. According to [3] the distribution of depending tasks among autonomous robots is an open field of research so far, only the article by Kalra & Stentz [4] is mentioned.

The research in the SCM domain evolved from distributed scheduling in the production planning context, therefor solutions where presented e.g. in [5] and [6]. An actual outline of the research done on the coordination of supply webs is presented in [7]. A lot of previous presented methods are based on auction mechanisms (e.g. [8]) or on a hierarchical structure among the agents (e.g.

T. Eymann et al. (Eds.): MATES 2005, LNAI 3550, pp. 222–228, 2005.

MUST [9]). Both approaches seem inadequate or functionally incomplete. A detailed discussion of the inadequacy of both groups can be found in [10]. A more promising technique may be bargaining processes. These methods base on the idea of self-interested agents trying to improve their local profit. Assignments are determined by agreements/contracts among the agents. Bargaining methods have been adopted to a number of requirements, respecting the autonomy of the entities, for instance. A review can be found in [7], too. The here presented ABACO method can coordinate autonomous entities, precisely their scheduling systems, maintaining a high level of autonomy for each entity.

2   Constraints for Coordination Methods

To be independent from any special scenario we first introduce the term *planning authority* (PA). A PA is an (autonomous) organisational entity, internally using a scheduling system. A set of planning authorities can form a production network. A sketch of two production networks is shown in figure 1. To fully cover

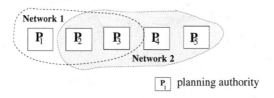

Fig. 1. A draft view of production network

the concept of production networks we assume that the planning authorities are autonomous in legal and economic sense. The following list of coordination constraints is mainly motivated by the autonomy of the planning authorities and an excerpt from [1] and are explained in detail in [10].

- No information disclosure: local sensitive knowledge is not used
- No hierarchy among the planning authorities is necessary
- A PA can participate in more than one production network
- Network optimisation in respect to local autonomy
- Networks are dynamic
- Reactive scheduling is necessary
- Local scheduling systems as black boxes

As already stated, the coordination methods presented so far are not capable to solve the coordination problem under these constraints. The hierarchical methods are not applicable, because they rely on a hierarchy among the planning authorities. The methods based on simple market mechanisms are not sufficient, because they do not offer the possibility of reactive scheduling.

There is some research in the area of coordination scheduling systems of autonomous entities, for instance see [11] or [12], but these approaches can only cover some of the constraints stated above.

3   The ABACO Method

3.1   Modelling a Production Network

A PA is an autonomous entity, trying to achieve its individual goals while co-operating with other planning authorities in one or more production networks. To maintain this autonomy in the coordination model, every PA is represented by an autonomous agent, a so called *planning authority agent* (PAA). The local scheduling system of the PA is wrapped by the PAA.

As mentioned before a PA can participate in a number of networks simultaneously and can leave or enter networks at will. In respect to this flexibility of each PAA and to reduce the communication cost within a network we introduce another component called *communication server*(CS). The CS provides some significant infrastructure to the network. A network therefore consists of a set of PAAs and a CS, as sketched in figure 2. In contrast to the PAAs the CS acts

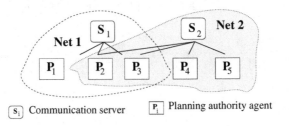

S_i Communication server P_i Planning authority agent

Fig. 2. Draft representation of a production network

only reactive and consequently is not autonomous. For that reason, we do not call the CF an agent[1].

3.2   Architecture of a PAA

The architecture of a PAA is shown in figure 3. All information for the initalisation process and the local schedule is stored in the database. The 'world model' represents the known world of the agent. The communication manager is responsible for sending and receiving messages to/from other agents. The agent control component is responsible for reasoning about the actions the agent performs. Every agent has to be customised to be able to represent its PA. Therefore some localisation modules exist, which are dynamically loaded when the agent is initialised. This modules have to

- implement an interface between the PAA and the local scheduling system.
- specify the bargaining strategy for the agent.
- make improvement proposals for the local schedule, this is needed during the improvement discussions described later on.

---

[1] Using the definition from [13] an agent is autonomous by definition.

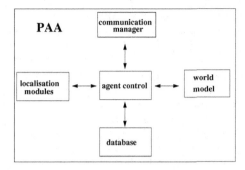

Fig. 3. Architecture of a PAA

3.3   Coordination Protocol

Several protocols are used for the coordination of predictive and reactive scheduling and schedule improvement. They are explained in detail in [10].

Initialisation. The CS is the first component which has to be run to initialise the network. Then agents can subscribe to the network by register themselves with their name and a list of activities the agent wants to offer within this network. A PAA can leave a network by un-register itself from the specific CS.

Predictive Scheduling. Predictive schedule for an order can start when all necessary activities to fulfil this order are offered by at least one agent. The network orders are scheduled sequentially. There could exist alternative activity sequences, which have to be evaluated. This is done by a method similar to the contract net protocol [14]. The CS functions as the manager trying to contract activities to the agents. During this process only information about the activity names and the associated time slots are exchanged.

After all possible sequences have been evaluated, the CS can choose the best alternative. All agents which where determined to accomplish activities of the chosen sequence are informed by the CS. Each agent that received an confirmation for an offer has to confirm its offer again. This is necessary, as the situation of the PAA may have changed during the contracting process. When confirming an offer the agent has to ensure that he can fulfil his offer towards to network.

Reactive Scheduling. Reactive scheduling becomes necessary when an event in the environment changes the situation the global schedule relies on. If such an event occurs, the existing global schedule can become partially invalid. Examples for such events are the quitting of an agent or the change of conditions of a network order. The reactive scheduling is started by the CS, which can initialise different reactive scheduling schemes, depending on the event that occurred. The rescheduling is based on the main idea of using an alternative PAA for a given activity when the originally assigned PAA can not fulfil its confirmation for whatever reason. If that strategy fails all scheduled orders which are affected by the occurred event are cancelled and these orders are scheduled again, using the predictive scheduling scheme described above[2].

Improvement Discussions. Improvement discussions are a special feature of the ABACO method. They allow to improve the global schedule by discussions among the PAAs. We only sketch the major aspects of improvement discussions here to give an impression of the abilities of this approach. Improvement discussions rely on the following two assumptions:

- Each PA wants to optimise its local schedule.
- The local optimisation potential for a PA is limited by its commitments towards the production networks it is participating in.

The second assumption is true, because a PAA generates its offers based on a given time slot, which has not to be optimal for the PAA. Beneath that the local schedule of a PAA can become suboptimal through changes in the environment.

To improve a local schedule, it can be necessary to change the actual commitments towards a production network. This can only be done with the confirmation of the other concerned entities within the production network. This is evaluated in the process we call an *improvement discussion.*

Before starting such a discussion a local improvement has to be found. This is done by a special localisation module. After a possible improvement was found the agent has to try to change its commitments to the network. This is done within an improvement discussion.

Discussion Rules: For the execution of an improvement discussion, some rules have to be respected. Discussions are forbidden as long unscheduled network orders exists. After all network orders are scheduled, the CS sends a message, telling every agent that they are now allowed to initialise discussions. When an agent has received such a message it starts to search for local improvements. If the necessity of reactive scheduling occurs, the CS has the opportunity to cancel ongoing discussions. During an improvement discussion undesired side effects can occur. For example one can think of situations where

- a discussion about all activities of a network takes place.
- some discussions could be based on not widely agreed changes.
- there may occur cyclic or contradictory change proposals within a discussion.

To avoid such side effects, there is the need for further discussion rules. The following very restrictive rule set prevents the occurrence of undesired side effects.

- Only one activity can be the topic of an improvement discussion.
- Only one discussion can take place at a time in a network.
- The number of agents allowed to participate in a discussion is limited to a maximum of three, namely the agent which starts the discussion and the agents assigned to the predecessor and successor activity in the activity sequence and the CS[3].

---

[2] This is a quite simple strategy but similar to the one presented in [11].

[3] A comparable limitation can be found in [4], too.

It has to be mentioned, that these rules are much more restrictive then necessary to prevent the side effects described. But, as far as we can see, the weakest sufficient discussion rule set to prevent such side effects is yet unknown.

Improvement Discussion Protocol: There exist two kinds of discussions:

1. Discussions about a change of the time slot for an activity.
2. Discussions about finding another PA for an activity[4].

The main idea of this protocols is, that every participating agent evaluates the consequences of the discussed changes on its local schedule and sends the result of this evaluation to the agent which initialised the discussion. If the positive effects outweigh possible negative effects and no agent rejects the change proposal then the change is done. This results in an overall improvement.

4   Conclusion and Further Work

In this article we described the coordination problem among autonomous scheduling entities, trying to achieve a common goal. We point out a number of constraints a coordination method has to respect to be applicable in such a scenario. We then presented the ABACO method, based on a MAS capable to coordinate the tasks among the agents and preventing the autonomy of each agent. The ABACO method was implemented prototypically.

Next steps should lead to benchmarks with conventional coordination approaches using real-world data. It can be expected that the performance of the ABACO approach is not as good as conventional approaches, but in contrast the ABACO approach is based on weaker preconditions and is applicable in a wider area of applications. Although a very challenging aspect is the participation of a PA in independent or even competing networks.

In a broader sense the ABACO approach deals with the coordination of different self-interested agents with dependent goals and activities, with the boundary constraint of maintaining the autonomy of each agent. We are convinced that ABACO is applicable in this broader sense as well.

References

1. Corsten, H., Gössinger, R.: Unternehmensnetzwerke: Grundlagen - Ausgestaltungs-formen - Instrumente. Schriften zum Produktionsmanagement 38, Lehrstuhl für Produktionswirtschaft Universität Kaiserslautern (2001)
2. Gancet, J., Lacroix, S.: Embedding heterogeneous levels of decisional autonomy in multi-robot systems. In: 7th Int. Symposium on Distributed Autonomous Robotic Systems. (2004)
3. Lemaire, T., et al.: A distributed tasks allocation scheme in multi-uav context. In: IEEE 2004 Int. Conf. on Robotics and Automation. (2004)

---

[4] In general this implies an additional discussion about changing the time slot.

4. Kalra, N., Stentz, A.: A market approach to tightly-coupled multi-robot coordination: first results. In: Proc. of the ARL Collaborative Technologies Alliance Symposium. (2003)
5. Smith, S.F.: OPIS: A Methodology and Architecture for Reactive Scheduling. In Zweben, M., Fox, M.S., eds.: Intelligent Scheduling. Morgan Kaufmann (1994)
6. Liu, J.S., Sycara, K.: Distributed scheduling through cooperating specialists. In: IJCAI-93 Workshop on Knowledge-Based Production Planning, Scheduling and Control. (1993)
7. Stockheim, T., et al.: Coordination of supply webs based on dispositive protocols. In: 10th European Conf. on Information Systems. (2002) 1039 – 1053
8. Schmidt, C.: Marktliche Koordination in der dezentralen Produktionsplanung Effizenz - Komplexität - Performance. Galber (1999)
9. Sauer, J.: Modelling and solving multi-site scheduling problems. In Jorna, R., van Wezel, W., Meystel, A., eds.: Planning in Intelligent Systems: Aspects, Motivations and Methods. Wiley (2005 (to appear))
10. Schumann, R.: Ein agentenbasiertes Verfahren zur Koordination von Planungssystemen. Diplomarbeit, Carl von Ossietzky Universität Oldenburg (2004)
11. Frey, D., et al.: Integrated Multi-agent-based Supply Chain Management. In: Proc. 5th. Int. Workshop on Enabling Technologies: Infrastructure for Collaborative Enterprise. (2003) 24 – 29
12. Kawamura, T., et al.: Development of a Distributed Cooperative Scheduling System Based on Negatioations between Scheduling Agents. Systems and Computers in Japan **31** (2000) 92 – 101
13. Wooldridge, M.: An Introduction to Multi Agent Systems. Wiley (2002)
14. Davis, R., Smith, R.: Negotiation as a metaphor for distributed problem solving. Artifical Intelligence **20** (1983) 63 – 109

Agent-Based Simulation for Testing Control Software of High Bay Warehouses

Cornelia Triebig*, Tanja Credner*, Peter Fischer°, Titus Leskien°,
Andreas Deppisch°, and Stefan Landvogt°

*University of Würzburg, Department of Artificial Intelligence
°SSI-Schäfer-Noell GmbH, Giebelstadt

Abstract. In this contribution we want to present a collaboration
project in which multiagent technology is applied to an industrial problem: testing the control software for automatic high bay warehouses.
Before the hardware will actually be accessible, a virtual warehouse represented as a multiagent system serves as an intelligent testbed. This
project is a cooperation between the Department for Artificial Intelligence at the University of Würzburg and SSI Schäfer Noell GmbH
(Giebelstadt).

1 Introduction

Simulation forms an important and well established method in scientific and
industrial applications for improving comprehension and increasing quality of
design and control of complex systems. Mainly the reduction of time and thus of
cost gained in industrial applications is an important aspect for the increasing
number of applications of simulation methods.

In the area of high bay warehouses and other material flow systems, simulation is applied mostly for generating performance measures or testing layout
design. There, established simulation technology like queuing systems or object-
oriented simulation is used rather successfully. However, there are additional
and attractive scenarios for using simulation supporting high bay warehouse
construction:

- testing control software using a virtual version of the high bay warehouse
  before the real system is implemented and in use.
- supporting requirement acquisition in discussion with the customer
- simulation of the warehouse and control system for user training
- generating reproducible error situations

Beyond appealing graphics, specific requirements are posed on the simulation
software used for these application scenarios. The simulation software should be
able to represent the warehouse on a high level of detail; current changes in the
warehouse configuration should be easy to adapt in the simulation and also fast
to perform. Due to high project pressure, the construction of a model should be

T. Eymann et al. (Eds.): MATES 2005, LNAI 3550, pp. 229–234, 2005.

speed up; modeling should not require simulation experts but should be manageable by warehouse experts themselves. These requirements are hardly fulfilled by standard simulation systems and languages. In the scope of our collaboration project we were able to show that the agent paradigm allows highly flexible modeling on a level of preciseness that is accomplishable without expensive training in modeling and simulation techniques.

2   Related Work

With this collaboration project we briefly refer to simulation as well as to agent-based technology. Therefore let us have a look at work concerning these subjects.

There are few simulation tools designed for the application field of production and material flow systems. One of them is the commercial simulation tool eM-Plant [1]. It can be used for visualization, planning and optimization of production and logistics. eM-Plant provides several building block toolboxes for various domains e.g. automatic guided vehicle systems, airport, assembly, etc.. These toolboxes contain different building blocks which can be adapted to the requirements of a specific project and combined together. Another commercial simulation tool is FlexSim [2]. FlexSim enables "fast and easy modeling, clear visualization as well as reuseability of models". FlexSim, like eM-Plant, can be applied in various domains. It can be used as vending tool, because of the visualization, as well as for planning, design and simulation of different systems.

There are many other simulation tools but they are all similiar to the tools presented above. However, for the choice of an appropriate simulation environment they were not considered.

The application field of agent-based technology is extensive and can be found in almost every domain. However, "although agent technology is an accepted research area, it has not gained wide-spread industrial acceptance until now"[3].

This research area is now drawing more attention on itself because it is being recognized a powerful tool for the development of large and complex systems and it is also beginning to gain industrial relevance [3]. In [4] Jennings, Sycara and Woolridge give a roadmap of agent research and development and an overwiew on agent-based industrial and commercial applications. The main areas in which agent-based approaches are already in use are e.g. manufacturing, process control, telecommunication, air traffic control, transportation systems, information management, electronic commerce, etc.. With regard to our project there are some interesting approaches in manufacturing and process control. Timm, Herzog, Woelk and Tönshoff engage in improvements of information logistics in the area of production engeneering [5]. They present an agent-based approach to the integration of process planning and production control and of making the workflow more flexible by using co-operative agents systems as described in [5]. They try to fill the gap which arises from "strong borderlines between process planning, production control and scheduling systems, caused by extreme specialization and independent historical paths of system evolution".

Another agent-based application on manufacturing was developed by a Daimler Chrysler-led consortium [6]. Bussmann and Schild present their auction-based approach to manufacturing line control in [7]. In this approach which is applied in the domain of automobile industry, workpieces auction off their current task, while machines bid for tasks.

3   The Simulation Environment SeSAm

For the our project we use the generic environment SeSAm (Shell for Simulated Agent Systems, *www.simsesam.de*) that allows high-level visual programming of multi-agent simulations. This open-source project is developed by the Department for Artificial Intelligence (University of Würzburg). SeSAm provides a generic environment for modeling and analyzing with agent-based simulation. The focus lies on providing a tool for easing the construction of complex models.

SeSAm offers several categories of objects that can take part on simulations. Naturally, agent classes can be implemented. Objects that don't act themselves but only are used to act with can be added as ressources. The so-called world represents the environment and is in fact a specialized agent. Each of these objects can handle a number of own variables, which are used to store the knowledge of the agent and for interactions. The behavior of an agent must be defined as an activity graph. The syntax is abutted to UML. Actions an agent should perform are defined by combining the atomic activities that are offered by SeSAm. Such actions are grouped into activities connected with directed edges that represent a condition. If this condition is evaluated as true during a simulation run the agent will continue with the next activity.

For creating a real simulation run, a situation for the model needs to be built. Instances of the agent classes are placed on the map, if desired the starting values of their variables can be edited. After this, the real simulation can be started. Additionally it is possible to define analyzing functions and to decide whether variables are logged during the simulation.

For defining ordinary simulations as described above, not a single line of Java Code needs to be written because everything is implemented via manipulating graphical elements. If special requirements arise, e.g the need for communication with external systems, SeSAm can easily be extended by Java-Plugins. Generic interfaces in the internal structure of the project allow new data types, atomic primitives and also new complex GUI elements to be added.

4   Agentbased Simulation for High Bay Warehouses

A high bay warehouse basically consists of transport routes for transport units, pallets or bins, and high bay storage and retrieval. In particular, there are different modules like variable conveyor elements, scales and scanners (with error probabilities), storage elements, but also human operators. Each of these elements may be treated as an agent with specific behavior. The modularity of warehouse components facilitates the mapping of warehouse components on agents: real component behavior is mapped to agent behavior.

Agents realized in this way are also layout independent. That means, these agents can be applied in any model. As each project requires an adapted combination of warehouse components, this property facilitates and accelerates the modeling of specific projects. This enables models with variable structures.

A further property of agents is that it is facile to build them in a generic way. Generic built agents make it possible to reuse them in all models of this domain. The generic-ness of agents maintaines the extensibility and also the adaption of agent behavior in succession of improvements or innovations.

One of the most important aspects of using agent-based technology for the simulation of high bay warehouses is the detailed simulation with the integration of involved persons. Human operators are employed as part pickers at picking stations or to manually control the conveyor lines. As a result of this, these human operators are also able to compensate errors or malfunctions with their natural intelligence. The agent-based approach makes it easier to simulate human behavior than other technologies. Typical agent properties enable a better and more detailed mapping of human intelligence, perception and thus the resulting and actual behavior in the simualtion than it is achieved by other technologies.

5   SeSAm-Based Models of High Bay Warehouses

Different modules like conveyor elements, scales and scanners, storage elements, but also human operators are the basic elements of a high bay warehouses. Each of these elements may be treated as an agent, that means, as a more or less autonomously intelligent building block with local sensors and effectors. Beyond communication within the virtual high bay warehouse - that is with other agents, there has to be also communication with the warehouse control software.

Until now the construction of eight actual high bay warehouse projects have been supported by agent-based simulation for testing the control software. The general procedure is that we develop a multi-agent model of the high bay warehouse in SeSAm. The real warehouse is concurrently built up. Thus, details of the real-world warehouse can be adapted almost synchronously.

As far as the use and functionality of the basic elements are concerned all warehouses are similiar, a fixed number of agents was implemented like different kinds of conveyors, shuttle vehicles, storage and retrieval machines or human part pickers. The use of these precasted agents speeds up the modeling. However, because of the requirements of specific virtual high bay warehouses, some adaptions of the applied agents must be conducted. Therefore we decided to design these agents as generically as possible. The fixed number of reusable agents should be minimized. This level of modeling is sufficient for the application scenarios in requirements engineering and training, but not for the primary application, namely the test of control software. Therefore a special adaption or connection between the virtual warehouse - represented with agents, and the specific software is required. This adaption is more or less easily to build, because of the Plugin-concept of SeSAm mentioned above. The generic-ness of the agents also supports the communication between control the software and agents. This communication is datagram-based, much like some proprietary ACL-messages. The control software to test sends commands in reaction to notifications or alarms the agent. This is implemented using the Plugin-concept.

Agents may be grouped to higher-level components with some fixed organizational structure that again may be integrated into the overall virtual high bay warehouse in the same way as "atomic" agents. We developed aggregates with complex synchronization protocols, like

- storage-and-retrieval machines within their working environment (There you can also observe the actual process of storage and retrieval in the warehouse.)
- carousels for transport and delivery (especially used in bin conveyor systems)
- complex conveyor lines, which can change their transport direction
- "intelligent" conveyor lines, which can route transport units in a new direction when accumulations on some routes occur
- vertical conveyors and (multi) shuttle vehicles

6   Example Project

In this section we want to present a successfully implemented project. In figure 1 you see the complete virtual warehouse. For better understanding we separated the illustration in two sections and added a legend showing the used agents: the Storage and Retrieval Area (1) and the High Rack Storage Area (2).

Section 1 of figure 1 shows Storage Points, conveyor line elements and Retrieval Points. On Storage Points Transport Units (TUs) enter the warehouse system. On Retrieval Points, they leave the system. The three Storage Points which you can see in this area are connected to a conveyor line. Conveyor lines consists of two different conveyor elements: Simple and Generic Conveyors. Simple Conveyors manage only one direction, Generic ones manage several directions in which TUs can be routed. Each of these agents is able to take only one TU at the same time. In this project, there are two ways for TUs arriving at the High Rack Storage, as the arrows show. The right side of section 1 is responsible for retrieval of TUs out of the system. This part of the system consists only of Simple and Generic Conveyors as well as of Retrieval Points. In the High Rack Storage (section 2 of figure 1) you can additionally see the Storage Retrieval Machines serving the actual storage. The representation of the storage is facilitated because there is no need in this project to show in which way and on which place TUs are stored. If TUs enter the storage they will be destroyed. In case of a retrieval request of stored TUs Storage Points reproduce them.

As soon as the warehouse system is represented and customized in a SeSAm-model software tests are started. To customize the model the initial agent variables ar adapted, e.g. the setting of the conveying direction. The software test consists of successive software unit tests. Each component of the whole warehouse control software is tested on its own. Therefor special datagrams are generated and TU orders are sent to see if the generated TUs take the specified destination and arrive at a given position. Thus, the warehouse control software is proofed and should work correctly after copious tests. In this model stadium the simulation is also used as presentation tool for customers.

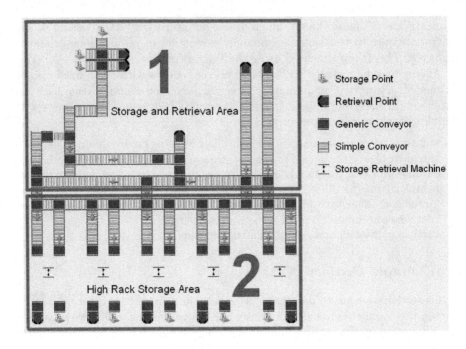

Fig. 1. Screenshot of a high bay warehouse simulated with SeSAm

7   Conclusion

At the moment eight projects are successfully completed, other four are in process and further projects are planned. Already with the first virtual warehouse we used, several errors in the control software could be found and fixed before the real-world warehouse was available. With each virtual warehouse the effort for its modeling decreased due to an improved set of agents. That way several ten thousands of Euros could be saved.

References

1. http://www.emplant.de
2. http://www.g-f.at
3. http://www.agentlab.de
4. Jennings, N.R., Sycara K., Woolridge, M.: A Roadmap of Agent Research and Development. Auto. Agents and Multi-Agent Syst., Vol. 1, No. 1, July, 1998, pp. 7-38.
5. Tönshoff, H.K., Woelk, P.O., Herzog O., Timm I.J.: Integrated process planning and production control - A flexible approach using co-operative agent systems. Proc. 10th Int. Conf. on Prec. Engineer., Yokohama, Japan, July, 2001, pp. 857-861.
6. Jennings, N.R., Bussmann, S.: Agent-based Control systems. IEEE Control Systems Magazine, Vol. 23, June 2003, pp. 61-73.
7. Bussmann, S., Schild, K.: Self-organising manufacturing control: an industrial application of agent technology. Proc. 4th Int. Conf. on Multi-Agent Systems, Boston, MA, 2000, pp. 87-94.

Collaborative Agent-Based Knowledge Support for Empirical and Knowledge-Intense Processes

Andrea Freßmann[1], Kerstin Maximini[1], Rainer Maximini[1], and Thomas Sauer[2]

[1] University of Trier, Department of Business Information Systems II,
54286 Trier, Germany
{andrea.fressmann, kerstin.maximini,
rainer.maximini}@wi2.uni-trier.de
[2] rjm Business Solutions GmbH, 68623 Lampertheim, Germany
t_sauer@rjm.de

Abstract. Independent from specific application domains, similar requirements can be identified regarding information needs during daily work. For coping with generality on the one hand and domain specificity on the other hand the Collaborative Agent-based Knowledge Engine CAKE is currently developed that combines agent and workflow technology in an innovative way. Agent technology is used for integrating various services, whereas workflow technology is used for coordinating collaboration among agents.

1 Collaborative Agent-Based Knowledge Engine (CAKE)

Motivated by requirements derived from different application domains like fire services, agile software engineering, medicine, and geographical information systems a domain-independent system called *Collaborative Agent-based Knowledge Engine (CAKE)* [1] is currently developed aiming at supporting empirical and knowledge-intense processes. *Empirical processes* [2] are mostly unpredictable, unrepeatable, and are subject to change as they are enacted. *Knowledge-intense processes* like identifying, creating, and sharing of knowledge require sophisticated knowledge management strategies.

For enabling domain-specific applications CAKE provides the possibility to expand a general data and process model individually. It makes use of workflow technology for facilitating knowledge intensive tasks required for context-based information support and agent technology for integration of various services.

CAKE requires a lot of flexiblity, e.g. for coping with changes during runtime on behalf of end-users. In particular, context-based information has to be adapted to changing situations of system users. Conventional software reaches the end of its capabilities here, requiring mostly predetermined paths. CAKE overcomes this challenge with the provision of *agile workflows*. Agile workflows offer the options of either modelling single tasks in detail or modelling abstractly, supporting late modelling as well. Technically, this kind of workflows is supported by *Case Based Reasoning (CBR)* [3] search technology: When proceeding to an abstractly planned task the workflow engine allows the corresponding user to retrieve a suitable workflow definition in a special workflow database. In that scope, ad-hoc planning is facilitated during runtime.

T. Eymann et al. (Eds.): MATES 2005, LNAI 3550, pp. 235–236, 2005.
© Springer-Verlag Berlin Heidelberg 2005

Besides widening the flexibility given by agile and knowledge-intensive workflows there is also a challenge to incorporate business-relevant information in form of integration of retrieval engines in order to access distributed knowledge sources. While access to distributed databases and retrieval engines is necessary, incompatibility is often a drawback. For coping with compatibilities CAKE also includes an *agent framework* that enables and mediates arbitrary access and communication to different agent-based services. From a conceptual point of view, CAKE does not only distinguish between *information agents* that provide knowledge and *user agents* that request knowledge, but knows a third kind, namely *collaboration agents* that manage the collaboration between other agents based on *collaboration patterns*. These patterns are technically described as workflow definitions and organise the agents' collaboration. In contrast to conventional agent-based approaches that provide agents to get in contact to other agents for pursuing their goals, CAKE makes use of collaboration patterns to exploit combinations of various information sources and best practices. Collaboration patterns encompass domain-specific and domain-independent search strategies with respect to potential types of agent collaborations. For enabling a convenient usage CAKE hides these strategies from users without the need of specification which agent users intend to request. In order to realise the concepts described above CAKE makes use of agent technology for combining services provided by the workflow engine manager and external services, e.g. retrieval engines. The flexibility of agile workflows is carried forward to the agent framework by providing a dynamic set of agents whereas agents are able to enter and leave the CAKE *agent society* based on the concept of network agent society as proposed by Dignum et al. [4].

In summary, CAKE consolidates both technologies basically: agent technology for providing the integration of various services and external technologies, workflow technology for both coordinating collaboration among agents and supporting context-based information. Particularly, the presented collaboration patterns facilitate the management of agent collaborations based on best practices or on configurable patterns. Furthermore, these patterns enable routing facilities for transferring knowledge within organisations which means high universality to CAKE.

Acknowledgements. The authors acknowledge the European Commission for funding AMIRA under grant number FP6, project IST-2003-511740.

References

1. Freßmann, A., Maximini, R., Sauer, T.: Towards collaborative agent-based knowledge support for agile projects. In Althoff, K.D., Dengel, A., Bergmann, R., Roth-Berghofer, T., eds.: WM2005: Professional Knowledge Management Experiences and Visions, Kaiserslautern, Germany, DFKI GmbH (2005) 383–388
2. Advanced Development Methods, Inc.: Control chaos: Living on the edge. the origins of scrum, http://www.controlchaos.com (1996)
3. Weber, B., Wild, W., Breu, R.: Cbrflow: Enabling adaptive workflow management through conversational case-based reasoning. In Funk, P., Calero, P.A.G., eds.: Advances in Case-Based Reasoning, Proceedings of 7th European Conference, ECCBR 2004. LNAI3155, Madrid, Spain, Springer Verlag, Berlin-Heidelberg (2004) 434–448
4. Dignum, V., Weigand, H., Yu, L.: Agent societies: Towards frameworks-based design. Lecture Notes in Computer Science **2222** (2002) 33ff

Experiments in Neo-computation Based on Emergent Programming

Jean-Pierre Georgé, Marie-Pierre Gleizes, and Pierre Glize

IRIT, Université Paul Sabatier, 118 route de Narbonne,
31062 Toulouse cedex, France
{george, gleizes, glize}@irit.fr

1 Emergent Programming

The general objective of this work is to develop a complete programming language in which each instruction is an autonomous agent trying to be in a cooperative state with the other agents of the system, as well as with the environment of the system. By endowing these *instruction-agents* with self-organizing mechanisms[2], we obtain a system able to continuously adapt to the task required by the programmer (i.e. to program and re-program itself depending on the needs). The work presented here aims at showing the feasibility of such a concept by specifying, and experimenting with, a core of *instruction-agents* needed for a subset of mathematical calculus. In its most abstract view, *Emergent Programming* is the *automated assembling of instructions of a programming language using mechanisms which are not explicitly informed of the program to be created*. We chose to rely on an adaptive multi-agent system using self-organizing mechanisms based on cooperation as it is described in the *AMAS* theory[1]. An important part of our work on *Emergent Programming* has been the exploration of the self-organization mechanisms which enable the agents to progress toward the adequate function, depending on the constraints of the environment but without knowing the organization to reach or how to do it.

2 The Elementary Example

The elementary example we choose is constituted of 6 agents: 3 "*constant*" agents, an "*addition*" agent, a "*multiplication*" agent and an "*output*" agent. A "*constant*" agent is able to provide the value which has been fixed at his creation (cf. Figure 1). The values produced by the system are results from organizations like $(A + B) * C$. *AgentOut* transmits the value he receives to the environment and is in charge of retrieving the feedback from the environment and forward it into the system. It is important to note that this information is not in any way an explicit description about the goal and *how* to reach it (it only informs that the value has to be higher or lower).

The size of the complete search space is 6^5, that is 7776 theoretically possible organizations, counting all the incomplete ones (i.e. where not every agent has all his partners). Among them, we have 6 types of different functional organization (they can actually calculate a value) (cf. Figure 1). The aim is to start without any partnerships between agents and to request that the system produces the highest value for example.

T. Eymann et al. (Eds.): MATES 2005, LNAI 3550, pp. 237–239, 2005.

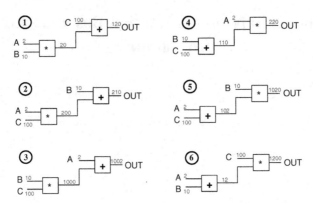

Fig. 1. The 6 different possible types of functional organizations for the elementary example

2.1   Reorganization Mechanisms

The agent's self-organizing capacity is induced by their capacity to detect *NCS* (*Non-Cooperative Situations*), react so as to resorb them and continuously act as cooperatively as possible. This last point implies in fact that the agent also has to try to resorb NCS of other agents if he is aware of them. We will illustrate this with the description of a simple NCS and how it is resorbed.

NCSNeedIn detection: the agent is missing a partner on one of his inputs. Since to be cooperative in the system he has to be useful, and to be useful he has to be able to compute his function, he has to find partners able to send values toward his input. Most NCS lead the agent to communicate so as to find a suitable (new) partner. These calls, because the agents have to take them into account, also take the shape of NCS.

NCSNeedIn resorption: this is one of the easiest NCS so resorb because the agent only has to find any agent for his missing input. The agent has simply to be able to contact some agent providing values corresponding to his own type (there could be agents handling values of different types in a system). So he generates an *NCSNeedInMessage* describing his situation and send it to his acquaintances.

NCSNeedInMessage detection: the agent receives a message informing him that another agent is in a *NCSNeedIn* situation (the sender is missing a partner on one of his inputs).

NCSNeedInMessage resorption: the agent is informed of the needs of the sender of the NCS and his cooperative attitude dictates him to act. First, he has to judge if he is relevant for the needs of the sender, and if it is the case, he has to propose himself as a potential partner. Second, even if he is not himself relevant, one of its acquaintances may be: he tries to counter this NCS by propagating the initial message to some acquaintances he thinks may be the most relevant.

It is important to note that the information which is given as a feedback is not in any way an explicit description about the goal and *how* to reach it. Indeed, this information does not exist: given a handful of values and mathematical operators, there is no explicit method to reach a specific value even for a human. They can only try and guess, and this is also what the agents do. That is why we believe the resolution we implemented to be in the frame of emergence.

3 Results

First, the internal constraints of the system are solved very quickly: in only a few re-organization moves (among the 7776 possible organizations), all the agents find their partners and a functional organization is reached. Then, because of the feedback from the environment, other NCS are produced and the system starts reorganizing toward its goal. Since the search space if of 7776 possible organizations, a blind exploration would need an average of 3888 checked organizations to reach a specific one. Since a functional organization possesses 4 identical instances for a given value (by input permutations), we would need 972 tries to get the right value. Experimentation shows that the system needs to explore less than a hundred organizations among the 7776 to reach one of the 4 producing the highest value. We consider that this self-organization strategy allows a relevant exploration of the search space. A noteworthy result is also that whatever organization receives the feedback for a better value, the next organization will indeed produce a better value.

4 Discussion

If we define all the agents needed to represent a complete programming language (with agents representing variables, allocation, control structures, ...) and if this language is extensive enough, we obtain maximal expressiveness: every program we can produce with current programming languages can be coded as an organization of *instruction-agents*. In its absolute concept, *Emergent programming* could then solve any problem, given that the problem can be solved by a computer system. Of course, this seems quite unrealistic, at least for the moment.

But if we possess some higher-level knowledges about a problem, or if the problem can be structured at a higher level than the instruction level, then it is more efficient and easier to conceive the system at a higher level. This is the case for example when we can identify entities of bigger granularity which therefore have richer competences and behaviors, maybe adapted specifically for the problem. Consequently, we will certainly be able to apply the self-organizing mechanisms developed for Emergent Programming to other ways to tackle a problem. Indeed, *instruction-agents* are very particular by the fact that they represent the most generic type of entities. The exploration of the search space, for entities possessing more information or more competences for a given problem can only be easier. For example, we think that problems like Ambient Intelligence or Autonomic Computing are ideal candidate for a problem solving by emergence approach.

References

1. M.-P. Gleizes, V. Camps, and P. Glize. A theory of emergent computation based on cooperative self-oganization for adaptive artificial systems. In *Fourth European Congress of Systems Science*, Valencia, Spain, 1999.
2. F. Heylighen. *Encyclopedia of Life Support Systems*, chapter The Science of Self-organization and Adaptivity. EOLSS Publishers Co. Ltd, 2001.

A Framework Based on Multi-agent Systems for Information Retrieval Through Mobile Devices

Angela Carrillo Ramos, Jérôme Gensel, Marlène Villanova-Oliver,
and Hervé Martin

LSR-IMAG Laboratory, SIGMA Team. B.P. 72,
38402 Saint Martin d'Hères Cedex, France
{carrillo, gensel, villanov, martin}@imag.fr

Abstract. In this paper, we describe *PUMAS*, a framework based on *Multi-Agent Systems (MAS)* for accessing *Web Information Systems (WIS)* through *Mobile Devices (MD)*. The goal of *PUMAS* is to provide nomadic users with adapted information taking into account, on the one hand, their preferences and history in the system and, on the other hand, the limited capacities of their *MD*. We describe the four *MAS* of *PUMAS* which handle the adaptation process. We also describe how the user's queries are redirected towards one or several *WIS* which contains the information for answering them.

1 Motivation

In order to provide the nomadic user only with *"the right information in the right place at the right time"*, a *Mobile Device (MD)* application must embed mechanisms for propagating the user's queries towards the *"right"* information sources which can answer these queries taking into account the user's preferences, the features of her/his *MDs*, her/his location, etc. For this purpose, we have defined *PUMAS*, a framework based on *Multi-Agent Systems (MAS)* for retrieving information distributed between several *WIS* and different types of *MDs*. Through *PUMAS*, our final objective is to build and propose a framework which is, beyond the management of accesses to *WIS* performed through *MDs*, also in charge of performing an adaptation of information. We briefly present the architecture of *PUMAS* as well as the *Query Routing* process [4] executed in *PUMAS* by a *Router Agent* in order to redirect the queries formulated by the user towards the different *WIS*.

2 The PUMAS Framework

The architecture of *PUMAS* [1] is composed of four *MAS*, each one encompassing several *ubiquitous agents*: First, the *Connection MAS* provides the mechanisms for facilitating the connection from different kinds of *MD* to the system. Second, the *Communication MAS* ensures a transparent communication between the *MDs* and the system. It also applies a *Display Filter* for displaying the information to the user according to the technical constraints of her/his *MD*. Third, the *Information MAS* which receives the user's query, redirects it to the *"right"* *WIS*, applies a *Content Filter* according to the user's profile and returns the filtered results to the *Communication MAS*. Finally, agents of the *Adaptation MAS* communicate with the agents of the three other *MAS* in order to exchange information about the user and her/his *MD*.

T. Eymann et al. (Eds.): MATES 2005, LNAI 3550, pp. 240–241, 2005.

The *Knowledge* managed by the *PUMAS* agents for achieving their adaptation tasks is stored in *Knowledge Bases (KBs)* in the form of *pieces of knowledge*. We call these pieces *"facts"* and define them using *JESS* (*http://herzberg.ca.sandia.gov/jess/*). A complete description of the *Knowledge Management* in *PUMAS* is presented in [2].

The *Query Routing* process in *PUMAS* is achieved by the *Router Agent* which receives the query together with the characteristics of the user and of her/his *MD*. In order to redirect the query to the *"right" IS(s)*, a strategy is chosen by the *Router Agent* and depends on several criteria: user's location, preferences, etc. The strategy can lead to the sending of the query to a specific *WIS*, or to the sending of the query in a broadcast way, or to the split of the query in sub-queries, each one being sent to one or several *ISAgents* (which execute on the *WIS* and search for the asked information). The *Router Agent* is also in charge of compiling the results returned by the *ISAgents* and of analyzing them to decide whether the whole set of results or only a part of it will be sent to the user. In *PUMAS*, the *Query Routing* process consists of three activities (based on the work of Xu *et al* [3]): First, the analysis of the query (related to the possible split of the query in sub-queries). Second, the selection of the *Information Sources* (the *Router Agent* computes the network of *neighbors,* based on ideas of Yang *et al* [4]). The last activity is the redirection of the query to the *neighbors*.

3 Conclusions and Future Work

In this paper, we have described *PUMAS,* a framework composed of four *MAS* (one *connection MAS,* one *communication MAS,* one *information MAS* and one *adaptation MAS*) which retrieves adapted information according to the user's characteristics and those of her/his *MD*. We also described the *Query Routing* process performed by the *Router Agent* which is composed of three activities: an analysis of the query, a selection of the information sources and a redirection of the query. We now aim at implementing each *MAS* of *PUMAS*. For this purpose, we have chosen *JADE-LEAP* (*http://jade.tilab.com/*).

References

1. Carrillo-Ramos, A., Gensel, J., Villanova-Oliver, M., Martin, H.: PUMAS: a Framework based on Ubiquitous Agents for Accessing Web Information Systems through Mobile Devices. In proc. of the 20th ACM Symposium on Applied Computing (SAC 2005) (Santafe, New Mexico, USA, March 13 - 17, 2005), ACM Press, New York, NY (2005) 1003-1008.
2. Carrillo-Ramos, A., Gensel, J., Villanova-Oliver, M., Martin, H.: Adapted information retrieval in Web Information Systems using PUMAS. To appear in 7th Int. Workshop on Agent-Oriented Information Systems (AOIS2005) (Utrecht, Netherlands, July 25, 2005).
3. Xu, J., Lim, E., Ng, W.K.: Cluster-Based Database Selection Techniques for Routing Bibliographic Queries. In proc. of 10th International Conference on Database and Expert Systems Applications (DEXA 99) (Florence, Italy, August 30 - September 3, 1999), LNCS, Vol. 1677, Springer-Verlag, Berlin Heidelberg (1999) 100-109.
4. Yang, D., Xu, L., Cai, W., Zhou, S., Zhou, A.: Efficient Query Routing for XML Documents Retrieval in Unstructured Peer to Peer Networks. In proc. of the 6th Asia Pacific Web Conference (APWeb 2004) (Hangzhou, China, April 14 - 17, 2004), LNCS, Vol. 3007, Springer-Verlag, Berlin Heidelberg (2004) 217-223.

CASCOM: Context-Aware Service Co-ordination in Mobile P2P Environments*

Heikki Helin[1], Matthias Klusch[2], António Lopes[3], Alberto Fernández[4], Michael Schumacher[5], Heiko Schuldt[6], Federico Bergenti[7], and Ari Kinnunen[8]

[1] TeliaSonera Finland Oyj, Finland
Heikki.j.Helin@teliasonera.com
[2] Deutsches Forschungszentrum für Künstliche Intelligenz (DFKI), Germany
klusch@dfki.de
[3] Associação para o Desenvolvimento das
Telecomunicações e Tecnicas de Informática (ADETTI), Portugal
antonio.lopes@we-b-mind.org
[4] Universidad Rey Juan Carlos (URJC), Spain
alberto.fernandez@urjc.es
[5] Ecole Polytechnique Fédérale de Lausanne (EPFL), Switzerland
michael.schumacher@epfl.ch
[6] University for Health Sciences, Medical Informatics and
Technology (UMIT), Austria
heiko.schuldt@umit.at
[7] FRAMeTech S.R.L., Italy
bergenti@cs.unipr.it
[8] EMA Group, Ltd., Finland
ari@ema.fi

Abstract. The research project CASCOM (Context-aware Business Application Service Co-ordination in Mobile Computing Environments) will implement, validate, and trial value-added support for business services for mobile workers and users across mobile and fixed networks. The vision of the CASCOM approach is that ubiquitous application services are flexibly co-ordinated and pervasively provided to the mobile users by intelligent agents in dynamically changing contexts of open, large-scale, pervasive environments.

1 CASCOM Overview

The essential approach of the research project CASCOM is the innovative combination of agent technology, semantic Web services, P2P, and mobile computing for intelligent P2P (IP2P) mobile service environments. The services of our environment are provided by agents exploiting the coordination infrastructure to efficiently operate in highly dynamic environments. The IP2P infrastructure

---

* This work has been supported in part by the European Commission under the project grant FP6-IST-511632-CASCOM.

T. Eymann et al. (Eds.): MATES 2005, LNAI 3550, pp. 242–243, 2005.

includes efficient communication means, support for context-aware adaptation techniques, as well as dynamic service discovery and composition planning.

Software agents will be a key technology to address the challenges of our architecture. IP2P networks provide an environment for agents to collaborate as peers sharing information, tasks, and responsibilities with each other. Agents help to manage the P2P network complexity, and they will improve the functionality of conventional P2P systems. Our innovations in this domain will concern the development of context-aware agent-based semantic Web services, and flexible resource-efficient co-ordination of such services in the nomadic computing field. Further, context-awareness is investigated in the context of IP2P environment and we will develop context-aware agents which provide various business application services.

Service co-ordination mechanisms of P2P systems can be applied to multi-agent systems to improve their efficiency. Although this may be accepted on a conceptual level, the combination of agents and P2P environments certainly deserves more innovative research, especially regarding nomadic environments. The dynamic topology of IP2P networks, characteristics of wireless network connections, and the limited capacity of mobile devices pose several challenges that have been addressed inadequately in service discovery architectures. In CASCOM, we will investigate mechanisms for service discovery algorithms for dynamic IP2P environments.

The problem of service co-ordination can be split into several sub problems: discovery, composition planning, execution monitoring, and failure recovery. CASCOM will advance the state of the art by carrying out innovative research on how these problems can be solved in IP2P environments. Especially CASCOM will provide flexible and efficient matching algorithms to be performed in large scale and resource limited IP2P environments.

Using AI planning formalisms in service composition and planning are developed for problems where the number of operators is relatively small but where plans can be complex. In Web service composition for open, large-scale IP2P environments planning methods dealing with huge number of possible service are required. However, plans are not necessarily very complex, and therefore planning methods must follow more closely the structure of the service directories. CASCOM will develop planning mechanisms that establish plan fragments directly on top of the service directory to solve this problem.

In general, it is expected that the outcomes of the project will have significant impact on the creation of a next-generation global, large-scale intelligent service environment. Both, research results on methods for service provision, discovery, composition and monitoring, and the deployed prototype of an open IP2P service environment in the context of nomadic computing will advance the state of the art of European and world knowledge in areas related to the deployment of services in open systems.

More information about CASCOM can be found from our homepage at http://www.ist-cascom.org/.

Author Index

Lecture Notes in Artificial Intelligence (LNAI)